Language, Symbols, and the Media

Communication in the Aftermath of the World Trade Center Attack

Robert E. Denton, Jr., editor

Transaction Publishers
New Brunswick (U.S.A.) and London (U.K.)

First paperback printing 2006

Copyright © 2004 by Transaction Publishers, New Brunswick, New Jersey.

This book is printed on acid-free paper that meets the American National Standard for Permanence of Paper for Printed Library Materials.

Library of Congress Catalog Number: 2004051767
ISBN: 0-7658-0265-1 (cloth); 1-4128-0551-1 (paper)
Printed in the United States of America

Library of Congress Cataloging-in-Publication Data

Language, symbols, and the media : communication in the aftermath of the
    World Trade Center attack / Robert E. Denton, Jr., editor.
        p. cm.
    Includes index.
    ISBN 0-7658-0265-1 (alk. paper)
    1. War on terrorism, 2001-2.   2. Terrorism and mass media—United
States. 3. Terrorism in mass media. 4. Signs and symbols—United States. I.
Denton, Robert E., Jr.

P96.W36L36   2004
303.6'25—dc22   2004051767

This book is dedicated to those who lost their lives on 9/11, to those who gave their lives in America's war against terrorism here at home, in Afghanistan, in Iraq, and elsewhere around the world as well as to those who continue to serve to make the world a safer place for us all.

Contents

Preface

"The World is not at all structured like a fairy tale... Evil must be confronted in its womb and, if there is no other way to do it, then it has to be dealt with by the use of force."—Vaclav Havel, September 19, 2002 to the Graduate Center of the City University of New York

At this writing, well over 100,000 American troops are in Iraq. It appears that Osama Bin Laden is still alive but on the run. Saddam Hussein is captured and awaits the trial and judgment of the Iraqi people. While building schools and hospitals, suicide bombers target hotels and embassies within Iraq. While working to provide electricity to all of Iraq, American convoys are hit with mortar fire. While repairing the oil pipelines and restoring refineries for Iraqi economic development, American Blackhawk helicopters transporting troops are fired upon from those hidden in buildings below. We continue to lose troops, now more than during the actual intense assault and drive to Baghdad; hundreds more than in first Iraq war.

We are now at war and in the post-Cold War period; "9/11" inaugurated a new Era in terms of foreign policy and our "war on terror." The rules that governed American foreign policy since World War II no longer apply. Our "friends" are no longer defined by their anti-communism and our "enemies" are no longer defined by their affiliation with the Soviet Union. "In the new era," according to Anne Applebaum (2002, 19), "we are no longer selling democracy for its own sake, but exploring security, both for our sake and for the sake of other potential victims."

On 9/11, terrorism left the domain of criminality and entered that of warfare. Just what are the implications? It means not only targeting foot soldiers, but also the organizations and governments behind the terrorists. It means relying on the armed forces, not policemen. It means defense overseas rather than on American soil and in our courtrooms. It means reasonable proof as sufficient evidence to deploy U.S. forces. It means using force and even pre-emptive strikes to deter future attacks.

We are indeed experiencing a "new world order," a new political landscape, a new era of warfare. A few thugs can terrorize an entire nation. Small nations can dominate international debate and diplomacy. A few ounces of anthrax can be more devastating to life than multi-ton explosives.

Of course, the connection between terrorism and religion is not new. However, until the 1990s we witnessed more ethnic, nationalist-separatist, or ideological motivated terrorism. By the middle of the decade, however, the rise of religious terrorism was evident. Ironically, although the total volume of terrorist incidents worldwide declined during the 1990s, the proportion of persons killed in such incidents increased. Thus, while terrorists were less active, they were certainly more lethal. Prior to the September 11 attack, over the preceding thirty-three years, fewer than 1,000 Americans had been killed by terrorists either overseas or within the U.S. In just ninety minutes, more than 3,000 Americans lost their lives at the hands of terrorists. (Hoffman 2002, 2-3, 7). Another 1,000 (and counting) are lost on the battlefields of Afghanistan and Iraq.

According to Bruce Hoffman (2002, 4), religious terrorism tends to be more lethal than secular terrorism because of the radically different value systems, mechanisms of legitimization and justification, concepts of morality, and worldviews that directly affect the "holy terrorists" motivation: "For the religious terrorist, violence first and foremost is a sacramental act or divine duty, executed in direct response to some theological demand or imperative and justified by scripture. Religion, therefore functions as a legitimizing force, specifically sanctioning wide scale violence against an almost open-ended category of opponents."

On that fateful day, little did we know what lay before us in terms of war and peace, friends and foes, or personal fear and national security. We did not know the current or future price in terms of human life or financial costs. With each passing day, month, and year, we gain insight into the impact and influence of 9/11 upon our cultural, social, and political life. Some influences are major and obvious, while others are subtle.

This collection of essays examines the language, symbols, and media of 9/11. Each chapter focuses on one or more elements of communication while investigating a wide range of topics from the media's portrayal and dilemmas of coverage to advertising and public relations strategies; from the use of humor and the role of sports in our healing process to the impact of the Patriot Act upon public discourse; from the use of religious sacred symbols to the meaning of patriotism as part of the political socialization of young adults. Although loosely arranged by the broad topic areas, each chapter addresses one or more aspects of language, symbols, and media of 9/11.

Ronald Lee and Matthew Barton analyze the challenge to religious pluralism in the aftermath of the attacks of 9/11. They explain the grounds for the immediate backlash against Islam and the relationship between civil religion and rituals of pluralism. Finally, they explore the ceremonies, speeches, and media coverage that enacted a ritualistic recommitment to American religious pluralism with several conclusions about the usefulness of ritual as a way of understanding American political culture.

For Wat Hopkins, free speech is not simply a convenience or even a right of citizens in our society. It is a mandate, essential to the proper working of our democratic republic. Hopkins reviews several crucial historical and contemporary Supreme Court rulings relevant to the limitations of free speech in times of war and national crises. In essence, citizen critics of governmental policies and actions should be encouraged, especially in times of national stress.

Now after more than two years since the passage of the Patriot Act, it remains suspect, controversial, and many provisions challenged in federal courts. Craig R. Smith puts the measures of the Patriot Act into historical context by comparing the legislation and its interpretation of it to other legislation passed in response to past American crises. His analysis provides insight into the roles played by our branches of government, the impact upon the First Amendment as well as other rights such as consulting with an attorney and to confront one's accusers.

After the attacks of 9/11, Roger Rosenblatt in *Time* magazine suggested that perhaps we witnessed an end to "the age of irony" and called for shift in the formation of American values. He called for a return to "traditional values" and a rejection of the "banality of popular culture." Daniel J. O'Rourke III and Pravin Rodrigues explores Rosenblatt's call for the rejection of irony and the ironic response of the weekly newspaper the *Onion* as counterpoints in a debate about the impact of irony as a rhetorical device in American culture.

Robert Brown looks at the role of sport in the post-9/11 healing process in America. After examining the role of sport during national crises, he focuses on the influence of the World Series and Super Bowl following the attacks in 2001. Brown finds that in times of crisis, sport can provide solemn opportunities to mourn the dead, patriotic messages to inspire, salutes to honor the life-saving efforts of those involved, and to reinforce a sense of unity. The two sporting events examined provided messages of healing and inspiration for many Americans.

Edward Horowitz and Johan Wanstrom examine the reactions and responses of young adults to the events of 9/11 on its one-year anniversary. Through their empirical study, they found emotions of fearfulness, sadness, suspicion, and anger among young adults. In addition, those who were more likely to display a flag were more religious, paid more attention to news coverage, engaged in more discussion with parents and friends about the attacks and the war on terror and, finally, expressed more dimensions of patriotism.

John Llewellyn investigates how both New York Mayor Rudolph Giuliani and California Congressman Gary Condit both benefited from the shift in pubic attitudes and attention resulting from the attacks of 9/11. Utilizing the theoretical concepts of agenda-setting and media framing, Llewellyn demonstrates how Giuliani and Condit received a public "makeover" or reframing of careers and reputations.

Katherine Kinnick finds substantive, stylistic, and situational characteristics of post-9/11 advertising functioning as a rhetorical genre. Using an overwhelming appeal to patriotism, national ads included expressions of grief, sympathy, and goodwill; images and language evoking American cultural values and icons; and preference for large display ads.

Virtually every business and industry was impacted by the attacks of 9/11. Perhaps none were hurt more than the tourism industry. Utilizing situational theory of publics and the relationship management perspective, Lisa Hall examines how messages were redesigned and primary publics refocused as well as communication tactics utilized by convention and visitors bureau managers. In general, she found less reliance upon traditional advertising and more on Internet and Public Relations media tactics. More specifically, communication tactics should encourage relationship-building opportunities among target audiences.

At the philosophical heart of the freedoms of the press is the notion of the "Marketplace of Ideas," in which it is assumed that a robust and unrestrained dialogue on significant issues is essential to public policy formation. Of course, the media has an important role in this process. At no time is this role more important than during war or social upheaval. Bruce Drushel examines several instances of media self-censorship following the attacks of 9/11. He also discusses the impact of self-censorship as it relates to the First Amendment and the implications for the policymaking process during times of crisis. Drushel concludes with an argument for greater regulation of the marketplace of ideas to ensure the representation of unpopular points of view.

Editing a volume can be a challenge, for many reasons. However, I find the collaboration with colleagues focusing on a single topic or an area of common interest rewarding and informative. This collection of essays began as a panel program at the National Communication Association in November 2002. Other colleagues investigating the impact and lessons of the attacks of 9/11 were invited to join the project. I enjoyed the process of discussing chapter ideas with such wonderful colleagues and learn from their insights and analyses. Thankfully, the contributors made this a rewarding and enjoyable endeavor. I genuinely appreciate their participation in this volume and their insightful contributions. But more importantly, I value their friendship.

I wish to thank my colleagues in the Department of Communication at Virginia Tech. A faculty committed to scholarship productivity provides encouragement, even for an "older" colleague with administrative responsibilities. I also want to thank Jerry Niles, Dean of the College of Liberal Arts and Human Sciences; Richard Sorensen, Dean of the Pamplin College of Business; and Major General (retired) Jerrold Allen, Commandant of the Corps of Cadets for their continued support of administrative, professional, and scholarly activities. For more than fifteen years, they have understood the importance of the right "mix" that makes my job a privilege and pleasure. They have supported me professionally, financially, and personally. I am very fortunate to work for such outstanding administrators who continue to serve as role models in every way.

Finally, I wish to thank members of my family who tolerate the long hours in the endeavors of teaching, research, and outreach. They sustain me, encourage me, and provide a sense of belonging and security that frees me to read, write, and pursue projects of interest. Rachel, Bobby, and Chris provide the joys of my life well beyond academe.

This book is dedicated to those who lost their lives on 9/11, to those who gave their lives in America's war against terrorism and to those who continue serve to make the world a safer place for us all.

References

Applebaum, A. 2002. "The New World Order." In *Our Brave New World*, edited by Wladyslaw Pleszczynski, 1-20. Stanford, CA: Stanford University Press.
Hoffman, B. 2002. *Lessons of 9/11*. Santa Monica, CA: Rand Corporation.

1

The Language, Symbols, and Media of 9/11: An Introduction

Robert E. Denton, Jr.

On that bright, clear, and fateful day of September 11, 2001, nineteen Saudis and al-Qaida operatives, wielding knives and box-cutters, hijacked four American aircraft. At 8:45 A.M. American Airlines Flight 11 departed Boston, Massachusetts in route to Los Angeles, California crashed into the North Tower of the World Trade Center with eighty-one passengers and eleven crewmembers on board. Just eighteen minutes later, United Airlines Flight 175, also in route from Boston to Los Angeles, with fifty-six passengers and nine crewmembers hit the South Tower. At nearly 9:30 A.M., another flight headed toward Los Angeles, American Airlines Flight 77, departed Dulles International Airport with fifty-eight passengers and six crew members and crashed into the Northwest side of the Pentagon. Thirty minutes later, United Airlines Flight 93 departed Newark, New Jersey, this time in route to San Francisco, California with thirty-eight passengers and seven crewmembers. The flight crashed in a field in Pennsylvania resulting from a struggle between the hijackers and brave passengers. Many speculate the target of this flight was the U.S. Capital or even perhaps the White House.

The attacks upon America on September 11, 2001 are being characterized as this generation's Pearl Harbor. The comparison is powerful. Especially since the fiftieth anniversary of D-Day, there is a plethora of books and films commemorating the heroics of those who fought with courage, commitment, and sacrifice during World War II. In the words of Tom Brokaw (1998), they stayed true to the values "of personal responsibility, duty, honor, and faith" (XX). Quite

1

simply, as he proclaims in his best selling book, they are the "greatest generation any society has produced" (XXX). The surprise attack upon our forces on the morning of December 7, 1941, characterized by President Roosevelt as "a day that will live in infamy," changed the course of history and the lives of a generation of Americans. It took three hours before news reached the mainland of the bombs dropping on Pearl Harbor and more than a week before the *New York Times* carried the first pictures (Nacos, 39). The surprise, horror and magnitude of the attack forced America into a four-year war far away from the shores of the homeland.

For most Americans and many others around the globe, life was suspended on September 11, 2001. The perpetrators gained our attention and that of the world. They took control of our public agenda and even our private lives. Fighter jets flew over major cities; Air Force One flew evasive patterns throughout the day and the Secret Service kept Vice President Cheney in virtual hiding.

On the evening of September 11, 2001, President George W. Bush (2001) acknowledged that "Today, our nation saw evil, the very worst of human nature" (738). Nine days later before a joint session of Congress, President Bush (2001) proclaimed

> on September the eleventh, enemies of freedom committed an act of war against our country. Americans have known wars—but for the past 136 years, they have been wars on foreign soil, except for one Sunday in 1941. Americans have known the casualties of war—but not at the center of a great city on a peaceful morning. Americans have known surprise attacks—but never before on thousands of civilians. All of this was brought upon us in a single day—and night fell on a different world, a world where freedom itself is under attack. (760)

We were "at war." President Bush announced that "our war on terror begins with al-Qaida, but it does not end there. It will not end until every terrorist group of global reach has been found, stopped, and defeated" (761).

Not since the assassination of President John Kennedy did so many Americans and others around the world stayed glued to their television sets. For the first five days after the terrorist attack, television and radio networks covered the aftermath around the clock. All four of the major networks (i.e., ABC, CBS, FOX, and NBC) suspended regular programming and provided ninety hours of "wall-to-wall" coverage, exceeding the amount devoted to President Kennedy's assassination in 1962 and the first Iraq war in 1991 (Glass 2002, 4). We followed the horror and minute-by-minute destruction of the

World Trade Center buildings, people jumping to their deaths and running for their lives, the flames engulfing the Pentagon, and the Pittsburgh crash site of United Flight 93. The wall-to-wall coverage of events by the networks closely followed President Bush's war rhetoric. The various networks competed for known celebrity talking heads. Within hours they were calling the attack "America's New War," "War on Terror," and "War Against Terror," to name just a few.

All the subsequent "war talk" by President Bush and members of his administration set the serious tone of the actions and form of our response. Forget the fact that only Congress has the constitutional power to declare war and that war is traditionally waged between states. The word—taken either literally or metaphorically—provided President Bush several advantages. In times of war, the public places more trust in elected officials. The idea of a nation under attack buys a level of goodwill for presidents that they otherwise would not enjoy. Presidents also become more protected from political infighting and personal attacks. Criticism by members of the opposing political party is usually silenced; we easily and mistakenly jump to the conclusion that it is unpatriotic to challenge the wisdom of political or military operations against a foreign foe. And citizens are asked to make personal sacrifices, which, after September 11, meant the inconvenience of tighter security and new restrictions on some civil liberties.

To be "at war" demands some form of action. At home, President Bush's early pronouncements acknowledged our shock, anger, and promise of justice. Abroad, his war rhetoric generated cause for concern. French President Jacques Chirac, while visiting the White House just a week after the attacks to show solidarity with America, stated, "I don't know whether we should use the word 'war,' but I would say that now we are faced with a conflict of a completely new nature" (Herbert 2001, E-1).

Bush's early use of the word "crusade" to describe the fight against terrorism caused alarm among those in the Islamic world. For them, the term evoked images of Christian soldiers battling against Islam during medieval times. The White House even apologized for the word insisting that Bush intended the word to mean only "a broad cause." The name the military chose for its anti-terrorism campaign was changed from "Infinite Justice" to "Enduring Freedom" because the former offended Muslim allies. To Muslims, only God can provide infinite justice (Herbert 2001, E-1).

The news media was also dealing with language issues. Should the attackers be described as "terrorists" or "freedom fighters?" There was even a debate within newsrooms across the nation whether or not anchors and reporters should wear flag pins or ribbons. Reuters news service instructed reporters to preface any descriptions of attackers with "so-called" (Irvine and Kincaid 2001). The major networks, except Fox News, decided that anchors should not wear flags or ribbons. After all, the news media are supposed to be "neutral," "objective," "non-biased" in perspective. The dilemma was real for the press. Did their patriotic duties override their more professional duties? Especially in a time of crisis?

The human and financial costs were real as well. The consequences and impact are with us today and will be so for years to come. The immediate loss was over 3,000 lives, many more thousand families impacted by lost mothers, fathers, brothers, sisters, aunts, and uncles. From an economic perspective, billions were lost in the stock market, in company revenues, in retail sales, in insurance liability, and in tax intakes by state and federal authorities. Billions more required in clean-up costs, security and defense measures, supporting select industries and to stimulate the economy.

This volume examines the language, symbols and media of 9/11. Each chapter focuses on one or more elements of communication while investigating a wide range of topics from ranging from the use of humor and the role of sports in our healing process to the impact of the Patriot Act upon public discourse; from the use of religious sacred symbols to the meaning of patriotism as part of the political socialization of young adults; from the media's portrayal and dilemmas of coverage to advertising and public relations strategies post-9/11. Although loosely arranged by the broad topic areas, each chapter addresses one or more aspects of language, symbols, and media of 9/11.

Human communication is the vehicle for political and social thought, debate, and action. Language serves as the agent of social integration; as the means of cultural socialization; as the vehicle for social interaction; as the channel for the transmission of values; and as the glue that bond people, ideas, and society together. Language, therefore, is a very active and creative process that does not reflect an objective reality but creates a reality by organizing meaningful perceptions abstracted from a complex world. Language becomes a mediating force that actively shapes one's interpretation of the environment.

Terrorism as Communication

Interestingly, more than two decades ago, Alex Schmid and Janny deGraaf (1982) argued simply that terrorists' acts of violence are really acts of communication. In effect, terrorists' acts should be viewed as "violent language" (1). "Without communication there can be no terrorism" (9). For them, the genuine power of terrorism is that it functions as propaganda. The result is behavior modification of the target audience by both coercive and persuasive means. In effect, terrorism uses violence against one to obtain an effect upon others. The immediate victim(s) is/are merely an instrument or tool of communication. For terrorists, message matters, not the victim(s) (14). Thus, in essence, "terrorism can best be understood as a violent communication strategy. There is a sender, the terrorist, a message generator, the victim, and a receiver, the enemy and/or the public" (15). In the words of an ancient Chinese proverb, "Kill one, frighten ten thousand." In addition to communicating messages of fear to the mass audience, terrorists also may polarize public opinion, make converts, mislead the enemy by spreading false information, win publicity, advertise causes and movement, and discredit victim(s), to name just a few.

The Language and Symbols of 9/11

I have already noted the power of language to influence our perceptions and subsequent behavior. The president, of course, has the special power of definition, defining and labeling an act, providing context for interpretation. Key phrases or symbols evoked by a president have two primary effects. Key audiences begin to use the term or characterization as well as evoke ancillary symbols and images. Key phrases or symbols also create expectations of action, solutions, and visions of the future.

The war metaphor that came to frame the attacks was most powerful. The war metaphor defines the objective and encourages enlistment in the effort, it identifies the enemy, and it dictates the choice of weapons and tactics with which the struggle will be fought (Zarefsky 1986, 29). There are additional assumptions and implications with the act of rhetorically evoking the war metaphor. For us, most wars are unconditional in terms of mounting all means necessary, as much time as required to be victorious, as much funds as necessary to complete the task. The metaphor and label requires a lower standard of burden of proof for action or to establish guilt. Finally, the metaphor suppresses opposition to subsequent actions or response. Ironically, to declare war is to unify the nation in a sense of purpose, commitment and sacrifice.

Is terrorism a form of war? Most scholars say no. War, especially a "just war," "is conducted between armies who recognize the legitimacy of targeting their uniformed enemies, but endeavor to limit violence against civilians and, more generally, to keep their use for force proportionate to the ends in question" (Carruthers 2000, 163). In contrast, terrorism utilizes "extra-normal" violence, most often in peacetime with no regard to civilians or conventional targets. Reprehensible forms of violence designed as much to gain publicity as to rectifying ideological or political grievances.

Throughout the ordeal, key words and phrases were formulated and took on special meaning. For example, saying 9/11 (and not 911) is sufficient to refer to the attacks. Law enforcement officers and firefighters became heroes. Not since the Cold War have we confronted an "evil empire." We soon learned of the dangers pending from the "axis of evil" compromised of Iran, Iraq and North Korea. We discovered the range of devices comprising "weapons of mass destruction." Three years later, the letters "WMD" suffices.

Of course, the very label "terrorist" implies negative judgment. The term has been attached to "enemies" since the French Revolution (Carruthers 2000, 163). The label has become more common since World War II. The semantic battle over the term has ideological and political implications. As the cliché goes, "one man's terrorist is another man's freedom fighter." Historically, the American government has been rather quick to label "leftist guerrillas" as terrorists while labeling "right-wing" U.S. supported mercenaries as "rebels (Carruthers 2000, 165).

It was the Reagan administration that initiated the first "war against terrorism" in the wake of the TWA hijacking and within the shadows of Carter's "Iran hostage situation." They framed terrorism as a threat to international security thus replacing Carter's "human rights" concerns at the heart of American foreign policy. At the time, some American media commentators suggested that "terrorists" replaced "communists" as our number one enemy. Susan Carruthers (2000) argues that by elevating terrorism as a concern, the Reagan Administration was well served by the U.S. media. The mainstream media duplicated our own partial view of labeling specific acts and countries as terrorists; in doing so, provided some cover for our own actions in such countries as Nicaragua and Angola, to name just a few; and through its reporting, actually built consensus for counter-terrorism measures (193). As a result, the Reagan administration enjoyed widespread support for the 1986 bombing of Tripoli and other actions directed at Libya's Colonel Gaddafi.

The attacks of 9/11 targeted some of the primary symbols of America's strength, power, and world status. The World Trade Center stood as the symbol of our financial wealth and enterprise. The Pentagon is the center of America's military power and the suspected target of the White House stands as the symbol of the world's political power. The attacks brought down the symbol of *our* financial wealth, seriously damaged the home of *our* military fortress, and caused the evacuation of the center of *our* political power.

The American flag became the primary symbol of unity, commitment, determination, and our values of democracy and freedom. Immediately following 9/11, consumer demand for flag-themed merchandise sky-rocketed. Now three years later, demand is still very strong. Traditionally, flag displays and themed items are in use primarily between Memorial Day through Labor Day. However, upon the events of 9/11, demand became year round. Almost any item now sports the flag in one way or another: pens, pencils, calculators, Christmas tree ornaments, towels, birdhouses, dinnerware, home furnishings, you just name it. Virtually any kind of clothing for every season sports the flag. Jeffrey Bergus, corporate product development director for Arizona Jean Company, observes, "Patriotism has turned into a lifestyle since 9/11. A trend is a trend, but a lifestyle stays around for a long time" (*Roanoke Times* 2003, A11).

We make sense of events by the use of narratives. Narrative metaphors and images help us understand the social and political worlds in which we live. They also can sanction some kinds of actions and not others. Narratives are explanations for events in the form of short, commonsense accounts or stories. They contain images and judgments about the motives and actions of our own groups and those of others. Groups with very different beliefs and values construct very different narratives of an event. They are grounded in selectively remembered and interpreted experiences. Within a community, a narrative may emerge and gain easy consensus. Finally, narratives provide a sense of community and connectedness.

As already mentioned, to portray the attacks as analogous to the "sneak attack" at Pearl Harbor justified a military response, punishment for those responsible and actions to prevent future attacks. Compare this view to one that America now knows what it is like to live in physical terror, as with the Palestinians, Iraqis, and others in the Middle East who have done so for years. From this perspective, America has ignored the Arab world, abandoned the region after Gulf War I and provided virtually unconditional support for Israel. The contrasting views between Americans and Muslims in general is best expressed by the statements issued on the day the Afghanistan war started, October 7, 2001. President George Bush referred to the "sudden terror" that had descended on the United States just twenty-seven days earlier. Osama bin Laden asserted that the Muslim world had experienced more than eighty years of "humiliation and disgrace" at the hands of Americans. In the two and a half weeks following the attacks, the major television networks and NPR broadcast thirty-three stories that addressed the question, "why do they hate us?" (Nacos 2002, 45). The first narrative encourages a strong, military response and images of justice. The second views the attacks as a wake-up call for America and our role in the Arab world. This rationale would argue America should not seek revenge, but greater understanding and attention to the plight of Arabs.

Another narrative emerged viewing America as the "great Satan." We represent "the West," the epitome of global exploitation and injustice. We need to recognize our historical capitalist exploitation of the World, being destructive to cultures and environments. Our capitalistic system contributes to the growing gap between the rich and poor. Our ever-increasing demand for the world's natural resources endangers the environment for all nations. In effect, the terrorists may be bad, but we are worse. America is the original sinner who keeps thugs in power, consumes far more than its share of the world's resources, and spreads a culture of drugs, sex, and egoism.

One of the more controversial narratives that emerged viewed the attacks on America as punishment for our own greed, pride, arrogance, and continual decay of morals and values. This view was best expressed by Jerry Falwell: "I really believe that the pagans, and the abortionists, and the feminists, and the gays and the lesbians who are actively trying to make that an alternative lifestyle, the ACLU, People For the American Way, all of them who have tried to secularize America. I point the finger in their face and say 'you helped this happen.'" He concluded that we had created an environment "which possibly has caused God to lift the veil of protection which has allowed no one to attack America on our soil since 1812" (CNN, 2001).

Finally, another major narrative that emerged was the view that as individuals or members of the world community, you were either "with us or against us." In Bush's speech on September 20, 2001, to the Joint Session of Congress with British Prime Minister Tony Blair in the audience, he proclaimed "Every nation in every region now has a decision to make: either you are with us or you are with terrorists" (761). Within our boarders, it was difficult to challenge a military response without appearing as unpatriotic.

The various narratives that emerged in the aftermath of 9/11 provide collective understanding of what happened, why it happened, who we are and where we are going. They provide a context for the attacks and justification for response. The attacks became part of a larger allegory, a tale of good versus evil, order versus chaos.

The Media of 9/11

Because the United States is the most media-saturated nation, Schmid and deGraaf (1982) predicted that we are "the country most open to terrorist use of the media" (33). In a more recent study, Brigitte Nacos (2002) explores the notion of "mass-mediated terrorism" where the media become instruments of terror. Mass violence becomes a political statement and the media images of violence evoke terror among the general public. "Groups and individuals who commit or simply threaten political violence understand their deeds as a means to win media attention and news coverage for their actions, their grievances, and their political ends" (10). From this perspective, "when terrorists hurl a rocket into Great Britain's foreign spy headquarters, bomb the hull of the USS Cole, hold hostages in a remote part of the Philippines, or hijack an Indian airliner, they do not simply commit violence—they execute premeditated terrorism that virtually assures a great deal of news coverage" (10). The visuals of media coverage spread fear and anxiety in their targeted societies.

On 9/11 and days following, the televised pictures and news photography served the purpose to bear witness to the horror, magnitude, and destruction of the attacks. Millions of Americans saw the first plane hit the World Trade Center, millions more the second plane. Who will ever forget the image of the plane almost gracefully turning toward the towers, crashing into the building and exploding in a fireball. We witnessed the metamorphosis of a commercial plane into a weapon of mass destruction. Then the frantic looks on the faces and voices of those running for safety while firefighters and police ran toward the towers. Who will soon forget the moment the buildings fell, the thick dust covering everything for miles and miles. At the same time, we witnessed the dark smoke rising from the Pentagon while workers were helping those injured on the ground. In the aftermath, our hearts were with the firefighters raising a flag at "ground zero," searching the rubble, and standing still with head bowed and hat removed as each fallen comrade was removed.

On that fateful day, Richard Drew, on assignment for AP shooting a maternity fashion show was drawn to the twin towers soon after they were engulfed in flames. Soon upon arrival, he heard people on the ground gasping because people in the Towers were jumping. Drew started shooting pictures; his camera found a falling body and followed it for a twelve-shot sequence. The unidentified body was traveling 150 miles per hour. The next morning one shot appeared on page seven of the *New York Times*, then hundreds of newspapers all around the world.

In the photograph, the man

> appears relaxed, hurling through the air. He appears comfortable in the grip of unimaginable motion. . .His arms are by his side, only slightly outriggered. His left leg is bent at the knee, almost casually. His white shirt, or jacket, or frock, is billowing free of his black pants. His black high-tops are still on his feet. . . The man is perfectly vertical, and so in accord with the lines of the buildings behind him. He splits them, bisects them: Everything to the left of him in the picture is the North Tower; everything to the right, the South. . . There is something almost rebellious in the man's posture, as though once faced with the inevitability of death, he decided to get on with it; as though he were a missile, a spear, bent on attaining his own end. (Junod 2003, 177)

The photo became known as "the Falling Man." In most American papers, the photograph ran just once and never again. Public reaction was quick to criticize the exploitation of a man's death, invasion of his privacy, turning a tragedy into "pornographic voyeurism."

It appears that of all the images of 9/11, those of people jumping were the ones that became "taboo." At CNN, for example, such footage was shown live, then after intense discussions within the newsroom, it was shown only if the people were blurred and unidentifiable. Within hours, no such footage was aired. The same was true for the other networks. Even archival footages of "the jumpers" were cut years later from several documentaries (Junod 2003, 180).

In actuality, officials estimate that more than 200 people jumped on that fateful day. People began jumping soon after the first plane hit the North Tower and continued for nearly two hours until both buildings fully collapsed. They jumped from all sides, in a continual stream, some with tablecloths and other fabrics as makeshift parachutes, but to no avail. Witnesses still report having nightmares. The images and the sounds of "the jumpers" they cannot get out of their head. "Those tumbling through the air remained, by all accounts, eerily silent; those on the ground screamed" (Junod 2003, 179).

Newspapers displayed a higher percentage of photos than normal for well over a month after the attacks. The attacks produced more pictures, bigger pictures, and more prominent pictures. In the first days of the attack, photos primarily focused on the sites of the attacks. Later, the focus was on the people and families of the victims. According to Barbie Zelizer (2002, 55), the post-9/11 photography functioned to ease the dissonance caused by the public trauma of the attacks and facilitate the accomplishment of certain military and political strategic ends, in effect helping to mobilize support for war against Afghanistan.

During this crisis, for the first time, millions, even billions of people across the world could access and exchange information in real time utilizing the Internet. Even today, our "War on Terrorism" is the world's first war in the Internet age. It raises additional issues of security, access to sensitive information and international coordination of attacks, not to mention basic outlets for propaganda and misinformation.

For a week following the 9/11 attacks, nearly 12 million Americans visited online news sites daily (Glass 2002, 3). For example, during the week following the attacks, unique visitors to CNN's web site increased 23 percent and MSNBC's site 20 percent. The television networks all experienced over 6 percent increase (Glass 2002, 4).

Fifteen percent of Internet users sent email messages to family members on 9/11, 36 percent sought news online in the aftermath of the attacks. Within the first forty-eight hours of the crisis, 13 percent of Internet users joined "virtual meetings" or participated in chat rooms or discussion groups. At the very least, the Internet played a supplemental role for individuals via the use of email, instant messaging and as a source of news (Glass 2002, 5).

We know that visual images are language. As J. Hartley (1992) observes, "No picture is pure image; all of them, still and moving, graphic and photographic, are 'talking pictures,' either literally, or in association with contextual speech, writing or discourse. Pictures are social, visual, spatial, and sometimes communicative" (28).

War is now engaged in the "media age." There is instant and live access to battlefields, to the views of friends and foes alike. With experts galore, instant predictions, opinions and criticisms abound.

We have witnessed a subtle but very important evolution of media coverage, not only in times of national crises but also in times of war. The White House becomes a full partner in providing and controlling access to officials, to critical sites, and to battlefields. The Bush administration worked in harmony with the military in developing a strategy of media access and control during and after 9/11, followed by the Afghanistan invasion and the imbedding of members of the press with military units during the assault on Iraq. For some, the "cozy" relationships among the administration, the press and the military resulted in unparallel access and coverage. For others, the relationships resulted in bias reporting sympathetic to the military and administration views, operations and policies. The classic "watchdog" function of the press providing a balance against the government transformed to the "lapdog" function relying so heavily on the official sources for information and access, the media actually served to promote the interests and policy positions of both the current administration and the military. At the very least, the long running feud between the military and the press was abated, at least for the current conflict in Iraq.

Susan Carruthers (2000) articulates well the dilemma for war correspondents. "The war zone may jolt correspondents into an awareness that they themselves are a part of the proceedings and thus can never satisfactorily be apart from them in the manner 'objective journalism' prescribes" (272). She notes an irony in today's coverage of war and tragedies. "It appears that states and reporters alike over the course of the twentieth century inclined to show less, even as technology permitted more accurate imagistic capturing of moving subjects in motion. Ironically, perhaps, the nineteenth-century dawn of the photographic age exposed American civilians to unflinching portraits of the Civil War dead—immobile corpses forming the best subjects for early battlefield photography—of a starkness rarely encountered now (certainly not during one of 'our wars')" (277).

Conclusion

At the time and even more pronounced now, the attacks on the World Trade Center and the Pentagon mark the end of one era in our history and the start of another. Our way of life changed that day in so many ways; guns at airports, greater latitude of government surveillance activities, and the second Iraq war, to name just a few. We find ourselves, as Michael Hoyt (2001) observed, "in a part of the world we barely understand where every action has an unknown and potentially deadly reaction. At a balancing point between a new engagement with the world or a new xenophobia, between a new appreciation of our freedoms and a willingness to trade some of them away for security, between blind vengeance and calculated justice. And with unknown numbers of terrorists out to kill us" (5).

Nearly three years since the attacks of 9/11, Americans still feel an intense patriotism. Seventy percent say they are "extremely proud" to be Americans, up from 55 percent on the fourth of July 2001. Sixty percent of Americans think that the U.S. Constitution has a great deal of impact on their lives. Fifty-five percent think Americans are more patriotic than they were twenty-five years ago (*Roanoke Times* 2003, A7).

Terrorism is virtually a way of life for some nations and religious sects. Terrorist motivations are intense, emotional, religious, historical and cultural. Our dilemma is obvious. We value religious tolerance, but Islamic extremists reject it and embrace violence. To complicate matters more, there is no single "type" of terrorist. Unlike the Cold War managing deterrence between two major powers, terrorism involves many groups, not just nations.

What makes al Qaeda difficult is that the organization is not a single entity, it is a system comprised of many leaders, "soldiers," facilitators, and supporting population segments. Thus, there is no organizational center whose destruction would bring down the organization.

Also, to endure a long, consistent, sustained effort for a war on terrorism must be similar to our decades long Cold War. It will involve targeting multiple nations and using a variety of economic and military strategies (Davis and Jenkins 2002, xiv). It will also cost hundreds of billions of dollars. Paul Davis and Brian Jenkins (2002, 39-58) suggest deterrence by threatening anyone who even tolerates WMD-related terrorism, "political warfare" (use of information and propaganda campaigns), and putting at risk what the terrorists hold dear.

Such strategies and tactics raise many troubling issues for America. As we witnessed in the more recent Iraq war, we must now use preemptive force when threaten with weapons of mass destruction. For our national security, we may well be forced to lower standards of evidence in ascribing guilt and may violate international sovereignty. We are forced to work with nations lacking our qualities of democracy and freedom. We are forced to change our own laws restricting or impacting individual freedoms.

Unfortunately, to deal with terrorism, it appears that our best options revolve around increasing levels of violence. In the past, deterrence by persuasion and threat were effective. Now it appears our options, in increasing order of violence, include deter by defeating/ preventing attacks, by punishing rogue nations with various sanctions, and by defeating such nations, even with preemptive military actions.

Bruce Hoffman (2002) argues that we should first recognize that terrorism is, always has been and will be "instrumental:" that is, planned, purposeful and premeditated. Second, we need to recognize that terrorism is fundamentally a form of psychological warfare. Terrorism is designed to instill fear, intimidation and undermine confidence in the target government. Third, all democratic countries that value freedom and civil liberties will remain most vulnerable to terrorism. Fourth, the hatred and negative feelings toward the United States throughout the world are not likely to diminish any time soon. We have become to the enemy to new generation of terrorists. Finally, terrorism is a perennial, ceaseless struggle, although a somewhat new direct threat to our nation. For him, the struggle is likely to be never-ending (25-26).

The following essays are diverse by topic but all share a communication perspective or focus. Within each essay, issues of language, symbols and media are addressed. Much has already been written about the causes and impact of 9/11 upon American life. Much more will be written in the future as we attempt to understand the triggering event that sparked our "war on terror," new concerns about national security, and the realignment of international allies. With the benefit of limited hindsight, this collection provides additional views and perspectives of the role of communication and understanding of the attacks of 9/11.

References

Brokaw, Tom. 1998. *The Greatest Generation*. New York: Random House.

Bush, George W. 2001a. "Address by George W. Bush, President of the United States Delivered to the Nation, Washington, D.C., September 11, 2001." *Vital Speeches of the Day* LXVII:738-739.

_____. 2001b. "Address by George W. Bush, President of the United States Delivered to a Joint Session of Congress and the American People, Washington, D.C., September 20, 2001." *Vital Speeches of the Day* LXVII:760-763.

Carruthers, Susan. 2000. *The Media at War.* New York: St. Martin's Press.

CNN.Com. 2001. Falwell apologizes to gays, feminists, lesbians. September 14. Retrieved July 11, 2003, from *http://www.cnn.com/201/US/09/14/Falwell.apology*

Davis, Paul and Brian Jenkins. 2002. *Deterrence & Influence in Counterterrorism*. Santa Monica, CA: Rand Corporation.

Glass, Andrew. 2002. The war on terrorism goes online (Working Paper Series #2002-3). Cambridge, MA: Shorenstein Center on the Press, Politics and Public Policy.

Hartley, J. 1992. *The Politics of Pictures: The Creation of the Public in the Age of Popular Media*. New York: Routledge.

Herbert, James. 2001. Reigning words: Leaders, media can cause a storm of debate in the labels they use. *San Diego Union-Tribune*, October 4.

Hoffman, Bruce. 2002. *Lessons of 9/11*. Santa Monica, CA: Rand Corporation.

Hoyt, Michael. 2001. Journalists as patriots. *Columbia Journalism Review*, Nov/Dec: 4-5.

Irvine, Reed and Cliff Kincaid. 2001. Is Reuters Kowtowing to Terrorists? *Accuracy in Media*, November 22, retrieved July 13, 2003 from *http://www.aim.org*.

Junod, Tom. 2003. The falling man. *Esquire*. September, 177-81, 198-99. Nacos, Brigitte, L. 2002. *Mass-Mediated Terrorism*. Lanham, MD: Rowman & Littlefield.

Roanoke Times. 2003a. Patriotic-themed merchandise remain popular. July 4.

Roanoke Times. 2003b. Polls say intense feelings of patriotism still persist. July 4.

Schmid, Alex and Janny deGraaf. 1982. *Violence as Communication*. Beverly Hills, CA: Sage.

Zarefsky, David. 1986. *President Johnson's War on Poverty*. University: University of Alabama Press.

Zelizer, Barbie. 2002. "Photography, journalism and trauma." In *Journalism after September 11*, edited by Barbie Zelizer and Stuart Allen, 48-68. New York: Routledge.

2

September 11, 2001 and the Rituals of Religious Pluralism

Ronald Lee and Matthew Barton

On the morning of September 11, 2001, nineteen men hijacked four airliners departing from American airports. They crashed two of the planes into the north and south towers of the World Trade Center; a third into the Pentagon; and a fourth in rural Somerset County, Pennsylvania, southeast of Pittsburgh. In all, the attacks claimed 3,062 lives.

Of the nineteen hijackers, fifteen were from Saudi Arabia, two were from the United Arab Republic, one was from Egypt, and one was from Lebanon. All were Muslim. The men were identified as part of the al-Qaeda terrorist network. The network's leader, Osama bin Laden, had issued a *fatwa* on February 23, 1998 calling for Muslims to "kill the Americans and plunder their money wherever and whenever they find it" (Bin-Laden et al., 1998).[1]

This *fatwa* has two recognizable parts: the first is a list of American "crimes and sins" and the second defines the Muslim religious duty, given these particulars. Bin Laden organizes the "crimes and sins" around "three facts known to everyone." First, he claims that the United States "has been occupying the lands of Islam in the holiest of places, the Arabian Peninsula." Second, he argues that "despite the great devastation inflicted on the Iraqi people . . . and despite the huge number of those killed, in excess of 1 million," the Americans "are once again trying to repeat the horrific massacres." Third, he asserts that the American aim is "to serve the Jews' petty state" and, thus, "divert attention from its occupation of Jerusalem" and the "murder of Muslims." The text characterizes American transgressions in religious terms. They are "sins." They constitute "sins" because Americans have occupied the "holiest" of Islamic places; they have entered into military activity that has killed "Muslims"; and they have done the work of the "Jews."

In the *fatwa's* second part, bin Laden explains the Muslim obligation in the face of such an affront to the faith. "In accordance with the words of Almighty God," he writes, "'fight [the pagans] until there is no more tumult or oppression, and there prevail justice and faith in God.'" According to the sacred word, those who do not respond to God's call will be punished and those who carry out God's command shall be rewarded in heaven.

> O ye who believe, what is the matter with you, that when ye are asked to go forth in the cause of God, ye cling so heavily to earth! Do ye prefer the life of this world to the hereafter? But little is the comfort of this life as compared with the hereafter. Unless ye go forth, He will punish you with a grievous penalty, and put others in your place; but Him ye would not harm in the least. For God hath power over all things.

The religious language of the *fatwa* is repeated in two other al-Qaeda documents. In the recovered luggage of Mohamed Atta, the final instructions to the hijackers were found. The text "deploys familiar and evocative Quranic terminology to construct al Qaeda's chosen adversary not in terms of national, racial, or political alterity, but as people to whom one is opposed on strictly religious grounds. They are infidels, nonbelievers, and allies of Satan, while the text construes its readers and authors as believers, the faithful, allies of God, and God's faithful servants" (Lincoln 2003, 13).

Following President Bush's October 7, 2001 national address commencing Operation Enduring Freedom, al-Qaeda released a videotaped message. On the tape, Osama bin Laden calls President Bush the "the head of international infidels" and the United States "the modern world's symbol of paganism." He says that Americans are "killers who toyed with the blood, honor and sanctities of Muslims" (Lincoln 2003, 22).

The attacks on Anglo-European imperialism have all been heard before. What is distinctive in these texts is the absence of references to modern nationhood. Bin Laden neither constitutes Americans as citizens nor Muslims as national subjects. The clash is not nation versus nation but between the faithful and the infidel, the believer and the pagan, and the people of God and the allies of Satan. Americans, as progeny of the Enlightenment, founded a secular state with a proscribed role for religion. Over two centuries, Americans have developed a refined pluralist sensibility in matters religious. Religious discourse may be brought into the public square, but in a form that forgoes its absolutist character. It may come as a set of reasons, among many others, for moral action (Hart 1977; Kennedy 1983; Neuhaus 1984).

Yet, what Bruce Lincoln (2003) has termed the "minimalist" religious tradition is just what bin Laden finds so offensive. The al-Qaeda network "understands and constructs itself as simultaneously the militant vanguard and the most faithful fragment of an international religious community." As such, "the goal it articulates is the restoration of Islam in a *maximalist* [our emphasis] form and its consequent triumph over its internal and foreign enemies" (75). There is in this discourse no distinction between church and state, the personal and the political, or the secular and the sacred. If we think of September 11 in this way, the terrorist attacks were an assault on American religious pluralism. For bin Laden, Islam, rightly understood, cannot accommodate modern Christianity and Judaism. For such religious minimalism is for him the "paganism" of the "infidel."

This external attack on American secular society and the value of religious pluralism set in motion a series of domestic fissures in the national political culture. Ironically, a number of the responses to September 11 undermined the very values that al-Qaeda so despises. Yet, at the same time, a series of ritualized rhetorical gestures were performed that reinforced religious pluralism. This dance between the anti-pluralist and pluralist reactions in the wake of September 11 is our focus. "Pluralistic politics . . . ," Robert Ivie (2002) argues, "is foremost a matter of figuring out how a necessarily conflicted polity can bridge its divisions sufficiently for people to live together without sacrificing a healthy degree of diversity" (277).

In what follows, we detail the domestic challenge to religious pluralism by describing the often virulent backlash against Islam. Second, we explain the grounds of these discursive violations. Third, we examine the relationship between civil religion and rituals of pluralism. Fourth, we explore the ceremonies, speeches, and media coverage that enacted a ritualistic recommitment to American religious pluralism. Finally, we draw some conclusions about the usefulness of ritual as a way of understanding American political culture.

September 11 and the Domestic Challenge to Religious Pluralism

September 11 sent a shudder through the conventions of American civil religion. To use Roderick Hart's (1977) language, the terrorist attacks led to numerous violations of the "church-state contract." Religious tolerance is more than an evocative condensation symbol; it is a set of rhetorical practices. It places responsibilities on ordinary citizens, religious leaders, and political elites to follow certain rules of decorum when speaking of matters of faith in public. These norms were violated by criticism of Islam by other faiths, by a Christian revivalist interpretation of September 11, and by suggestions that American Muslims are a subversive threat to national security.[2]

Criticism of Islam by Other Faiths

The negotiation of public and private spheres of rhetorical action is especially important in the maintenance of religious pluralism. Certainly within particular private confines, it is permissible to criticize other faiths. However, a peaceful pluralist society depends on the restriction of public pronouncements undermining the legitimacy of other religions. In the present case, Islam is an established and influential world religion.[3] To denounce it publicly is a threat to the decorum of American religious pluralism.

In the aftermath of September 11, a number of well-known religious figures engaged in just such a violation. We have selected two widely publicized examples of this rule violation. These incidents represent far more than just the occasional inappropriate remark by a local pastor.

Reverend Franklin Graham. The Reverend Franklin Graham is the son of America's most beloved religious figure, Dr. Billy Graham. Franklin Graham is the president of the Billy Graham Evangelistic Association and, in recent years, has increasingly assumed his ailing father's role as the most prominent public face of American civil religion. He spoke in Littleton, Colorado at the memorial for the victims of the Columbine High School shootings; he delivered the benedictions at the Republican National Conventions in 1996 and 2000; and he gave the invocation at President Bush's 2001 inauguration (Cooperman 2003a, A2).

When such a prominent religious figure—someone whose role has been intertwined with representing the broad face of American religiosity—makes a grievous violation of political-religious decorum, it is especially noteworthy. It demonstrates the extent to which September 11 rocked the nation's commitment to religious pluralism.

On November 16, 2001, the NBC *Nightly News* broadcast an interview with Rev. Franklin Graham. During the course of the interview, Graham called Islam "a very evil and wicked religion" (Wilson 2002, A14). "It wasn't Methodists flying into those buildings, it wasn't Lutherans," Graham told NBC. "It was an attack on this country by people of the Islamic faith" (Jackson, Duke, and Brown 2001). In a recently published book, entitled *The Name*, Graham writes, "The God of Islam is not the God of the Christian faith. The two are different as lightness and darkness." "Much is said and published today about how peace-oriented Islam is," he continues. "A little scrutiny reveals quite the opposite" (Rosin 2002, A3). Graham (2002) adds, "The Bible teaches that individuals have a free will in making decisions about God; Islam often relies on force, intimidation, or conquering of entire nations to recruit converts" (72).

These remarks brought sharp replies from the American Muslim community. It was especially evident in two episodes. Franklin Graham was scheduled and did preach a Good Friday sermon at a religious service at the Pentagon. Several Muslim workers at the Department of Defense went to the chaplain's office to urge that Graham be disinvited (Cooperman 2003b, A4). They wrote a letter urging officials to find "a more inclusive and honorable Christian clergyman" (Cooperman 2003a, A20). Ibrahim Hooper of the Council on American-Islamic Relations said that Graham's Pentagon appearance "sends entirely the wrong message to Muslims in this country and around the world. This is a man who has repeatedly asserted that Islam is evil and it seems to convey a government endorsement, whether or not that is the case" (Marquis 2003, B10).

Franklin Graham heads a humanitarian relief organization called Samaritan's Purse. Samaritan Purse is one of a number of faith-based organizations expected to play a role in rebuilding Iraq. Although Samaritan Purse has a record of building hospitals all over the Middle East, it also brings with it an evangelical fervor. "In the Persian Gulf War," *Newsday* reports, "Graham provoked the ire of Gen. Norman Schwarzkopf by sending 30,000 unsolicited Arabic-language Bibles to U.S. troops in Saudi Arabia, in violation of an understanding between the U.S. and Saudi governments" (Eisenberg 2003, A40). Muslim leaders called these actions a "latter-day Crusade" and said it strengthened the perception that the war was against Islam itself (Eisenberg 2003, A40).

Dr. Jerry Vines. Dr. Jerry Vines is a former president of the Southern Baptist Convention, a widely published author of religious books, and the pastor of the 25,000-member First Baptist Church of Jacksonville, Florida.[4] On June 10, 2002, the day before the national Southern Baptist Convention, Dr. Vines spoke at the pre-convention pastors' conference in St. Louis.

In this address, Rev. Vines said, "Christianity was founded by the virgin-born Lord Jesus Christ. Islam was founded by Muhammad, a demon-possessed pedophile who had twelve wives, and his last one was a nine-year-old girl." "Allah," he continued, "is not Jehovah. Jehovah is not going to turn you into a terrorist that'll try to bomb people and take the lives of thousands and thousands of people." In saying this, he drew the lesson that the contemporary American commitment to religious pluralism had gone too far. "Today, people are saying all religions are the same. They would have us believe Islam is just as good as Christianity. But I'm here to tell you . . . that Islam is not as good as Christianity" (Jones 2002, A5). When asked, the Rev. Jack Graham, the new Southern Baptist Convention president, and the Rev. James Merritt, the immediate past president, endorsed Dr. Vines' remarks (Vara, 2002, 1).

Vines comments were widely reported in the news media (e.g., "Baptist Intolerance" 2002; Breed 2002; Brokaw 2003; "Brotherly Hate" 2002). In an *NBC Nightly News* story, correspondent Bob Faw reported from Jacksonville, Florida. "Jacksonville Muslims, devout and thoughtful," he said, "complain the atmosphere has been poisoned." Faw interviewed one Muslim parent who told her daughters, "Don't go out dressed like a Muslim." Monica Lunt, a Muslim woman, is quoted as saying, "It incites unrest. It incites an us-against-them type of mentality" (Brokaw 2003).

Christian Revival and the Interpretation of September 11

In addition to the public denunciation of Islam, a second form of violation occurred. In this offending discourse, the secular-pluralist character of the United States is faulted for the September 11 attacks. Here religious figures appear to call for something resembling an American theocracy.

Two days after the attacks, on September 13, Rev. Jerry Falwell was a guest on Pat Robertson's nationally broadcast program the *700 Club*. During their televised interview, Robertson and Falwell agreed that the September 11 attacks had occurred because the United States had offended God.

Their exchange is worth quoting at considerable length:

PAT ROBERTSON: . . . We have allowed rampant secularism and occult, etc. to be broadcast on television. We have permitted somewhere in the neighborhood of 35 to 40 million unborn babies to be slaughtered in our society. We have a court that has essentially stuck its finger in God's eye and said we're going to legislate you out of the schools. We're going to take your commandments from off the courthouse steps in various states. We're not going to let little children read the commandments of God. We're not going to let the Bible be read, no prayer in our schools. We have insulted God at the highest levels of government. And, then we say "why does this happen?"

Well, why it's happening is that God Almighty is lifting his protection from us. And once that protection is gone, we all are vulnerable because we're a free society, and we're vulnerable. We lake naked before these terrorists who have infiltrated our country. . . . And, the only thing that's going to protect us is the umbrella power of the Almighty God.

JERRY FALWELL: Well, as the world knows, the tragedy hit on Tuesday morning, and at 2:00 in the afternoon, we gathered 7,000 Liberty University students, faculty, local people together, and we used the verse . . . Chronicles II, 7:14, that God wanted us to humble ourselves and seek his face.

PAT ROBERTSON: . . . I think we've just seen the antechamber of terror.

JERRY FALWELL: The ACLU's got to take a lot of blame for this.

PAT ROBERTSON: Well, yes.

JERRY FALWELL: And, I know that I'll hear from them for this. But, for throwing God out successfully with the help of the federal court system, throwing God out of the public square, out of the schools. The abortionists have got to bear some burden for this because God will not be mocked. And when we destroy 40 million little innocent babies, we make God mad. I really believe that the pagans, and the abortionists, and the feminists, and the gays and lesbians who are actively trying to make that an alternative lifestyle, the ACLU, People For the American Way, all of them who have tried to secularize America. I point the finger in their face and say: "You have helped this happen." (quoted in Lincoln 2003, 104-106).

Bruce Lincoln (2003) in his analysis of the Robertson-Falwell exchange argues that the reference to II Chronicles 7:14 is an important clue to understanding this theological perspective on the hope for a Christian "revival." The verse reads: "If my people who are called by my name humble themselves, and pray and seek my face, and turn from their wicked ways, then I will hear them, and will forgive their sin and heal their land" (Revised Standard Version). "God anticipates," Lincoln writes, "future difficulties in his dealings with Israel but promises to play his part in reconciliatory processes that follow a regular, predictable sequence: (1) Israel sins and falls away from him; (2) He visits woes on his chosen, but fallible people, as a reminder and chastisement; (3) Israel repents, prays, and humbles itself; and (4) He restores their well-being." "This is the scenario," he continues, "that Falwell, Robertson, and their regular listeners refer to as 'revival,' a process that can work at both a personal and collective level" (41).

Surprisingly, this interpretation of September 11 mirrors both bin Laden's religious vision and his indictments of the West. Robertson and Falwell agree that God has removed his protection from the United States because it is a secular society with a minimalist religious tradition. In order to regain the favor of the Almighty, the nation must repent and then work to create a more maximalist religious state. Like bin Laden, they see the enemy as the "pagans" of secularism. To put this in the starkest of terms, Robertson and Falwell want a Judeo-Christian state that mirrors in many respects bin Laden's Islamic state.

American Muslims as Political Subversives

In a final example of a discursive violation of the norms of religious pluralism, some political commentators argued that the tenets of Islam are incompatible with American democracy. They argue that its theology precludes adherents from embracing religious diversity. They suggest that Americans have been naïve if they believe that such an aberrant religious tradition can comfortably assimilate into American society. In short, they advance the claim that Muslims are unsuitable as American citizens.

Cal Thomas (2003), a particularly pugnacious syndicated columnist, made these claims explicit. He is worth quoting at length:

> Suppose our enemies have invaded the United States through immigration for the express purpose of organizing themselves politically? Supposed they present themselves as benign and seek to register voters, becoming politically active in order to elect their people to office and change U.S. policy in the Middle East? What if their intentions are the eventual destruction of this nation through democratic processes and the imposition of a theocratic state? Would that be enough to get our attention? (19A)

As the column continues, Thomas writes, "In at least 16 states, Muslim groups, by their own admission, are organizing voter-registration drives and political consciousness-raising events for this express purpose." Thomas argues that no one will speak up because "we fear being labeled 'bigots' more than we fear the intentions of those who hate us, and so we are reluctant to speak ill of another person's faith, unless it is the majority faith." As the column progresses, Thomas refers to a newspaper story, which quotes Omar M. Ahmad, chairman of the Council on American-Islamic Relations, saying to a crowd of California Muslims in July 1998, "Islam isn't in America to be equal to any other faith, but to become dominant. The Koran . . . should be the highest authority in America and Islam the only accepted religion on Earth." Cal Thomas warns, "When Muslims gain political power, the historical and contemporary record is not encouraging for people who hold democratic values and are of the 'Judeo-Christian' persuasion" (19A).

To summarize, Thomas finds the normal democratic activities of registering, voting, and organizing a threat to national survival when American Muslims engage in these practices. He believes the United States is threatened by Muslims who are American citizens. For Thomas and others who champion this argument, they begin by identifying with bin Laden's first premise—Islam cannot exist in a modern, secular state. So, the hope of creating a world of religious tolerance is doomed. In this vision, Islam is the enemy and the Judeo-Christian societies of the West are in a zero-sum battle for survival.

Grounds of Rhetorical Violation

For speakers raised in the American culture, the sense of rhetorical impropriety is palpable in each of these episodes. Now the task is to specify the grounds that generate this feeling of violation. Because these rhetorical acts were not illegal—Graham, Vines, Falwell, Robertson, and Thomas are not government agents and thus did not violate the Constitution's "establishment" clause—the offenses were a violation of decorum rather than law.

Public/Private Decorum. There was a mismatch between utterance and circumstances. There was nothing inherently improper in the production of three of these speech acts. The violation stems from the public nature of the settings. If we re-situate these episodes, then the sense of impropriety would be muted. If Graham, Vines, Falwell, or Robertson had spoken to their own congregations, then the requirements of decorum would have been significantly different. Within the confines of denominational walls, we find nothing unusual about provocative Scriptural interpretations or pointed theological criticisms of other religions. In nearly any Catholic Church, for example, the faithful may hear a homily detailing the errors of Protestantism. Likewise, Protestants will offer intellectual defenses of the Reformation and explain the errors of the Roman church. Analogously, we trust that most of us would find nothing surprising in a sermon by Christian or Jewish clergy that detailed the errors of the Muslim faith.

Yet, in each of these cases, it is the sense of the message as *public*—thus intended for a *heterogeneous* audience—that creates the pointed sense of violation. Three of the episodes were disseminated through media that reaches broad audiences—Franklin on NBC's *Nightly News*, Robertson and Falwell on CBN's *700 Club*, and Thomas in a syndicated newspaper column. The case of Jerry Vines is somewhat more complicated. The Pastors' Conference, preceding the Southern Baptist Convention, appears in some respects like a *private* gathering of a *homogeneous* audience. Yet, the Southern Baptist Convention has become a public event covered by the working press. When the nation's second largest denomination conducts its annual meeting, it creates national interest. Just as private companies have public faces, so, too, do the pronouncements of American churches as corporate institutions carry beyond the narrow private interests of the given denomination.

In saying that we believe the sense of violation could be removed in three of the four cases, we cannot conceive of any obvious way in which Cal Thomas's discourse could be salvaged. There was probably a time when words like "nigger," "colored," or "boy" could be uttered without a sense of violation in some private contexts, but that time has hopefully passed. No right-thinking person would find such private speech anything but bigoted. Likewise, it is hard to place this deeply anti-democratic discourse in any supportive context, whether private or public. Even if we let our imaginations run free, we still find it indecorous. One could envision a meeting of FBI agents concerned with domestic terrorism discussing the danger presented by Muslim Americans. Even in such a context, the assertion that voting was a threat to national security would be chilling. Put differently, the Thomas violation is so foreign to the American democratic culture that it cannot find comfort in a private setting.

If the definition of circumstances turn on a tension between *public as heterogeneous audience* versus *private as homogeneous audience*, then what characteristic of the utterance itself prevents the smooth crossing between these two spheres of rhetorical activity.

After all, we could all think of countless discourses that could move uneventfully from the church pulpit to the pages of the newspaper or the television interview. Graham and Vines represent one type of violation, Falwell and Robertson a second type, and Thomas a third.

Denying the Legitimacy of an Accepted Religious Faith. The key element of this cultural rule has to do with the shifting conception of "accepted religious faith." Over time the nation has changed its religious character and broadened its conception of tolerance. Forty years ago, John Kennedy (1960) addressed the Houston Ministerial Association to answer what he characterized as legitimate questions about his Roman Catholic faith. The presence of Mormonism as a mainstream American denomination is another recent development. Islam, certainly one of the world's largest and most important faiths, is an "accepted" religion. If Graham or Vines had attacked the Unification Church of Reverend Moon or a New Age religion like Wiccan, we doubt that there criticism would have been viewed as a violation of public decorum.

Moreover, the nature of their remarks makes no distinction between the legitimate and illegitimate practice of Islam. More careful commentators condemned the radical use of Islam to justify terror, while carefully phrasing their criticism to exclude mainstream practices of the faith. To call Islam "evil" or its founder a "demon-possessed pedophile" is to claim a wickedness at the very foundation of the tradition. Such utterances are incapable of drawing distinctions.

Conflating Religion and Citizenship. Cal Thomas, Jerry Falwell, and Pat Robertson conflate religion and citizenship. They do it, however, in quite different ways. Thomas questions the fitness of Muslims to be good citizens. Falwell and Robertson attribute American political troubles to the secular nature of the state—they reject present understanding of the Constitution's "establishment" clause. We examine each episode in turn.

Cal Thomas's criticism of Islam is nearly a mirror image of the Protestant challenges to John Kennedy's candidacy. Protestants disputed the Catholic commitment to pluralism; they questioned the ability of a Catholic who belongs to a hierarchical church (papacy) to adhere to the Constitution and act in the national interest; and they believed that Catholics had a hidden agenda directed by Rome. Lurking behind these criticisms was the Protestant resentment that Catholics believed their religion to be the one true faith. Although Islam is far different from Catholicism in structure, Thomas articulates the same arguments. Muslims cannot be pluralist because they view anyone apart from Islam as an infidel. Muslims, despite what they say, want power for undemocratic ends. Just like the evidence arrayed against Catholicism, Thomas offers evidence against Muslims that come from other parts of the world. Thomas treats religious faith as a litmus test for American citizenship. In the American tradition, a charge of unfitness for citizenship much always be directed at an individual and based on behavior rather than faith.

The Falwell/Robertson violation is more complex. Certainly, it is permissible to bring a religious sensibility to arguments over moral controversies (Carter 1993; Neuhaus 1984). There may be widespread disagreement over gay rights, for example, but people of faith may weigh in on the morality of gay unions or the wisdom of sodomy laws. These arguments will certainly generate heated public debate and those who present cases on either side will be subject to biting criticism (Hunter 1991). Falwell and Robertson have made public statements on these issues for years, but they were of a different quality than their remarks following September 11.

On their September 14 broadcast, they blamed domestic secular enemies for foreign terror. In at least this one respect, this discourse fits the form of McCarthyism. The success of a foreign enemy was blamed on domestic ideological foes. Unlike McCarthyism, this was essentially a theological argument. Yet, it blamed others with different liberal religious beliefs for the deaths of 3,000 citizens. More pointedly, it focused on civil liberties as the source of God's anger. During a period in which a rhetoric of national unity is expected, this fractious discourse was an indecorous match of utterance with circumstance.

Summary. The rhetorical contours of pluralism are a product of such a complex of relationships between circumstances and utterance that it is difficult to imagine an exhaustive set of regulative rules. Or, at least we cannot imagine a small set of rules that were not encumbered with dozens of exceptions.

With this said, we will argue that the three grounds specified here are constitutive to any satisfactory rendering of the rhetorical rules of religious pluralism. The judgment of propriety/impropriety will always turn on a public versus private frame; the accepted legitimacy of the religion in question will always matter; and the linkage of religion to citizenship will always be determinative. How these grounds manifest themselves in any given controversy is too complex to lay down in any set of general rules.

Civil Religion and the Rituals of Pluralism

So far, we have described a series of unsettling episodes and explained the grounds upon which they may be considered discursive improprieties. These preliminaries set the backdrop for tackling the heart of the matter. What recurring rhetorical performances bolster the social value and correct the violations of religious pluralism? Given the threats to pluralism that accompanied the September 11 tragedy, how did government officials and other opinion leaders respond? Understanding the answer depends on both an examination of public discourse and an appreciation of the American civil-religious culture.

The scholarship on civil religion begins with the incontrovertible observation that "in no society can religion and politics ignore each other." "Faith and power," Robert Bellah (1980) argues, "must always, however uneasily, take a stance toward one another" (vii). The overlap will necessarily come to involve the question of "whether existing moral authority is moral and right or whether it violates higher religious duties" (viii). Stable societies find ways to deal with this potential tension. In the United States, the society has developed a "distinct set of religious symbols and practices," which "address issues of political legitimacy and political ethics but that are not fused with either church or state" (xi). It is this set of symbols and practices that has been termed "civil religion."

Civil religious discourse stands between church and state as the lubricant that permits a secular government to preside over a religious people. It provides the symbolic structures that simultaneously acknowledge a transcendent God and nourish tolerance and pluralism. A unique form of religious discourse is required that can underwrite the moral legitimacy of the state without promoting any particular faith tradition. The inventional *topoi* that mark this discourse are simultaneously transcendent and pragmatic. These messages appeals to God as the ultimate moral authority while addressing the exigencies of a secular state by eschewing particular theological commitments. Roderick Hart (1977) explains the pragmatic dimension as an implied "contract" between the "United States Government" and "Organized Religion." The key provision of the contract states that the "First party [government] rhetoric will refrain from being overly religious and second party [church] rhetoric will refrain from being overly political" (44). The contract, Hart argues, is enforceable because there are serious sanctions. If members of the church become too political, they lose their privileges as honored members of the national community and lose their access to political leaders. If, on the other hand, politicians become too religious in public matters, they will appear out of step and lose their influence (62-63). Of course, this is an ongoing negotiation. Circumstances, especially in times of crisis, may dictate a more political tone from religious leaders and a more religious tone from governmental authorities. Yet, there are implicitly understood and enforced boundaries even in these stressful times, as we shall see.

Hart's discussion of the mechanisms by which the "contract" is enforced lacks both empirical support and rhetorical specificity. To say that religious leaders, who become too political, lose influence is hardly obvious from the contemporary record. The prominent religious figures associated with the Christian Coalition, for instance, despite their frequent transgressions, continue to have considerable influence, especially within the Republican Party (Edsal 1998; Milbank 2001). The recent episode of Chief Justice Roy Moore, who refused a federal judicial order to remove the Ten Commandments monument from the Alabama Supreme Court, suggests that transgressions by government officials may bring considerable popular support to the violator (Spencer 2003). The reason is obvious. There are political strategies for which such violations create useful wedge issues. The dynamics of political influence are too convoluted to lend incontrovertible support for Hart's account of the contract's enforcement mechanisms.

Hart (1977), also, does not explain by what rhetorical mechanisms such sanctions are enforced. In his discussion of civic piety, he argues that "the content of 'official' civil-religious rhetoric is nonexistential," by which he means that "an active, behavioral concern for the tangible exigencies of the moment is not generally characteristic of such discourse." This form of rhetoric, he suggests, "is richly symbolic, reveling in a world of images rather than with practical policy" (75). Like us, he is struck by its "ritualistic presence" (87). Yet, he has a narrower conception of civil-religious ritual. Hart focuses exclusively on civic events that call forth God and nation (see Hart, 87-98) and writes not at all of the rituals that reinforce the boundaries of religious pluralism.

"Social drama," Victor Turner (1982) writes, "is initiated when the peaceful tenor of regular, norm-governed social life is interrupted by the breach of a rule controlling one of its salient relationships." This interruption leads to a state of crisis, "which, if not sealed off, may split the community into contending factions and coalitions." To deter this destructive split actions are taken by those considered the "most legitimate or authoritative representatives of the community" (92). This redress, Turner argues, involves ritualized action, often of a religious nature. These rituals are the "performance of something, for someone" and these rhetorical acts are "always action according to pre-existing conceptions." These rituals are not essentially about providing information, but about communicating that some ideas are so important that they "deserve to be set aside and protected" (Rothenbuhler 1998, 9).

As will become clear in our analysis, actors representing a variety of social institutions perform in this ritualized drama. Political figures come together and pray for guidance to an ecumenical God; religious figures interpret the Almighty as casting a wide and inclusive religious tent; clergy rebuke their brethren who foster dissention; and the national press performs its function as the public conscience by chastising violators of religious pluralism.

This ritualized drama presents an ideal public square (scene) in an inconsistent relationship with a violator (agent) and a violation (act).[5] To use Burkean language, agent and act are put in a discordant relationship with scene. In this sense, the drama plays out in comedic ways. The audience is introduced to an ideal society in which some blocking characters, often presented as buffoons, are center stage. The audience recognizes the imperfection in the scene and the action during the course of the drama leads to the disposing of the blocking characters and the reign of the hero. Typical of comedy, the blocking characters are often converted more than deposed.[6] The scene may end with a moment of reconciliation (see Frye 1957; White 1973, 7-11).

Bolstering: The Presentation of the Ideal American Scene

In numerous civic exercises, an idealized America is presented for public edification. After September 11, ecumenical events occurred all over the country. At the City Hall Plaza in Boston, "people of all different faiths, Jewish, Muslim, Christian, Sikhs, Hindus [came] together with one voice in prayer . . . and then to say we stand together as Americans against terror" ("National Conversation" 2001,

16). Catholic Bishops and Muslim leaders issued a joint statement saying, "We believe that the one God calls us to be peoples of peace" and that "we entreat Catholics and Muslims to join together . . . in services of prayer and community programs promoting peace" (Catholic, 2001). In San Jose, California, the city held an "interfaith prayer vigil at Cesar Chavez Plaza" (Heredia and Lelchuk 2001, A1). In Yankee Stadium, representatives of various faiths—Christian, Jewish, Muslim, Hindu, and Sikh—stood side by side. "Together these leaders underscored," the *Christian Century* reported, "a commitment to one of the boldest and most important of the nation's experiments in freedom—the U.S. will be a place where all may worship in the integrity of their own religious traditions, and where all will endeavor to live together in peace as they practice their faith in their day-to-day lives" ("Habit of Ministry" 2001, 5).

Three days after September 11, a particularly powerful spectacle of religious pluralism was performed at the National Cathedral in Washington, DC. What was carried out in cities and towns all over the country was encapsulated here. This service is worth exploring in detail, because it displays the rhetorical markers that depict the ideal American religious scene. This event was deemed sufficiently important to justify live coverage by all three major networks. For the sake of the present analysis, we will focus on the transcribed text of the ABC broadcast. The coverage is sufficiently conventionalized that there is little significant variation among the various televised presentations.[7]

The Political Actors

Thirty minutes before the beginning of the prayer service, the ABC anchor came on air to set the stage for the event. Peter Jennings and three correspondents—John McWethy, George Stephanopoulos, and Terry Morgan—identified those attending the service as they entered the sanctuary of the National Cathedral. They drew the audience's attention to an impressive array of political leaders—Colin Powell (secretary of state), Dennis Hastert (speaker of the House), Trent Lott (Republican leader in the Senate), Donald Rumsfeld (secretary of defense), General Henry Shelton (chairman, Joint Chiefs of Staff), Christie Whitman (EPA administrator), Paul O'Neill (treasury secretary), John Ashcroft (attorney general), Spencer Abrams (energy secretary), Elaine Chao (labor secretary), and Tommy Thompson (secretary of health and human services).

In this opening segment, there was a special emphasis on leaders of the political opposition. In describing their presence, the commentators made a point of constructing moments of reconciliation. "An interesting story . . . ," Jennings said, ". . . because we talk about these as being a moment of national reconciliation. And it is, as we'll undoubtedly see this morning, a moment of quite extraordinary political reconciliation, . . . at least in the public sense, between former President Clinton and former Vice President Gore" (ABC 2001, 2). Then, Jennings describes the arrival of Senator Hillary Clinton with her Senate colleagues. She joins her husband, along with Thomas Daschle, the Democratic Party leader in the Senate. In the most obvious moment of reconciliation, "Senator Lott [and] Senator Clinton" are described as "saying good morning to the Bushes" (ABC 2001, 5). Other prominent members of the opposition were also identified, including Senator Charles Schumer of New York, Senator Joseph Lieberman of Connecticut, and former members of the Clinton national security team (Anthony Lake and Sandy Berger).

As a way of encapsulating this opening segment of the broadcast, Jennings remarked, "What you are seeing in bits and pieces is the political and military and, to some extent, the bureaucratic superstructure of the country." To put this simply, the most powerful public figures in the United States presented themselves at a religious ceremony to pray for the dead and injured and to seek the guidance of the Almighty.

At the conclusion of the service, as the dignitaries departed, Jennings returned to his theme of unity and reconciliation. He described the "President saying goodbye and thank you to his opponent in the last election campaign, or one of them, Joe Lieberman." Then, he portrayed the departures by pairing up old political adversaries—former President Carter and former President Ford, former President Clinton and former President Bush. He mentioned the exchange of pleasantries between former Senator Dole and former President Clinton, opponents in the 1996 presidential election.

The Religious Actors

The clergy included the Right Reverend Jane Holmes Dixon (Episcopal bishop pro tem of Washington), Reverend Nathan D. Baxter (Episcopal dean of the Cathedral), Dr. Billy Graham, Dr. Muzammil H. Siddiqi (imam of the Islamic Society of North America),[8] Rabbi

Joshua O. Haberman (rabbi emeritus of the Washington Hebrew Congregation), Reverend Kirbyjon Caldwell (United Methodist Church of Houston), and Cardinal Theodore McCarrick (archbishop of Washington). This ecumenical gathering represents the Abrahamic faiths that dominate the American religious landscape.

These religious figures were each called for different reasons. Some were leaders in the Washington, DC religious community—Rabbi Haberman and Cardinal McCarrick. One was a national leader of Islam, Dr. Muzammil Siddiqi. Another was the most familiar face of American Protestantism, Dr. Billy Graham. Reverend Kirbyjon Caldwell is the president's personal friend. Bishop Dixon and Reverend Baxter are associated with the National Cathedral, which is run under the auspices of the Episcopal Church.

The Scene

The National Cathedral is nearly a perfect representation of American religious pluralism. It is a Christian edifice, which was built with a congressional charter to the Protestant Episcopal Cathedral Foundation of the District of Columbia. The Cathedral was constructed for "national purposes, such as public prayer, thanksgiving, funeral orations, etc., and assigned to the special use of no particular Sect or denomination, but equally open to all" ("History" 2001, 1).

Over the last sixty years, the National Cathedral has been the backdrop for scenes of collective worship. It held monthly services "On behalf of a united people in a time of emergency" during World War II, was the site of Dr. Martin Luther King's last Sunday sermon, was the building in which Dwight Eisenhower's funeral was held, and was the place where the nation gave thanks for the freeing of the American hostages in Iran ("History" 2001, 1).

Nationalism, politics, and religion meet in every scenic feature of the September 14 prayer service. The service begins with the presentation of the flag by the Joint Armed Forces Color Guard. The U.S. Army Orchestra and U.S. Navy Chanters provide the music. The orchestral prelude includes "God, Bless America," and the mezzo-soprano Denyce Graves sings "America the Beautiful."

The other familiar Christian music—"God of Our Fathers," "Father in Thy Gracious Keeping," "O God, Our Help in Ages Past," the singing of the Twenty-Third Psalm and the Lord's Prayer, "The

Mighty Fortress Is Our God"—are characterized in an interesting way in the ABC broadcast. "And we'll hear all those great Christian hymns," Jennings says, ". . . that have, in their own way—one might argue—[become] so essential to the Christian faith and to Christian religion, but have *become more widely accepted as simply evocative and familiar hymns which are sung by people, Christian or not*" [our emphasis] (ABC 2001, 4).

The Ceremony

Welcome. The welcome by the Right Reverend Dixon is a perfect execution of the American civil religious tradition. She emphasizes the inclusiveness of the occasion three separate times in a brief four paragraph message. She thanks President Bush for "calling for this service . . . where people of many faiths have gathered." She elaborates in saying that "those of us who are gathered here—Muslim, Jew, Christian, Sikh, Buddhist, Hindu—[are] all people of faith." In the next paragraph and again in the final paragraph, she refers to the National Cathedral as a "house of prayer for all people" (ABC 2001, 7).

Bishop Dixon unites all of these faith traditions around love and justice. "All people of faith," she tells the congregation, "want to say to this nation and to the world that love is stronger than hate, and that love lived out in justice will in the end prevail." She continues in the following paragraph, "We want you to know that the light that burns here—the light of love, the light of justice, the light of hope—shines brighter than any light in the world. So come often, pray to God here, and let us be united that we will make that message of love, the message that world needs to here in this time of tragedy" (ABC 2001, 7).

Invocation. Reverend Baxter, dean of the Cathedral, offers the Invocation. In this opening prayer, he asks for the "healing of our grief-stricken hearts, for the souls and sacred memory of those who have been lost. Let us pray for divine wisdom as our leaders consider the necessary actions for national security—wisdom of the grace of God that as we act, we not become the evil we deplore" (ABC 2001, 7). He directs this petition to the "God of Abraham, Mohammed, and Father of our Lord Jesus Christ" (ABC 2001, 8). In asking for God's intervention, Reverend Baxter includes a plea to "save us . . . from random prejudice" (ABC 2001, 8).

The skeleton outline of the remainder of the ceremony follows the standard Christian liturgical tradition—a prayer, an Old Testament reading, a psalm, a reading from the Epistles, a Gospel reading, a sermon, and a closing prayer. The two additions are a prayer for leadership and remarks by President Bush. The ceremony, like the National Cathedral itself, is Christian in design but adapted to a more broadly ecumenical purpose.

Opening Prayer. The prayers and scripture readings that follow construct a single God—manifested in four religious traditions (Islam, Judaism, Catholicism, and Protestantism)—who is called on to protect America. Dr. Siddiqi's prayer is especially interesting because of its use of passages from the Qu'ran to support a petition to God to "Help us in our distress, keep us together as people of diverse faiths, colors and races, keep our country strong for the sake of good and righteousness, protect us from evil" ("National Day of Prayer" 2001). In the tradition of this supposedly alien faith, the audience hears a prayer that is at once ecumenical and nationalistic. The faith of bin Laden is used here neither to urge the destruction of the infidels nor to condemn those who live under secular government, but to articulate a fervent request for religious tolerance and national protection.

Old Testament Reading. Following immediately the Imam, the Jewish representative, Rabbi Haberman, reads from the Old Testament book of Lamentations. These verses refer to God's mercy, love, and compassion. The imagery of Muslim and Jew—echoing the central unresolved Palestinian-Israeli conflict that sits at the heart of terrorism—participating together in a joint American appeal to God is the contemporary restatement of Israel Zangwill's (1914) message in *The Melting Pot.* Come to America and leave behind Old World hatreds and begin a new and peaceful life.

Epistle. The Christian clergy follow. Reverend Caldwell reads from St. Paul's second letter to the Corinthians. This reading from chapters 4 and 5 focuses on the afflictions of this world as momentary compared with the "eternal weight of glory beyond all measure" coming in the next. These verses refer to "God" and "Lord" but without using the Christian term "Jesus."

Gospel. Cardinal McCarrick reads the Gospel passage from the fifth chapter of Matthew. Verses 3-10 are the Beatitudes from the Sermon on the Mount. They contain the essence of Christian ethics and values; often held to be on "a level with the Decalogue in the Old, and the Lord's Prayer in the New Testament" (Van Kasteren

1913, 372). The meek are rich; the hungry are filled; and the perse-
cuted are righteous. The outward appearance belies the spiritual reality. In historical context, this message points to the emptiness of
the legalistic pharisaic tradition without the internal spiritual commitment to God. These poetic passages refute the Islamist notion of
Christian imperialism; they explain the Christian concern for the
downtrodden; and they speak of a universal ethic that transcends
the Christian faith.

Sermon. Dr. Graham, the famous Christian evangelist, personi-
fies civil religion. Although himself a Protestant, he preaches without regard to Christian sect and has been called innumerable times
to speak as the face of American religion. Few understand better the
requirements of such a pluralist occasion. "We come together today
to reaffirm," he begins, "our conviction that God cares for us, whatever our ethnic, religious or political background may be."

Yet, like nearly everything else about this event, Christianity en-
velopes the ceremony, while admitting of other religious traditions.
Near the end of Graham's remarks, he says, "Here in this majestic
National Cathedral, we see all around us symbols of the cross." He
continues, "For the Christian—I'm speaking for the Christian now—
the cross tells us that God understands our sin and our suffering, for
he took upon himself, in the person of Jesus Christ, our sins and our
suffering" (ABC 2001, 12).

The themes of the sermon, although steeped in Christian theology and supported by Biblical references, are universal. Graham
offers a meaning for death, consoles those who are left behind, at-
taches God to pursuits of a just America, and grapples with the mystery of why God permits evil to befall the faithful. All of this enacts
the central commitment of civil religion—God is the ultimate source
of meaning and morality. However this one God is understood, He
remains our national foundation. Without Him, these events lead us
to nihilism. We may not understand the mystery of God, but we can
trust that all of this suffering has some final significance.

President Bush. In this speech, the president speaks as the nation
itself. In using the collective "we," he tells us who we are, what are
purposes are, and how we relate to God. There is no presence of
the singular—no reference to himself as president or leader of an
administration; there is only the voice of national sovereignty
without any suggestion that this voice does not speak for all without
division.

Bush speaks of God without reference to any religion. The president speaks repeatedly of prayer. "We learn in tragedy," he says, "that His purposes are not always our own, yet the prayers of private suffering, whether in our homes or in this great cathedral, are known and heard and understood" (ABC 2001, 16). He also assures the audience that this "world He created is of moral design. Grief and tragedy and hatred are only for a time. Goodness, remembrance and love have no end. And the Lord of life holds all who die and all who mourn" (ABC 2001, 16). This is the assurance that God bends history toward justice and that He cares for those who have been hurt and lost. Like Graham's sermon, this discourse asserts that morality and meaning are ultimately transcendent. The contingencies of politics are anchored in something permanent and, therefore, accountable to a final moral arbiter.

Correcting: The Repudiation of Civil Heresy

If we are right, then the idealized public square, as portrayed in civic exercises like the September 14th prayer service at the National Cathedral, provides the dramatic background against which violations of religious pluralism are prosecuted. Sometimes this scene is explicitly evoked and at other times it is implicitly presented through the presentation of its opposite.

Irony of Scene

The rhetoric of correction involves the irony of scene. In Burke's (1969) famous formulation of irony as a master trope, he writes that it may be understood as "what goes forth as A returns as non-A" (517). In particular, these discourses of correction are closely related to Burke's observation that we should "ironically" note "the function of the disease in 'perfecting' the cure, or the function of the cure in 'perpetuating' the influences of the disease" (512). For in the repudiation of violations of religious pluralism, the vocal criticism of a violator is simultaneously evidence of the "cure" and confirmation that there are those scoundrels who are motivated to perpetuate the "disease." Violations are never treated simply as the harmless exception. Each case defiles the scene of the ideal public square and thus must be eradicated. The fear of contagion always hovers over these discourses. A comment by Dr. Jerry Vines or Rev. Franklin Graham may represent a deeper and frightening vein in the American psyche. It may become the new extremist and intolerant "ism."

Over the months following September 11 there were many stories, commentaries, and editorials about religious tolerance. Many
of these reported on the prophylactic function of American pluralist
virtues. The editorial board of the *Dallas Morning News*, for example, reports on "ecumenical groups across the nation are discovering that Islam, with its strong emphasis on charity, is a natural fit
with other religious groups that are seeking common ground and
understanding." In a favorable commentary on the new term
"Abrahamic," the paper observes that the "new terminology . . .
never may catch on, but the underlying psychology inevitably will."
"Every religion," the editorial continues, "adapts to American political culture when it becomes entrenched here. In America, religions
don't battle for domination because civil law holds precedence over
religious law" ("Judeo-Christian-Islamic" 2003). Thomas Oliphant
(2003) of the *Boston Globe* describes a series of episodes in which
Americans were reaching out to one another across the faith lines of
Jewish, Christian, and Muslim. Many newspapers reported the surprising survey finding that Americans were increasingly accepting
of Muslims in the wake of September 11 (Raasch 2001). "The Sept.
11 attacks have increased the prominence of religion in the United
States to an extraordinary degree," while "at the same time, the public has a better opinion of Muslim-Americans than it did before the
attacks." In particular, "nearly two-thirds of conservative Republicans (64%) feel favorably toward Muslims in this country, up 29
percentage points" in seven months ("Post September 11 Attitudes"
2001).

In stark contrast, violators are constructed as progenitors of a vile
scene. "Cal Thomas' syndicated column," the *Baton Rouge Advocate* argues, ". . . was a propaganda piece worthy of . . . Joseph
Goebbels. . . . [I]f you want to get a handle on what Cal Thomas has
in mind for American Muslims, go read the Nazi Nuremberger laws
on citizenship and race passed by the Nazis in 1936. Go read about
Kristallnacht" ("Thomas spouts propaganda" 2003).

The irony rests in the constant argumentative pattern that "A returns as non-A." In the violators' fervor to protect America against
its enemies, they may turn America into what they claim to despise.
"Now we have preachers," Richard Cohen (2002) writes, "who do
not counsel toleration and understanding, but a sort of bigotry—an
ugly and sweeping vilification of a whole people, in the manner of
the very Islamic radicals they condemn" (A25). The editorial board

of the *Winston-Salem Journal* argues, "The terrorists to whom Vines made reference are examples of what can happen when religious faith is perverted into zealotry that loses sight of the original religious principles. Vines' intolerant and divisive statements are an example of such zealotry" ("Baptist intolerance" 2002, A18). "We have to wonder," the *Arkansas Democrat-Gazette* editorialist writes, "whatever the good Reverend hoped to accomplish by that kind of ugliness. Just change the name of the religion and the prophet, alter a phrase or two, and his statement could have come straight out of one of the more hate-crazed Arab dailies on the subject of Jews or Christians." The editorial asks, "Are we now going to overcome our enemies by imitating them? . . . Those who would turn this conflict into a religious war, a crusade, a jihad, are doing what the enemy wants" ("Brotherly hate" 2002, B8). In a similar vein, Nicholas Kristof (2002) of the *New York Times* observes, "Since 9/11, appalling hate speech about Islam has circulated in the U.S. on talk radio, on the Internet and in particular among conservative Christian pastors—the modern echoes of Charles Coughlin, the 'radio priest' who had a peak listening audience in the 1930's of one-third of America for his anti-Semitic diatribes" (A21).

Upon reflection, one can recall this argumentative pattern of rhetorical policing again and again in the history of American public discourse. McCarthyism is a species of fascism. Anti-Semitism is anti-Christian. Pressing too hard always reverses the scene.

Irony of Agent

Virtue is a dispositional quality of an agent who works on behalf of the good. So, to say that someone had courage would be to ascribe a quality of character that permitted that person to persevere in the face of danger. Moreover, when "courage" is used as a virtue, it supposes that such perseverance was done for a just end. Although a villain—say members of the Gestapo—may have endured in the face of physical danger, those who found their purposes reprehensible would hardly be expected to label such a quality "courage." Instead, they probably would be identified with terms of vice—fanatical, brutal, or ruthless. Each of these may suggest a kind of fearlessness, but this would not be identified with the language of virtue.

The comedian and political commentator Bill Maher, former host of the late-night, ABC program *Politically Incorrect*, created a firestorm of negative comment for an utterance that associated the September 11 terrorists with courage. On Monday, September 17, 2001, Maher and Dinesh D'Souza were discussing the use of the term "cowards" to describe the terrorists. Maher argued that they were not "cowards" because they gave their lives for the cause. Then he added, "But also, . . . we have been the cowards lobbing cruise missiles from 2,000 miles away. That's cowardly. Staying in the airplane when it hits the building, say what you want about it, it's not cowardly" ("Transcript" 2001). This resulted in Sears and FedEx pulling their advertising and in several ABC affiliates dropping the show. As a result, *Politically Incorrect* was cancelled.

The criticism of Maher is a near perfect example of the *irony of agent*. The meaning of the virtue-vice pairing of courageous-cowardly, what Burke might call the dialectic of irony, is determined by a controlling sense of the good. Maher's commentary played on the contrast in acts—choosing to die for the cause by crashing an airplane into a building versus safely firing cruise missiles from 2,000 miles away from the enemy—but failed to account for the controlling sense of moral purpose featured in the scenic terms "terrorism" and "national defense." So, the irony is that the "courageous" become "cowardly" and the "cowardly" become "courageous."

In the repudiation of the violators of religious pluralism, this same irony of the agent occurs. The civic virtue of patriotism is ironically reversed. Cal Thomas, for instance, characterizes his column as a patriotic warning against the domestic Muslim threat. In its repudiation, the critic contends that any anti-pluralist sentiment is contrary to the good and, thus, Cal Thomas is actually unpatriotic.

In the religious context, Graham and Vines all claim to bear essential witness to Christ. As part of this witness, they must tell the truth about Islam. The criticism they receive from the Christian community ironically reverses the virtue of witnessing. To show the face of hate to another faith is to undermine the Christian message. They are scolded for their failure to be Christ-like. In their attempts to promote Christianity, they are accused of undermining Christianity. For instance, Dr. Clive Calver, president of World relief, an agency of the National Association of Evangelicals, said, "It's very dangerous to build more barriers when we're supposed to be following one[Jesus] who pulled the barriers down" (Goodstein 2003, A22).

Journalists played on the same dialectic tension between virtue and vice. "If Falwell hopes to bring more people to the Christian faith," Courtney Rice (2002) writes, "he should be speaking about Jesus' love to the Muslim people, not condemning Muhammad with inflammatory and false allegations." She continues, "Christian leaders should be telling Falwell to hit the books; the Bible has a few things to say about this hateful speech. In Luke 6:37, Jesus tells his disciples, 'do not judge and you will not be judged; do not condemn, and you will not be condemned.'" In this commentary, the virtue of love is in a dialectic relationship with the vice of hate. "It is time," Rice concludes, "to challenge the haters who claim to be advocating Christian faith and to, with extreme love, reclaim Christianity for the majority of believers."

The irony of agent constantly warns that pushing too far reverses the virtue-vice pairing. Advocacy becomes bigotry; witnessing becomes heresy; loving becomes hating. This ritual warns us to take the middle course.

Correction as Ritual

The ironic reversal of scene and agent is a constitutive rhetorical form of liberal democracy. We cannot imagine the American political culture without the official, the editorial board, the columnist, and the newspaper letter writer as performers, who turn the tables on the zealot. They say, "You have gone too far and now become that which you most fear." This is inescapable in the tension between freedom and tolerance. The liberty to press one's case always is always in tension with the limits necessary for respecting others. So, people may witness their faith but they must do it while considering the followers of other traditions. In pressing a position to its Malthusian limits, you create the ironic reversal. This point of reversal is the line between democracy and tolerance.

Not surprisingly, Americans have constructed rituals for signaling the point of danger. For telling people to turn back is not a simple rational process. There are no legal restrictions preventing a Christian from publicly criticizing the basis of the Islamic faith. To say that Muhammad married a 9-year-old girl is a matter of the historical record. To talk about the relationship between Islamic nations and war is an issue for historical interpretation. Even if it were possible, refuting the substance of these claims is essentially beside the point. "A ritual view of communication," James Carey (1975) argues, "is not directed toward the extension of messages in space but the main-

The Rituals of Religious Pluralism   43

tenance of society in time; not the act of imparting information but the representation of shared beliefs" (6). The ritual puts again before the public the image of the ideal public square by performing ceremonies of bolstering and by enacting a rhetoric of correction.

One way to read Burke's (1984) *Attitudes toward History* is as a statement about the inherent irony of liberalism. If one follows a particular perspective to its rational conclusion, the results may well be tragic. So, if freedom of religion were fully realized in unfettered Christian witness, then the result would surely destroy religious pluralism. As we observe in the examples of Graham, Vines, Falwell, Robertson, and Thomas, pressing against the boundaries of pluralism generates scapegoats. If unchecked, these discourses would eventually lead to a rhetoric of violence. Burke's "comic corrective" calls us to embrace the humility of irony. It asks us to counter our perspective with opposing perspectives (Ivie, 2001). In so doing, we place limits on how far we will push our view. We ultimately have to just try and muddle through and get along with one another. What we have termed the irony of scene and the irony of agent celebrates just this humility of restraint.

Conclusions

The aftermath of the September 11 tragedy brought with it some moments of cultural reassurance. The United States was attacked by terrorists who employed an interpretation of Muslim teachings to justify their actions. This use of Islam incited a number of prominent Americans to make remarks contrary to the tenets of the national commitment to religious pluralism. Yet, despite the gravity of the circumstances, the pluralist rituals of bolstering and correcting were efficiently performed. These rituals are so engrained in the political cultural fabric that they were not shaken by the intensity of the September 11 experience.

If the national response to discursive violations of religious pluralism were merely a pragmatic response to situational exigencies, then we would expect the trauma of September 11 to have altered American discourse. Lance Bennett (1978), writing about the 1976 presidential campaign in the wake of Watergate, made a similar observation. Even though the candidates said these new circumstances changed everything about politics, the rituals of the campaign were more powerful than the immediate situational exigencies. Likewise, the exigencies of terrorism did not overwhelm the rituals that convey symbolically "that some things are more important than others, and that some ideas, symbols, and activities are so important that they deserve to be protected" (Rothenbuhler 1998, 24).

We worry that some who read this essay will find it lacks balance. After all, every example of a violator and violation is connected with evangelical Protestantism. Even Cal Thomas, who we described in his secular role as a columnist, came to prominence as the spokesman for Jerry Falwell's Moral Majority (Thomas and Dobson 1999). This outcome was unintended. We were looking for any prominent example of a rhetorical violation of religious pluralism. In retrospect, we suppose that it is not surprising that this would be a particularly troubling problem for evangelicals. Their tradition places great emphasis on Christian witness. Among their more conservative adherents, the ecumenical emphasis of many of the so-called mainline denominations has always been problematic. Also, evangelical churches are far less likely to be organized hierarchically. So, the measured words of the U.S. Conference of Catholic Bishops are replaced by the individual reactions of prominent Baptist pastors. Yet, even within the evangelical tradition, there were numerous voices of correction.

Finally, we suggest that the relationship among pluralism, irony, and humility is more than theoretical. It is part of the American discursive reflex that is always ready to say "you have gone too far" and "you have turned into what you criticize." This is a powerful check on the citizenry's legally unfettered freedom of speech and religion.

Notes

1. A fatwa is an "Islamic religious decree issued by the 'ulama.'" The "ulama" refers to the "doctors of Muslim religion and law" (Fatwa 2001).

2. Following the terrorist attacks, American Muslims suffered through frequent and often severe episodes of harassment. Incidents ranged from ethnic profiling to verbal and physical assault (e.g., Fahim 2001; James 2001; Labbe 2001; Rothstein 2001; Sachs 2001; Woods 2001). During the twelve months following September 11, the American-Arab Anti-Discrimination Committee documented over 700 violent incidents targeting Arab Americans, including several murders; over eighty cases of illegal and discriminatory removal of passengers from aircraft; a 400 percent increase in employment discrimination; and numerous instances of denial of service (ADC 2003). These individual incidents are not part to our analysis, but they do provide an emotional backdrop to the messages we analyze.

3.   Islam has more than 1.3 billion adherents worldwide. Depending on the source, estimates range from 1.4 to 7 million American Muslims (Woodward 2001, 102). According to the State Department, one of very four Muslims in the United States is African American (Parish 2001).
4.   Recent books by Jerry Vines include Spirit Life (1998), Power in the Pulpit (1999), Spiritfruit (2001), and Pursuing God's Own Heart: Lessons from the life of David (2003). For an overview of his ministry, see the web site of the First Baptist Church of Jacksonville, Florida (http://www.fbcjax.com).
5.   In talking of the relationship between consonant and disconsonant scenes, we are reminded of Burke's (1984) discussion of frames of acceptance and rejection in the first chapter of Attitudes toward History.
6.   Franklin Graham, for example, clarified his views in saying, "I do not believe Muslims are evil people because of their faith. I personally have many Muslim friends. But I decry the evil that has been done in the name of Islam" ("Amen corner" 2001, 1B). This statement follows the traditional rhetorical posture of distinguishing between legitimate mainstream Islam and illegitimate radical interpretations of the faith's teachings. Also, Jerry Falwell also apologized for his remarks on the 700 Club (Carlson 2001, F1).
7.   For comparison, see the transcript of the NBC broadcast (NBC 2001; Today 2001).
8.   An Imam is the spiritual leader of a Muslim congregation and is usually the most learned member.

References

ABC news. "National Day of Prayer memorial service." September 14, 2001, Lexis-Nexis via http://web.lexis-nexis.com/universe/

ADC Research Institute. 2003. Executive summary. In "Report on hate crimes and discrimination against Arab Americans: The post-September 11 backlash," http://www.adc.org/hilal/web/executive.htm

Amen corner. 2001. *Atlanta Journal and Constitution*, 1B, December 8.

Baptist intolerance. 2002. *Winston-Salem Journal*, A18, June 16.

Bellah, R. N. 1980. Introduction to *Varieties of civil religion*, by R. N. Bellah and P. E. Hammond. San Francisco, CA: Harper & Row.

Bennett, W. L. 1978. The ritualistic and pragmatic bases of political campaign discourse. *Quarterly Journal of Speech* 63:219-238.

Bin-Laden, S. U.; A. al-Zawahiri, A. R. A. Taha, S. M. Hamzah, and F. Rahman. 1998. Jihad against Jews and crusaders: World Islamic front statement, February 23, http://www.efreedomnews.com/News%20Archive/ Terrorists/Fatwah2_ BinLaden.htm

Breed, A. G. (2002, July 2). Convert brothers take heat for message that Islam is hardly a peaceful faith. *Associated Press*, July 2, 2002, Lexis-Nexis, via http://web.lexis-nexis.com/universe/

Brokaw, T. 2003. *NBC nightly news.* New York: National Broadcasting Corporation, February 25.

Brotherly hate: How to lose a war—and our souls. 2002. *Arkansas Democrat-Gazette*, B8, June 20.

Burke, K. 1984. *Attitudes toward history* (third edition). Berkeley: University of California Press.

Burke, K. 1969. *A grammar of motives.* Berkeley: University of California Press.

Campbell, K. K. and K. H. Jamieson. 1990. *Deeds Done in Words: Presidential Rhetoric and Genres of Governance.* Chicago: University of Chicago Press.

Carey, J. W. 1975. A cultural approach to communication. *Communication* 2:1-22.

Carlson, P. 2001. Jerry Falwell's awkward apology. *Washington Post,* F1, November 18.
Carter, S. L. 1993. *The Culture of Disbelief: How American Law and Politics Trivialize Religious Devotion.* New York: Basic Books.
"Catholic bishops and Muslim leaders issue joint statement." *Communications: United States Conference of Catholic Bishop,* September 14, 2001, http://www.usccb.org/comm/archives/2001/01-163.htm
Cohen, R. 2002. Imams of inanity. *Washington Post,* A25, December 3.
Cooperman, A. 2003a. Graham invitation irks Muslims at Pentagon. *Washington Post,* A2, April 15.
Cooperman, A. 2003b. At Pentagon, Graham lets controversy sit silently. *Washington Post,* A4, April 19.
Edsal, T. B. 1998. Wooing the Christian Coalition. *Washington Post,* A2, September 20.
Eisenberg, C. 2003. A controversial crusade. *Newsday,* A40, April 21.
Fahim, K. 2001. Backlash and counter-backlash. *Village Voice,* 42, September 25.
Frye, N. 1957. *Anatomy of Criticism: Four Essays.* Princeton, NJ: Princeton University Press.
Goodstein, L. 2003. Top evangelicals critical of colleagues over Islam. *New York Times,* A22, May 8.
Graham, F. 2002. *The Name.* Nashville, TN: Thomas Nelson.
Habit of ministry. 2001. *Christian Century,* 118:5, October 10.
Hart, R. P. 1977. *The Political Pulpit.* West Lafayette, IN: Purdue University Press.
Heredia, C., and I. Lelchuk. 2001. A nation bows its head in prayer. *San Francisco Chronicle,* A1, September 14.
"History." *A national house of prayer for all people: Washington National Cathedral.* (n.d.), http://www.cathedral.org/cathedral/index.shtml
Hunter, J. D. 1991. *Culture Wars: The Struggle to Define America.* New York: Basic Books.
Ivie, R. L. 2001. Productive criticism then and now. *American Communication Journal, 4.* http://acjournal.org/holdings/Vol4/iss3/special/ivie.htm (accessed October 18, 2003).
Ivie, R. L. 2002. Rhetorical deliberation and democratic politics in the here and now. *Rhetoric and Public Affairs* 5:277-285.
Jackson, F., J. Duke, and J. Brown. Evangelist Graham in presidential hot water over comments: White House hosts Ramadan gathering. *Agape Press,* November 20, 2001, http://www.familypolicy.net/nf/franklin-11-20-01.shtml
James, R. 2001. College leaders target bigotry; Arab-American and internal students say they have been victims. *Syracuse Post-Standard,* B1, September 25.
Jones, J. 2002. Baptist calls Islam founder "pedophile"; church leaders agree, Muslims outraged. *Pittsburgh Post-Gazette,* A5, June 13.
Judeo-Christian-Islamic? A growing population prompts new thinking. *Dallas Morning News,* May 27, 2003, Lexis-Nexis via http://web.lexis-nexis.com/universe/
Kennedy, E. M. 1983. Truth and tolerance in America. http://www.americanrhetoric.com/speeches/edwardkennedytruth&tolerance.htm
Kennedy, J. F. 1960. Address to the Greater Houston Ministerial Association. http://www.americanrhetoric.com/speeches/johnfkennedyhoustonministerialspeech.html
Kristoff, N. D. 2002. Bigotry in Islam – and here. *New York Times,* A21, July.
Labbe, T. S. 2001. Muslims endure season of suspicion. *Albany Times Union,* A9, September 30.
Lincoln, B. 2003. *Holy Terrors: Thinking about Religion after September 11.* Chicago: University of Chicago Press.
Marquis, C. 2003. A nation at war: Religious services. *New York Times,* B10, April 18.
Milbank, D. 2001. Religious right finds its center in oval office. *Washington Post,* A2, December 24.

National conversation. 2001. *Boston Herald*, 16, December 7.

National day of prayer and remembrance. *A national house of prayer for all people: Washington National Cathedral*. September 14, 2001, http://www.cathedral.org/cathedral/programs/wtc9.11/PresPrayer.html

NBC News special reports: America mourns. (2001, September 14). *NBC News transcripts*, May 28, 2003, Lexis-Nexis via http://web.lexis-nexis.com/universe/

Neuhaus, R. J. 1984. *The Naked Public Square: Religion and Democracy in America*. Grand Rapids, MI: Eerdmans.

Oliphant, T. 2003. Bridging the gap among religions. *Boston Globe*, A15, September 9.

Parish, N. 2001. Area black Muslims fear backlash, help fund recovery. *St. Louis Post-Dispatch*, A4, October 1.

Post September 11 attitudes: Religion more prominent; Muslim-Americans more accepted. Pew *Research Center for the People and the Press*, December 6, 2001, http://people-press.org/reports/display.php3?ReportID=144

Raasch, C. Tolerance for Muslims in U.S. rises since Sept. 11, survey says. *Gannett News Service*, December 6, 2001, Lexis-Nexis via *http://web.lexis-nexis.com/universe/*

Random House Unabridged Dictionary (second edition). 2001. Fatwah. New York: Random House.

Rice, C. 2002. Falwell's rhetoric hateful, inciting. *Johns Hopkins News-Letter*, November 1, 2002, Lexis-Nexis via http://web.lexis-nexis.com/universe/

Rosin, H. 2002. Younger Graham diverges from father's image. *Washington Post*, A3, September 2.

Rothenbuhler, E. W. 1998. *Ritual Communication: From Everyday Conversation to Mediated Ceremony*. Thousand Oaks, CA: Sage.

Rothstein, R. 2002. Lessons: The other war against intolerance. *New York Times*, D8, September 26.

Sachs, S. 2001. In the search for suspects, sensitivities about profiling. *New York Times*, D7, September 26.

Spencer, T. Voters split on Moore, like display, poll says. *Birmingham News*, September 7. 2003, Lexis-Nexis, via http://web.lexis-nexis.com/universe/

Thomas, C. 2003. It's time to confront the threat from within. *Baltimore Sun*, 19A, May 21.

Thomas, C. and E. Dobson. 1999. *Blinded by Might: Can the Religious Right Save America?* Grand Rapids, MI: Zonderovan.

Thomas spouts propaganda. *Baton Rouge Advocate*, May 26, 2003, Lexis-Nexis, via http://web.lexis-nexis.com/universe/

Today – NBC. *NBC News transcripts*, September 14, 2001, Lexis-Nexis via http://web.lexis-nexis.com/universe/

Transcript of the show *Politically Incorrect* telecast on ABC on September 17, 2001: Panel Discussion. http://www.geocities.com/vadi2000/pi/pi_transcript.html

Turner, V. 1982. *From Ritual to Theatre: The Human Seriousness of Play*. New York: Performing Arts Journal.

Van Kasteren, J. P. 1913. Beatitudes. In *The Catholic Encyclopedia* (Vol. 2, pp. 371-372). New York: Encyclopedia Press.

Vara, R. 2002. "Gentler image" takes a beating at Baptist meeting. *Houston Chronicle*, sec. Religion, 1, June 15.

Washington National Cathedral. (n.d.). "History." http://www.cathedral.org/cathedral/discover/history.shtml

White, H. 1973. *Metahistory: The Historical Imagination in Nineteenth-Century Europe*. Baltimore, MD: Johns Hopkins University Press.

Wilson, M. 2002. Evangelist says Muslims haven't adequately apologized for Sept. 11 attacks. *New York Times*, A14, August 15.

Woods, J. 2001. City's Islamic legal community voices concerns. *New York Law Journal*, 1, September 26.

Woodward, K. L. 2001. Religion: How should we think about Islam? *Newsweek*, 139:102-103, December 31.

Zangwill, I. 1939. *The Melting-Pot: Drama in Four Acts*. New York: Macmillan.

3

Uninhibited, Robust, and Wide-Open Debate: Reclaiming the Essence of Democracy in the Wake of 9/11

W. Wat Hopkins

In March 1964, Justice William J. Brennan, Jr., possibly the Supreme Court's most ardent and effective advocate of free speech, wrote that in the United States, there is "[A] profound national commitment to the principle that debate on public issues should be uninhibited, robust, and wide-open," even if those criticisms include "vehement, caustic, and sometimes unpleasantly sharp attacks on government and public officials" (*New York Times* 1964, 270). That recognition, Justice Brennan wrote, is at "[T]he central meaning of the First Amendment," and, therefore, citizens have more than a right to criticize their government and their governors, they have a duty to do so—as much a duty as it is the duty of government officials to administer (*New York Times* 1964, 273, 282).

It was a remarkable assertion, particularly since Justice Brennan was writing for a unanimous Court. In many ways, in *New York Times Co. v. Sullivan,* a history of relatively jumbled First Amendment jurisprudence coalesced into a cogent theory of the meaning of the First Amendment in a democratic society.

In the mid-1960s, free speech jurisprudence was still in its infancy. By early 1964, for example, the Court had decided barely 100 free expression cases and many of those dealt with regulatory issues, like copyright. The Court had settled the issue of prior restraint—ruling that it was unconstitutional—and had ruled that certain kinds of speech, fighting words and obscenity, for example, lay outside the protection of the First Amendment. Though it had ruled that obscene material was unprotected, however, the Court had not yet settled on a cogent definition of obscenity (Miller 1973, 24). And, while fighting words might not be protected, the Court was five years away from its landmark ruling that the advocacy of violence is protected, so long as the speech is not designed to produce "imminent lawless action" (Brandenburg 1969, 447-48). In addition, the Court had not developed a template for deciding cases involving expressive conduct, and commercial speech was still considered unprotected by the First Amendment, a rule that would not change for another twelve years (Virginia State Board 1976). The status of First Amendment protection for students was uncertain, and the Court, while granting First Amendment protection to movies, had barely scratched the surface in jurisprudence involving broadcasting, much less cable or new communication technologies.

And, most significantly, the Court had not considered in a substantive way how the constitutional mandate of free speech and a free press related to the experiment of the democratic republic. There had been hints, of course, but not until 1964, when Justice Brennan delivered his majority opinion in *Times v. Sullivan,* did those hints coalesce in a cogent way to delineate the role of free expression in the United States.

While considerable debate continues over the meaning of the First Amendment, two principles have emerged upon which there is almost universal agreement. First, at a minimum the First Amendment was designed to prohibit prior restraint. Second, expression that is important to the democracy, that is, expression that is of self-governing importance, receives almost absolute protection. Philosopher Alexander Meiklejohn proposed that the Constitution was designed to give virtually absolute protection to speech related to matters of self-governing importance, which he defined broadly (Meiklejohn 1961). Justice Brennan very nearly adopted Meiklejohn's proposal in *Times v. Sullivan.* "Uninhibited, robust and wide open debate," he wrote, is essential to the operation of the democracy and must be protected (270). The government, therefore, may not prohibit speech from entering the marketplace of ideas, because to do so erodes the fabric of the democratic society. The paradigm is simple: The democracy is dependent upon an active citizenry; to govern themselves effectively, the citizens must be informed; to be informed, citizens must have access to both government information and to a wide range of ideas related to the choices they must make.

Without a guarantee that a wide range of ideas is available, therefore, the essence of the democratic society is undermined. Unfortunately, that is what is happened in the wake of the terrorist attacks in New York and Washington on September 11, 2001. Almost immediately, government agencies moved to limit access to information—sometimes innocuous information. Similarly, persons who questioned the methods being used by the government to restrict access and to uncover suspected terrorists were painted with the broad brush of anti-patriotism. "Information that had been sensitive became sinister," noted Paul McMasters, ombudsman for the Freedom Forum in Arlington, Virginia (McMasters 2002). Possibly the two most visible examples are the quick passage by Congress of the USA Patriot Act and the efforts by Attorney General John Ashcroft to limit access by the public to many federal documents.

The Patriot Act became law with President George W. Bush's signature on October 26, 2001. It gives law enforcement agencies increased authority when dealing with suspected terrorists, but has also caused increasing concerns among civil libertarians. And critics of the act—or of any aspect of the so-called "war on terror"—have often found themselves victims of harsh criticism and other forms of verbal abuse. Members of the city council of Berkeley, California, for example, received death threats when the council suggested that the bombing in Afghanistan be curtailed (Elias 2001). And a political science professor in California received death threats for criticizing the Bush administration for its policies toward the Arab world (Kurtz 2001). They are accused of not being patriots—and how could they be if they question the "Patriot Act?"

Shortly after the events of 9/11, Attorney General Ashcroft, sent a memorandum to all federal agencies encouraging those agencies to be more circumspect in answering Freedom of Information requests. "Any discretionary decision by your agency to disclose information protected under the FOIA," the memorandum read, "should be made only after full and deliberate consideration of the institutional, commercial, and personal privacy interests that could be implicated by disclosure of the information" (Ashcroft memorandum 2001). The memorandum reminded agencies that the Department of Justice would defend those decisions. The action was part of an overall plan by the Bush administration to reverse the policy that had been adopted by the Clinton administration that openness, rather than secrecy, was the rule (Homefront Confidential 2002).

In many ways, these events—or events like them—were to be expected. Throughout history, the government has attempted to squelch both access to public information and commentary on official activities during times of stress on society (Blanchard 2002). There is a difference between efforts to stifle debate in the wake of 9/11 and similar attempts during earlier times of crisis. More than ever before, the attacks of 9/11 impacted in a passionate and dramatic way debate about public policy. Critics were seen, not as patriots who cared about what was going on among government and military leaders, but very nearly as traitors. Indeed, Attorney General Ashcroft made just such a claim. Speaking to the Senate Judiciary Committee on December 6, 2001, he attacked critics of the administration's techniques in responding to the terrorist acts of 9/11. Critics who attacked efforts by the administration to limit civil liberties were aiding terrorists, he said, by creating a "fog of war." Those criticisms, he said, "[E]rode our national unity and diminish our resolve. They give ammunition to America's enemies, and pause to America's friends" (Ashcroft statement 2001).

What the Attorney General fails to realize is that the health and welfare of the republic is just as dependant upon the marketplace of ideas and the robust debate it ensures as is the capture of Osama bin Laden. Regardless of whether that outlaw is captured, the republic will remain. That assurance may not be so if the first freedoms of the republic are trammeled and eventually forgotten.

The Mandate for Uninhibited, Robust Debate

There is very little evidence as to what the framers of the Bill of Rights meant by the assurance that "Congress shall make no law. . . abridging the freedom of speech or of the press." That language was not part of the bill of rights proposed by James Madison of Virginia in the First Congress, but, rather, it came out of a conference committee and combined what Madison had proposed in two separate amendments (Debates 1789, 451). And there was little discussion as to the meaning of the guarantee, at least until the adoption of the Alien and Sedition Acts of 1798. The Sedition Act, which provided a $2,000 fine, two years imprisonment, or both, for anyone who criticized members of Congress or the President prompted the first legislative debates on the meaning of the First Amendment.

Supporters of the law argued that freedom of the press did not include freedom to publish abusive commentary, false statements of fact, or material that could damage the government. "[T]he publication of false, scandalous, and malicious writings against the government, written or published with intent to do mischief" could be prohibited and punished, they argued (Debates 1789, 2987). Opponents, however, argued that misdeeds of government should be revealed to the populace; only then will the people have "important and necessary information" needed for self-government (Debates 1789, 3003-04). Even if a distinction could be made between "liberty of the press and abuse of the press," they argued, the Constitution prevents legislation designed to inhibit the press, which is as it should be: In a democracy there must be "a free investigation of all public acts" (Debates 1789, 406).

The vigorous debate over the Sedition Act did not last. Though attempts to repeal the act failed in February of 1799, it expired in 1801, and newly elected President Thomas Jefferson pardoned the handful of publishers who had been convicted under its provisions. Years would pass before debate over the meaning of the First Amendment and the relationship between free expression and a democratic government revived in significant measure.

Hints of a profound and direct relationship between the First Amendment guarantees of free expression and the operation of a democratic republic surfaced in Supreme Court jurisprudence for the first time in 1919. In March of that year, the Court decided what it would later assert to be the first important free speech case, *Schenck v. United States.* It would be another seven months, however, in *Abrams v. United States,* before the Court, through Justice Oliver Wendell Holmes, began exploring the significance of free expression to the democracy.

In *Schenck,* the Court, with Justice Holmes writing for the majority, upheld the convictions of Charles T. Schenck and Elizabeth Baer, officers in the Socialist Party, for violating the Espionage Act of 1917 by distributing circulars designed to interfere with military recruitment and operations. The Espionage Act contained no provisions for punishing words—only for punishing actions—but the Court found that the convictions could stand on the ground that Schenck and Baer were guilty of conspiracy to obstruct recruitment. Key to Holmes's resolution of the case was the *intent* of the conspirators, which was determined based upon the *content* of the publication.

Wrote Justice Holmes (Schenck 1919, 52):

> We admit that in many places and in ordinary times the defendants, in saying all that was said in the circular, would have been within their constitutional rights. But the character of every act depends upon the circumstances in which it was done. . . . The most stringent protection of free speech would not protect a man in falsely shouting fire in a theater, and causing a panic. It does not even protect a man from an injunction against uttering words that may have all the effect of force. . . . The question in every case is whether the words used are used in such circumstances and are of such a nature as to create a clear and present danger that they will bring about the substantive evils that Congress has a right to prevent. It is a question of proximity and degree. When a nation is at war many things that might be said in time of peace are such a hindrance to its effort that their utterance will not be endured as long as men fight, and that no court could regard them as protected by any constitutional right. It seems to be admitted that if an actual obstruction of the recruiting service were proved, liability for words that protected that effect might be enforced. The Statute. . . punishes conspiracies to obstruct as well as actual obstruction. If the act (speaking, or circulating a paper), its tendency, and the intent with which it is done are the same, we perceive no ground for saying that success alone warrants making the act a crime.

In *Schenck,* then, the convictions were upheld because the publishing of certain words was determined to be an act of conspiracy, which the law prohibited. Holmes made it clear that the uttering of words must have "all the effect of force."

Abrams was also an Espionage Act case, but Justice Holmes found that the facts were significantly different from those in *Schenck* and used the case to begin laying a foundation upon which would be built a paradigm for significant protection of expression. First Amendment scholar Vincent Blasi has called Justice Holmes's *Abrams* dissent, possibly "the single most influential judicial opinion ever written" on free speech (p. 1343). Justice Holmes did not retreat from the opinions affirming the convictions of Schenck, Baer and others who were convicted under the Espionage Act. The government, he reaffirmed, may constitutionally punish speech "that produces or is intended to produce a clear and imminent danger" of "substantive evils." And, he noted, "The power undoubtedly is greater in time of war than in time of peace because war opens dangers that do not exist at other times" (Abrams 1919, 627-28).

But, Justice Holmes added, the government must be wary not to go too far. Speech producing a clear and imminent danger of substantive evils may be punished, not exhortations or opinions, even if they attack the government. Indeed, Justice Holmes asserted that seditious libel, that is, criticisms of the government—even harsh criticisms—had not been left intact by the First Amendment. Free speech,

Justice Holmes indicated in the key passage to his dissent, is too important to be subject to such regulation (Abrams 1919, 630):

> Persecution for the expression of opinions seems to be perfectly logical. If you have no doubt of your premises or your power and want a certain result with all your heart you naturally express your wishes in law and sweep away all opposition. To allow opposition by speech seems to indicate that you think the speech impotent, as when a man says that he has squared the circle, or that you do not care whole heartedly for the result, or that you doubt either your power or your premises. But when men have realized that time has upset many fighting faiths, they may come to believe even more than they believe the very foundations of their own conduct that the ultimate good desired is better reached by free trade in ideas—that the best test of truth is the power of the thought to get itself accepted in the competition of the market, and that truth is the only ground upon which their wishes safely can be carried out. That at any rate is the theory of our Constitution.

It was a remarkable assertion—that *the best test of truth* is its ability to be accepted in the *competition of the market*—and it has caused considerable debate. The debate has centered both over the reasons for Justice Holmes's apparent turn-around since *Schenck,* and on whether the so-called "marketplace of ideas" theory is workable.

The marketplace of ideas theory wasn't original with Justice Holmes. While it traces its origins at least to sixteenth century political discourse, poet and essayist John Milton is generally credited with being its most eloquent early advocate. In 1644 Milton published *Areopagitica,* an essay responding to criticism of an earlier tract in which he had advocated a loosening of English divorce laws. Milton had a vested interest—he hoped to escape an unhappy marriage. While far from catholic in his opinion of who had free expression rights, Milton criticized licensing laws, advocating free expression as a means of discovering truth (646-47):

> And though all the winds of doctrine were let loose to play upon the earth, so Truth be in the field, we do injuriously, by licensing and prohibiting, so misdoubt her strength. Let her and Falsehood grapple; who ever knew Truth put to the worse in a free and open encounter.

The marketplace metaphor became popular in the American colonies in the eighteenth century, but nineteenth century English essayist John Stuart Mill is credited with nurturing the theory into full flower. In his 1859 work *On Liberty,* Mill argued for almost unrestricted freedom of expression: "If all mankind minus one, were of one opinion, and only one person were of the contrary opinion, mankind would be no more justified in silencing that one person, than he, if he had the power, would be justified in silencing mankind" (6). Mill found free expression necessary "to the mental well-being of mankind" for four reasons: First, the opinion that is silenced might be true; second, the silenced opinion, though it may be in error, may contain some truth, and its expression might strengthen or fulfill true opinion; third, the false opinion, by its expression, will strengthen truth; fourth, the meaning of the true doctrine might be lost if not challenged (52).

It was Justice Holmes, however, who introduced the theory into Supreme Court jurisprudence. He did not use that specific term, but he came close, referring specifically to a "free trade in ideas" and to "the competition of the market." Justice Holmes, and later Justice Louis Brandeis, constructed a test for protecting speech that merged the marketplace of ideas theory and the clear and present danger test. Under the test, speech could be restricted by the government only if there was a clear and imminent danger that substantive harm would occur before the damaging speech could be corrected by other speech. The government was not required to wait until the spark caused by the speech "has enkindled the flame or blazed into the conflagration" before acting, but "If there be time to expose through discussion the falsehood and fallacies, to avert the evil by the processes of education, the remedy to be applied is more speech, not enforced silence" (377). The search for truth in the competition of the market is "the theory of our Constitution" Justice Holmes noted in *Abrams*. Therefore, he asserted that seditious libel was overridden by the First Amendment (630).

Much of the development work on the relationship between free expression and the democratic republic was in dissenting opinions, but eventually those principles moved from dissent to majority. Eight years after *Abrams,* for example, in *Whitney v. California,* the Court asserted that the founders of the United States "valued liberty both as an end and as a means" (375). Wrote Justice Brandeis in a concurring opinion:

> They believed that freedom to think as you will and to speak as you think are means indispensable to the discovery and spread of political truth; that without free speech and assembly discussion would be futile; that with them, discussion affords ordinarily adequate protection against the dissemination of noxious doctrine; that the greatest menace to freedom is an inert people; that public discussion is a political duty; and that this should be a fundamental principle of the American government.

Justices Homes and Brandeis, therefore, lay the foundation for the proposition that free speech is not simply a convenience or even a right of participants in a free society—it is a mandate; it is essential to the proper—if not effective—workings of the democratic republic. That precept, introduced by Holmes, then expanded by Holmes and Brandeis, was not fully developed until slightly more than forty years later in *Times v. Sullivan*.

Fulfilling the Mandate: *New York Times Co. v. Sullivan*

New York Times Co. v. Sullivan serves as the symbolic midpoint in this discussion of the relationship between free expression and democracy. It was delivered slightly more than forty years after Justices Holmes and Brandeis laid the foundation for protecting speech during times of stress, and it was delivered slightly less than forty years before the debate would be revived in dramatic fashion by the events of 9/11. And it very well may be the Court's most important statement on the topic.

The primary significance of *Times v. Sullivan* is generally considered to be in the area of libel law. The Court held, for the first time, that public officials who bring libel suits based on criticisms of them in their official roles must prove that the criticisms were made with actual malice, that is, with knowledge of falsity or with reckless disregard for the truth (279-80). Even false statements of fact are protected under the First Amendment in such circumstances, Justice Brennan wrote for the majority, in order to protect robust debate on matters of public concern. The opinion is clearly the Court's most important pronouncement on libel law.

Often overlooked in that opinion, however, is Justice Brennan's rationale for ruling that false statements of fact deserve constitutional protection and, ultimately, for his assertion, quoted at the outset of this chapter, that citizens have a duty to criticize their government and their governors. A linchpin for that rationale was his determination that the libel suit against the *New York Times* was a form of seditious libel, which, Justice Brennan wrote, was unconstitutional. "Although the Sedition Act was never tested in this Court," he wrote, agreeing with the similar assertion by Justice Holmes forty-six years earlier, "the attack upon its validity has carried the day in the court of history" (276). Justice Brennan quoted Justice Brandeis on the point, asserting that the previous justice had established the "classic formulation" of the argument (270):

Those who won our independence believed. . . that public discussion is a political duty; and that this should be a fundamental principle of the American government. They recognized the risks to which all human institutions are subject. But they knew that order cannot be secured merely through fear of punishment for its infraction; that it is hazardous to discourage thought, hope and imagination; that fear breeds repression; that repression breeds hate; that hate menaces stable government; that the path of safety lies in the opportunity to discuss freely supposed grievances and proposed remedies; and that the fitting remedy for evil counsels is good ones. Believing in the power of reason as applied through public discussion, they eschewed silence coerced by law— the argument of force in its worst form. Recognizing the occasional tyrannies of governing majorities, they amended the Constitution so that free speech and assembly should be guaranteed.

Arguably, however, the assertion that the Sedition Act in particular and seditious libel in general were unconstitutional was irrelevant to the *Times* case. Historically, a case of seditious libel was brought under criminal law. That is, the government prosecuted the publisher of a document that it found to be so critical of the government that it was of an "insurrectionary" or treasonous nature. *Times v. Sullivan* was brought by L.B. Sullivan, a commissioner of public welfare for the city of Montgomery, Alabama. It was a civil suit, therefore, not a criminal case and could not fall within the parameters of seditious libel. In addition, attorneys for Sullivan argued that, even if the Sedition Act were unconstitutional, such a finding would not impact the case before the Court: The prohibition of the First Amendment, they argued, is aimed at Congress, not the states.

The argument was flawed in two ways, Justice Brennan wrote. First, the Court had held that the Fourteenth Amendment of the Constitution applied the First Amendment prohibition against laws infringing free speech and a free press to the states as well as the federal government (276-77). Second, and equally important, civil lawsuits can sometimes take on the role of seditious libel and, when they do, they, too, are prohibited by the First Amendment. Wrote Justice Brennan (277):

What a State may not constitutionally bring about by means of a criminal statute is likewise beyond the reach of its civil law of libel. The fear of damage awards under a rule such as that invoked by the Alabama courts here may be markedly more inhibiting than the fear of prosecution under a criminal statute.

Indeed, had it been convicted under the Sedition Act, the New York Times Co. would have been required to pay a $2,000 fine. At the time *Times v. Sullivan* was decided, however, it was facing more than $2 million in damage awards, many of which were nullified, in effect, by the actual malice rule.

The "central meaning" of the First Amendment, therefore, Justice Brennan wrote, is that critics of the government or of governors may not be punished for their criticisms (273). The government grants to public officials protection against libel actions brought by private citizens based on the official actions of those public officials. The rationale behind such protection is that the threat of lawsuits "would otherwise 'inhibit the fearless, vigorous, and effective administration of policies of government' and 'dampen the ardor of all but the most resolute, or the most irresponsible, in the unflinching discharge of their duties.'" Analogous consideration should be given the "citizen-critic," Justice Brennan wrote, because, "It is as much his duty to criticize as it is the official's duty to administer" (282).

The assertion was also grounded solidly in marketplace-of-ideas theory. Indeed, *Times v. Sullivan* was arguably the Court's most dramatic reaffirmation of the marketplace of ideas theory. The citizen-critic is important to democracy, the Court held, because important decisions are better achieved through a multitude of voices. Justice Brennan wrote that the constitutional mandate of free expression "'was fashioned to assure unfettered interchange of ideas for the bringing about of political and social changes desired by the people'" (269).

Robust Debate after 9/11

Times v. Sullivan was not the Court's last word on the role of free speech in a democratic society. Indeed, the Court has repeatedly asserted that the marketplace of ideas theory should govern free speech jurisprudence. The Court—or members of the Court—have referred to the marketplace of ideas theory in nearly 150 opinions in more than 100 cases. The essence of that jurisprudence is the notion, the Court has said, that free expression is essential to the operation of a democratic society (*Hustler Magazine* 1988, 50-51):

At the heart of the First Amendment is the recognition of the fundamental importance of the free flow of ideas and opinions on matters of public interest and concern. "[T]he freedom to speak one's mind is not only an aspect of individual liberty—and thus a good unto itself—but also is essential to the common quest for truth and the vitality of society as a whole."

Indeed, speech and press are protected by the Constitution specifically "to assure unfettered interchange of ideas for the bringing

about of political and social changes desired by the people"
(Rosenberger 1995, 844). That is, the Court has said, speech concerning public affairs is more than self-expression, "[I]t is the essence of self government" (Dun & Bradstreet 1985, 759).

Under this paradigm, the government may regulate speech of self-
governing importance only when that speech is likely to cause direct, immediate, and irreparable harm to the government. While it's
true that the Court held in *Schenck* that many things that might be
said in times of peace cannot be said in times of war, it's also true
that the Court was only addressing itself to words that could take on
the role of action. Words themselves could not be punished, only
words that were likely to cause immediate and direct harm. The harm
must be tangible and identifiable—not supposed or hypothetical.
The words, Justice Holmes wrote, must have "all the effect of force"
(Schenck 1919, 52). In *Schenck,* the danger was not what was published, but that what published constituted a conspiracy to obstruct military recruiting.

In *Abrams* and later cases, Justice Holmes reiterated that the government has more power to limit speech in times of war than in
times of peace, but that power was based on the fact that "war opens
dangers that do not exist at other times" (627-28). Holmes, however, did not back off the proposition that words may be regulated
only if they are likely to cause what he came to call "a clear and
present danger." Words must still have "all the effect of force;" in
wartime, however, heightened tensions might cause the conflagration to be more easily ignited.

Critics of the government, under the model established by Justices Holmes and Brandeis and developed to maturity by Justice
Brennan, are not traitors, therefore. Indeed, they are performing a
patriotic duty, in that they are helping the republic come to the best
possible course for public policy. In the face of stressful times—
like those ignited by the terrorist attacks of 9/11—these citizen-
critics should be encouraged, not discouraged. They are performing tasks that are at the heart of the democratic republic. The uninhibited, robust, and wide-open debate in which they participate is at
the central meaning of the First Amendment. It is the essence of
democracy.

References

Abrams v. United States, 250 U.S. 616 (1919).

Ashcroft, J. 2001. DOJ Oversight: Preserving our freedoms while defending against terrorism, before the senate committee on the judiciary, 107th Congress (Ashcroft Statement).

Ashcroft, J. 2001. Department of Justice FOI policy memorandum, October 12, 2001 (Ashcroft Memorandum).

AT&T v. Iowa Utilities Board, 525 U.S. 366 (1999).

Baker, C. E. 1989. *Human Liberty and Freedom of Speech*. New York: Oxford University Press.

Barron, J. 1967. Access to the press—A new First Amendment right. *Harvard Law Review* 80: 1641-78.

Blackstone, W. 1969. 4 *Commentaries of the laws of England 1765-1769*. South Hackensack, NJ: Rothman Reprints.

Blanchard, M. 2002. "Why can't we learn?" Cycles of stability, stress and freedom of expression in United States history. *Communication Law and Policy* 7:347-78.

Blasi, V. 1997. Reading Holmes through the lens of Schauer: The Abrams dissent. *Notre Dame Law Review* 72 (July): 1343-60.

Blasi, V. 1977. The checking value in First Amendment theory. *American Bar Foundation Research Journal* 1977 (ssss): 548-

Brandenburg v. Ohio, 395 U.S. 444 (1969). Chaplinsky v. New Hampshire, 315 U.S. 568 (1942).

Debates and Proceedings in the Congress of the United States. 1789.

Dennis v. United States, 341 U.S. 494 (1951)

Elias, T. 2001. America's Ordeal; Berkeley Takes a Costly Stand. *Newsday*, 4 November, p. A49.

Debs v. United States, 249 U.S. 211 (1919).

Dun & Bradstreet v. Greenmoss, 472 U.S. 749 (1985).

Frohwerk v. United States, 249 U.S. 204 (1919).

Gitlow v. New York, 268 U.S. 652 (1925).

Hopkins, W. 1989. *Mr. Justice Brennan and Freedom of Expression*. Westport, CT: Praeger.

Hopkins, W. 1995. Reconsidering the "Clear and Present Danger" test: Whence the "marketplace of ideas"? *Free Speech Yearbook* 33:78-98.

Hustler v. Falwell, 485 U.S. 46 (1988).

Ingber, S. 1984. The marketplace of ideas: A legitimizing myth. *Duke Law Journal* 1984 (February): 1-91.

Joseph Burstyn, Inc. v. Wilson, 343 U.S. 495 (1952).

Kostyu, P. 2003. The First Amendment in theory and practice. In *Communication and the Law*. Northport, AL: Vision Press.

Kurtz, S. 2001. Free speech and an orthodoxy of dissent. *Chronicle of Higher Education*, 26 October, p. 24.

Los Angeles v. Preferred Communications, Inc., 476 U.S. 488 (1996).

Meiklejohn, A. 1961. The First Amendment is an absolute. *Supreme Court Review* 1961:245-66.

Miller v. California, 413 U.S. 15 (1973).

Milton, J. 1957. Areopagitica. In *Complete Poems and Major Prose*. New York: Odyssey.

Near v. Minnesota, 283 U.S. 697 (1931).

New York Times Co. v. Sullivan, 376 U.S. 254 (1964).

Rabban, D. 1982. The First Amendment in its forgotten years. *Yale Law Journal* 90: 514-95.

Ragan, F. 1971. Justice Oliver Wendell Holmes, Jr., Zechariah Chafee, Jr., and the clear and present danger test for free speech: The first year: 1919. *Journal of American History* 58 (June): 24-45.

Red Lion Broadcasting Co. v. FCC, 395 U.S. 367 (1968).

Reno v. ACLU, 521 U.S. 844 (1997).

Reporters Committee for Freedom of the Press. 2002. Homefront confidential: How the war on terror affects access to information and the public's right to know. White paper.

Rogat, J. and J.M. O'Fallon. 1984. Mr. Justice Holmes: A dissenting opinion—the speech cases. *Stanford Law Review* 36 (July): 1349-1406.

Rosenberger v. Rector and Visitors, University of Virginia, 515 U.S. 819 (1985).

Roth v. United States, 354 U.S. 476 (1957).

Schauer, F. 1982. *Free Speech: A Philosophical Enquiry.* New York: Cambridge University Press.

Schenck v. New York, 249 U.S. 47 (1919).

Sedition Act, 1 Stat. 596 (1798).

Smith, J. 1988. *Printers and Press Freedom.* New York: Oxford University Press.

Smith, S. 2003. Schenck v. United States and Abrams v. United States. In *Free Speech on Trial—Communication Perspectives on Landmark Supreme Court Decisions.* Tuscaloosa: University of Alabama Press.

Sweeney, B. 1984. The marketplace of ideas: An economic analogy for freedom of speech. Unpublished paper.

Tinker v. Des Moines Independent Community School District, 393 U.S. 503 (1969).

United States v. O'Brien, 391 U.S. 367 (1968).

USA PATRIOT Act, P.L. 107-56, 115 Stat. 272 (2001).

Valentine v. Chrestensen, 316 U.S. 52 (1942).

Virginia State Board of Pharmacy v. Virginia Citizens Consumer Council, 425 U.S. 748 (1976).

Whitney v. California, 274 U.S. 357 (1927).

4

The USA Patriot Act in Historical Context

Craig R. Smith

During the War of 1812, British troops landed near the nation's capital and proceeded to burn the Presidential Mansion, now known as White House. First Lady Dolly Madison barely escaped with a wagonload of public treasures and was not re-united with her husband for over twenty-four hours. By the end 1814 the war had stalemated, Andrew Jackson had scored his victory over the British at New Orleans, and a peace treaty was signed. The British were eventually forgiven for their unkind "act of war." On December 7, 1941 the naval installation at Pearl Harbor on the island territory of Oahu was bombed in a sneak attack by the Japanese. Over twenty-five hundred Americans lost their lives. The United States declared war on Japan and eventually extracted revenge.

Neither of these events compared to the evil of the attack on the World Trade Towers in New York City on September 11, 2001 since this strike constituted a sneak attack on a civilian population by terrorists activists trained on foreign soil. Their Al Qaeda network, situated mainly in Afghanistan, was protected by the reigning Taliban government and headed by Osama Bin Ladin, a known international outlaw of Saudi origin. Thus, the crisis that this bombing incited was one of the worst in the history of the United States. One of the questions the nation faced was what kinds of security measures would be necessary to deal with the crisis. What impact would these measures have on the civil liberties of American citizens?

This chapter attempts to put the security measures passed by the Congress and implemented by President George W. Bush into historic context by comparing the legislation and the interpretation of it to other legislation passed in response to past American crises.[1] The chapter reveals a pattern of events that not only place the current crisis in context, but demonstrate the role that each branch of the government has played in the past.[2] The chapter pays particular attention to the First Amendment since historically the freedoms contained therein tend to be the most affected; however, such other freedoms, as the right to consult with an attorney and to confront one's accusers, are also examined.

Inciting the Demos

A crisis is the result of a perceived threat, real or imagined. For example, by 1798, the year the Alien and Sedition Laws were passed, over 300 United States ships had been sunk or commandeered by the French. The nine-year-old French revolution had fallen into the hands of the radical Directory. Hundreds of nobles, including the king and queen of France, had been sent to the guillotine. The Directory vowed to spread its ideology across Europe by force.

Vice President Jefferson and members of his party debated Federalists about the extent to which that threat was real for the United States. Jefferson had been minister to France during its revolution. He had also been secretary of state of the United States. As vice president, he tried to dampen fears of a foreign invasion and openly opposed President Adam's call for a more stringent policy of immigration. The Federalists countered by arguing that the external threat of war with France was only one part of the story. The other was an internal threat from "Philosophes" and "Jacobins" who had infiltrated the country and, according to Congressman Otis, even served in Jefferson's State Department.[3]

The parallel to the McCarthy era is hard to miss. Again, America faced a foreign threat. Between 1945 and 1949, many Eastern European countries and China were taken over by Communist regimes. In 1950 the United States led a United Nations policing action against Communist North Korea. The Soviet Union aided that country with equipment and training. Eventually, the Communist regime on mainland China supported North Korea in the field with soldiers.

The internal threat of subversion had most dramatically appeared during hearings of the House Un-American Activities Committee in the summer of 1948 when Whittaker Chambers, a former editor of *Time* magazine, had accused Alger Hiss, a high-ranking official in the State Department, of having been a member of a communist cell in the 1930s. Hiss was eventually convicted of perjury for denying Chambers' charges. The embers of the HUAC charges had barely cooled when Senator Joseph McCarthy in a speech in Wheeling, West Virginia in 1950 claimed to have a list of over 200 subversive communists employed by the State Department. Before his fall from power in 1954, McCarthy would exaggerate his claim to include the Army.

In between the Alien and Sedition crisis and the McCarthy era, the pattern of expanding an external threat into an internal threat was readily apparent in most crises. By the time Abraham Lincoln took the oath of office, seven states had seceded from the Union. When war came, Lincoln claimed that the internal threat of subversion justified his suspension of *habeas corpus* and the jailing of "Copperhead" newspaper editors and others who opposed his policies.

Following Lincoln's death, the external threat that the South might rise again was enhanced by the charge that President Andrew Johnson was in league with Southerners. Alabama and Florida had passed vagrancy laws that required the poor to work for the state. Their income was given to widows and orphans, thereby returning many blacks to the status of state owned slaves. Other states passed laws denying the right of "negroes" to bear arms, denying business licenses to "negroes," and garnishing wages from "negroes" under various pretexts. On top of that, Alexander Stephens, in what must be seen as one the most arrogant acts in history, asked to be seated in the first postwar U.S. Senate. Stephens had been the vice president of the Confederacy and had spent four years trying to destroy the very Senate in which he asked to be seated. Southern editors infuriated Northerners by defending the reconstruction conventions. Moving quickly to "restore" the southern states to the Union, Johnson exacerbated his weak position, lost credibility, and increased suspicions that he was in league with the South.

Putting aside the unique threat to some by unionization and to others by turn of the century anarchists, the next major external crisis with internal ramifications came during America's entry into World War I. Woodrow Wilson's administration sent a force of U.S. troops to Archangel, Russia to join with other allies in support of the White Russian armies opposing Lenin and the Bolsheviks, who were perceived to be an external threat not only because of their ideology but because they negotiated peace with the Germans during World

War I. Throughout the time of America's direct intervention into World War I and its attempt to prop up the White Russians, Wilson and his administration conducted an unremitting campaign of suppression of free speech at home.[4] Once war had been declared, Wilson was only too aware of ethnic opposition to his policies, particularly among Irish, German, and other Central European immigrants. In fact, Wilson had sought to repress his critics as early as 1915, when Theodore Roosevelt had launched a withering attack on the president's conduct in the *Lusitania* affair. Like Alexander Hamilton during the quasi-war with France, Wilson claimed that foreign agents were subverting national will. During World War I and following the Russian Revolution, A. Mitchell Palmer, Woodrow Wilson's attorney general, justified the suspension of civil liberties on the grounds that "Reds" were engaged in subversive activities.

America returned to "normalcy" during the 1920s until its attention was drawn to the depression. Then, despite efforts to avoid involvement, America was drawn into World War II. The horror of Pearl Harbor was enhanced by the threat of alleged subversion on the part of Japanese Americans and Nazi infiltrators. The attorney general of California, Earl Warren, was one of the first to call for the internment of the Japanese. Over 120,000 Japanese Americans were eventually placed in camps. Having endured years of vilification by Republican-owned newspapers over such issues as trying to pack the Supreme Court, failing to end the depression, and plotting to get America into the war, Franklin Roosevelt was ready, as he wrote J. Edgar Hoover, to "clean up a number of . . . vile publications" (Roosevelt 1942). The president proceeded to criticize and call for investigations of the *New York Daily News*, Henry Luce of *Time* and *Life*, Drew Pearson, and Robert S. Allen, among others. He also tried to keep newspapers from acquiring ownership of radio stations, the first instantiation of the cross-ownership rules of the Federal Communication Commission.

If such civil libertarians as Lincoln, Wilson, and Roosevelt could trample basic rights, think how much more dangerous the situation would have been with a president less sympathetic to civil liberties. The pattern of taking an external threat and reinforcing it with an internal threat has been common in our history. Those who point it out are often attacked as giving sympathy to the enemy. It is to that pattern of suppression that this study now turns.

Condemnation of the Internal Opponent

While the Alien and Sedition Laws passed the Federalist-dominated Senate with ease, they faced tougher sledding in the House. In fact, fistfights broke out during the debates, and the margin of victory for the Federalists was very close, as little as three votes on the crucial bills. During the debates, members of Congress were not above questioning the patriotism of their opponents. One such attack was watched closely by members of the House and by citizens in a packed gallery. Federalist Jonathan Dayton rose to rebut a speech by Albert Gallatin, a Democratic-Republican leader who had originally come to the United States from Switzerland. Dayton himself was known to be a moderate Federalist, so his insinuations concerning Gallatin's foreign origin and his presumed friendliness to European radicalism were all the more striking. Said Dayton, "And why should that gentleman [Gallatin] be under no apprehension? Was it that secure in the perfect coincidence of the principles he avowed with those which actuated the furious hordes of democrats, which threatened the country with subjugation, he felt a confidence of his own safety, even if they should overrun . . . the states? He might indeed contemplate an invasion without alarm . . . he might see with calmness . . . our dwellings burning" (Levy and Peterson 1962, 199). There were many more such attacks.

On Washington's Birthday in 1866 in the midst of the reconstruction battle and while President Johnson was being feted at the White House by his friends, a crowd gathered outside and began to serenade him. Carried away by their adulation and his drinking, Johnson gave a long rambling speech that was interrupted by cries begging the president to name the "traitors" to whom he had alluded. "I have fought traitors and treason in the South," said the president. "I opposed Davis, Toombs, Slidell, and a long list of others whose names I need not repeat. And now, when I turn around at the other end of the line, I find men—I care not by what name you call them" (McCulloch 1889, 393). Johnson was interrupted again with cries of "Call them traitors." He continued saying that it was those who opposed his plan of "restoration." The crowd demanded names and finally the president gave way: "I say Thaddeus Stevens of Pennsylvania. I say Charles Sumner. I say Wendell Phillips and others of the same stripe among them. . . . They may traduce me, they may slander me, they may vituperate, but let me say to you that it has no effect upon me; and let me say in addition that I do not intend to be bullied by my enemies. . . . If it is blood they want, let them have the courage enough to strike like men" (McCulloch 1889, 393). It would not be long before the Republicans in the Senate and the House began to question the president's loyalty to the Union. They spread stories about Johnson being found hung-over the morning he was sworn in, allowing the public to infer that he had celebrated Lincoln's assassination. They cited the fact that John Wilkes Booth had left his card at Johnson's boarding house, a charge that ignored the report that a co-conspirator happened to be staying there (Trefousse 1989, 195-96).

During the McCarthy era, professors, even those with tenure, were fired for exercising their right to request Fifth Amendment protection. Writers in Hollywood were blacklisted and held in contempt of Congress for invoking First Amendment protection and refusing to reveal associates who had been or were members of the Communist Party.

During the Vietnam War, President Lyndon Johnson charged that news organizations undermined the chance to negotiate peace (Turner 1985, 253). News reporters left the impression that the Communists were victorious during the Tet Offensive (Small 1988, 82, 139). He called protesters cowardly, particularly given that U.S troops were spending holidays away from their families "in a lonely and dangerous land" (Johnson 1965, 1125-26). Two years later, Johnson claimed that American fighting men resented the cheap talk of these protesters (Johnson 1971, 1013). Ambassador Averill Harriman scolded the *New York Times* for promoting the view that the United States lacked dedication to the Vietnam cause.

President Nixon also questioned the patriotism of the news media and protesters. He claimed that resisters did not act on conscience; they deserted their country. Students "assault[ed] the processes of free inquiry which are the very life of learning" (Nixon 1969, 236). Vice President Agnew (1970, 38) claimed that the news media and protesters were not loyal to the United States.

Crafting Legislation

With the external crisis exaggerated through an internal threat, and the opposition demonized as disloyal, the leaders of the movement turn to legislation to achieve their goals. The executive branch has acted in two distinct ways regarding new laws and regulations during a crisis. In some cases the chief executive signs on to what the Congress initiates; in other cases, the executive branch itself moves the rules and regulations to the forefront.

When the Congress passed the Alien and Sedition Acts,[5] John Adams happily signed them. When newspaper editors, protesters, and even a congressman were jailed under the acts, Adams pardoned not a one of them. Ulysses S. Grant signed even the most draconian of the Reconstruction measures and kept the South divided into five military districts each governed by a different Union general for the whole of his presidency.[6]

In 1947, three years before Joseph McCarthy came to the fore, President Harry S. Truman supported congressional investigations of unions, including the Screen Actors Guild, then headed by Ronald Reagan. However, Truman's record on these issues was fogged by his partisan attacks on McCarthy and his veto of the McCarran-Walter Immigration Act. His record in the late forties matches that of many liberal groups clamoring to avoid the soft-on-communism label (Medhurst, et.al. 1990). In 1952, the McCarran-Walter Immigration Act was passed over President Truman's veto by a vote of 278 to 133 in the House and 57 to 26 in the Senate. It gave the State Department authority to prevent foreigners with alien political beliefs or affiliations from entering the country. This throwback to the Alien Act of 1798 remains in force.[7]

Despite the fact that McCarthy had slandered his good friend, George Marshall, Dwight Eisenhower appeared with McCarthy during the 1952 elections. During Eisenhower's administration, many private meeting halls, including Madison Square Garden, refused to rent to groups that his attorney general labeled as communist (Rashin 1953, E12). Suspected communists were denied low-income housing and could not obtain passports (Parmet 1972, 226-96). J. Edgar Hoover made uncovering communist spies his top priority.[8]

Rather than being complicit, several presidents have initiated action on their own or urged the Congress to act. President Andrew Jackson asked the Congress to forbid the mailing of abolitionist tracks into the South on the grounds they had a record of inciting violence. When Congress refused to do the president's bidding, he simply ordered his postmaster general to carry out the order. President Lincoln suspended *habeas corpus* not only in war zones, but to prevent the Maryland legislature from meeting. He feared it would vote to secede.[9] Once war was declared in 1917, Woodrow Wilson encouraged the Congress to pass the Espionage Act, the Trading with the Enemy Act, and, a year later, the Sedition Act.[10]

In the meantime, the Espionage Act's censorship provisions allowed postmaster general Albert Burleson to suppress journals, letters, or whatever he believed to be a threat to national security (Johnson 1962; Suter and Samosky 1994). Wilson often defended Burleson's judgment (Link 1979-91, 43:246, 44:420). The Trading with the Enemy Act allowed the president to create the Committee on Public Information, known as the Creel Committee after its head George Creel, a former muckraker who had supported Wilson in the elections of 1912 and 1916. The committee was charged with coalescing a divided public behind the war effort by putting out "information" and "correcting" disinformation (Creel 1972; Larson and Mock 1939, 5-29; Hollihan 1984, 239-51). Faced with the surprising growth of the motion picture industry, Creel initiated a policy of "benign censorship" that often crossed swords with Burleson's activism.[11] With Wilson's support, Burleson overruled or circumvented Creel and also assumed more powers under the Sedition Act. Though Burleson came under continued attack from the nation's press and such strong voices as Norman Thomas and Upton Sinclair, Wilson continued to back Burleson. In fact, at one juncture, Wilson sought the indictment of a newspaper editor for seditious treason (Scheiber 1960, 38-39). Even after the war, from his death bed Wilson continued to support Burleson suppressive tactics (Link 1979-91, 43:246; 44:420). Throughout this period, Burleson found a soul mate in the attorney general Wilson appointed in 1919 at the height of the internal crisis in the United States. The internal side of this crisis was supported by real events. On April 28, 1919 sulfuric acid poured out of a package mailed to the mayor of Seattle. In June the mayor of Cleveland was attacked; two bombs went off in Pittsburgh; a judge's home in New York City and a rectory in Philadelphia were attacked; worst of all, Palmer had his own home in the Capitol blown apart. In August, Palmer created the General Intelligence Division and named J. Edgar Hoover as its director. In November they coordinated a raid on the Union of Russian Workers in twelve cities and arrested 450 members. In December 249 aliens were arrested and so was "Red" Emma Goldman, whom the assassin of William McKinley had claimed inspired him. Palmer escalated his raids just as the new year began by arresting 5,000 persons in thirty-three cities. Just when things seem to be calming down, a bomb exploded on Wall Street in September of 1920. Of all the internal crises, the one Wilson faced was probably the most serious and the most to provide real evidence of violence.

There is a tendency to allow Franklin Roosevelt's internment of American citizens of Japanese descent to obscure other questionable policies initiated by Roosevelt during the war. Near the end of March, 1942, George Christians, the chief officer of the Fascist Crusader White Shirts, and Rudolph Fahl of Denver were arrested for disseminating material that could demoralize the army. In early April, five more seditionists were arrested. The president took pride in the operation during his "Fireside Chat" later in the month: "this great war effort . . . must not be impeded by a few bogus patriots who use the sacred freedom of the press to echo the sentiments of the propagandists in Tokyo and Berlin" (Washburn 1985, 722). All of those from the March-April group were convicted by the end of the summer of 1942 except Fahl. By the end of the year, 150 persons had been arrested for seditious statements or publications (Washburn 1985, 722).

Whether provoked or not, the North Vietnamese attack on American naval ships in the Gulf of Tonkin in August, 1964 gave President Lyndon Johnson an excuse to ask Congress for broader military power. After that he felt more secure in attacking the news media. When Johnson discovered that the film used by CBS of a U.S. soldier setting a fire to a peasant shack in Southeast Asia was a re-enactment, Johnson called on J. Edgar Hoover to begin an FBI investigation of Morley Safer, the reporter responsible (Small 1988, 65). Draft card burners were prosecuted; Martin Luther King suffered from rumors circulated by the administration that communists had infiltrated into the core of his organization (Small 1988, 100).

During the same war, President Nixon's monitoring and attempted intimidation of the press became legendary. For example, in 1972 the CIA initiated "Project Mudhen," to spy on columnist Jack Anderson and his staff (Spear 1984, 136). The executive branch also focused on such liberal reporters as Daniel Schorr and Cassie Mackin.

The Congress

The Congress, as we have seen in the current crisis, often follows the lead of the president. However, the Congress has also taken the lead in initiating restrictive legislation. That was certainly the case during the Alien and Sedition crisis, when Federalists under the direction of Hamilton produced an ambitious legislative package that resulted in the passage of the following laws: The Naturalization Act forbade aliens from being admitted to citizenship unless they had has resided in the United States for at least fourteen years. No native, citizen, subject, or resident of a country with which the United States was at war could be admitted to citizenship. The Alien Act allowed the president to order all aliens that he judged to be dangerous to the peace and safety of the United States to depart. The Alien Enemies Act held that when war is declared or invasion threatened, all natives, citizens, denizens, or subjects of the hostile nation, being males of the age of fourteen years and upwards, who shall be within the United States, and not actually naturalized, shall be liable to be apprehended, restrained, secured and removed, as alien enemies.[12] The Sedition Act held that any persons combining or conspiring with intent to oppose any measure or measures of the government of the United States shall be liable to fines up to $5,000 and imprisonment up to five years. Any person writing, uttering, or publishing any false, scandalous and malicious writing or writings against the government, the Congress, or the president shall be liable to fine up to $2,000 and imprisonment up to two years.

The Congress would not be so active again until the end of the Civil War. Facing a hostile president and an intransigent South, Radical Republicans passed legislation and amended the Constitution. While the Thirteen and Fourteenth Amendments are valorized in current jurisprudence, the method of getting them passed opened them to question for years. Because the Radicals could not obtain enough Union-supporting states to ratify the amendments, they conditioned re-entry into the Union upon ratification of the proposed Thirteenth and Fourteenth Amendments. President Johnson specifically objected to the treatment of his home state of Tennessee in this matter. However, when the 1866 election results came in, it was clear the nation did not stand with him.

Newly emboldened, the 40th Congress opened under the leadership of Senator Benjamin Wade and House Speaker Schuyler Colfax. The Second Reconstruction Act was soon passed. It gave specific orders to the Army on how to implement reconstruction. Yet another piece of legislation known as the Supplementary Act, giving even more power to the military, was passed on July 19, 1867, despite even Sumner's feeling that military force should not be used to achieve reconstruction aims. However, it was the feeling of the vast majority of Congress that the attorney general had watered down the previous Reconstruction Acts and that even more specific language was required. The Supplementary Act was passed and Johnson's veto was overridden. The new reinstatement process required: (1) registration of voters, including all adult black males; (2) the swearing of a loyalty oath by each voter; (3) the election of a convention to prepare a new state constitution providing for black suffrage; (4) the ratification of the new state constitution; (5) the election of all public office holders; (6) the ratification of the Fourteenth Amendment; and (7) once the Fourteenth Amendment was adopted by the mandated number of states, a state having fulfilled the other requirements would be readmitted to the Union.

Complicity of the Courts

The lower courts and the Supreme Court are in no position to initiate legislation, but they can rule on the constitutionality of legislation or of the actions of the executive branch. Since the Alien and Sedition Acts were set to expire the day before the inauguration of 1801, they were never tested by the Supreme Court. However, they were widely upheld by Federalist judges in the lower courts.[13] When Jefferson became president on March 4, 1801, he pardoned all of those incarcerated under the Sedition Act and returned fines to many of them.

During the Civil War, Chief Justice Roger Taney, who had written the infamous *Dred Scott* decision, challenged Lincoln's suspension of habeas corpus. On May 25, 1861, John Merryman, a secessionist from Maryland, was taken into military custody. He immediately appealed to the Supreme Court to be released under a writ of habeas corpus. In arguing for the president's power to suspend the writ, Attorney General Bates contended that the chief executive cannot rightly be subjected to the judiciary. The president, he maintained, is their preserver and protector as the defender of the Constitution (Randall 1951, 124). The president cannot be required to appear before a judge to answer for his official acts because the court would be usurping the authority of executive branch.[14] Bates contended that for any breach of trust, the president is answerable before the high court of impeachment and no other tribunal.

In ruling on *Ex parte Merryman* (1861, 17 Fed. Cas. 144), Taney responded that the president had no lawful power to issue such an order. Taney claimed that only Congress could suspend the privilege of the writ and that Lincoln, though sworn to "take care that the laws be faithfully executed," had broken the laws himself. Taney pointed out that the provision regarding habeas corpus appears in that portion of the Constitution that pertains to legislative powers; therefore, its suspension was a legislative, not executive prerogative. Taney argued further that the military authorities should reveal the day and cause of the capture of Merryman and explain the reasons for the detention of Merryman. Such requirements applied to civil courts but not to military tribunals. And so the military refused to comply.

As with the *Dred Scott* case, Taney stuck to the letter of the law and read the Constitution strictly. Lincoln sought refuge in a higher law: the law of survival. Furthermore, according to Lincoln, the Constitution was "silent as to . . . who, is to exercise the power" of suspension (*Ex parte Merryman*, 1861, 17 Fed. Cas. 144). He would not release Merryman, even in the face of Taney's writ.

Horace Binney (1862), a Philadelphia lawyer, came to the defense of the president through his widely circulated pamphlet, *The Privilege of the Writ of Habeas Corpus under the Constitution*. In the pamphlet Binney attacked Judge Taney's arguments. The controversy excited lawyers and politicians, resulting in a paper war consisting of more than forty published answers to Binney's pamphlet. In the midst of this debate, Lincoln consistently argued that his paramount duty as chief executive was to preserve the integrity of the government (Randall 1951, 123). In Lincoln's view, there had been no violation of the Constitution, since the Constitution permits suspension of habeas corpus in specific cases and does not specify which branch of the government is to exercise the suspending power. As the provision was plainly made for an emergency, he argued, the natural inference is that the president should use his discretion. Lincoln believed that the danger should not be permitted to run its course until Congress could be called together (Randall 1951, 123). The issue was never resolved.

Not so in the case of Lambdin P. Milligan, who was arrested on October 5, 1864, by order of General Hovey, in command at Indianapolis; he brought Milligan before a military commission on charges of (1) conspiring against the government of the United States; (2) affording aid and comfort to the Rebellion against the authorities of the United States; (3) inciting an insurrection; (4) disloyal practices; (5) violation of the laws of war. Milligan, along with others, was a suspected member of Clement Vallandigham's secret anti-war society, the Sons of Liberty.[15] The military commission sentenced Milligan to be hanged on May 19, 1865. Milligan petitioned the United States Circuit Court for a writ of habeas corpus. The controversy over congressional versus presidential power was re-ignited. Attorney General Stanbery and Benjamin F. Butler (1866) argued that:

> The Commander-in-Chief has full power to make an effectual use of his forces. He must . . . have the power to arrest and punish one who arms men to join the enemy in the field against him; one who holds correspondence with the enemy; one who is an officer in an armed force organized to oppose him; one who is preparing to seize arsenals and release prisoners of war taken in battle and confined within his military lines . . . During the war his powers must be without limit, because if defending, the means of offense may be nearly illimitable (2).

Milligan insisted, however, that the Military Commission had no jurisdiction to try him upon the charges preferred, or upon any charge whatever, because he was a citizen of the United States and the state of Indiana. Moreover, he contended that the right of trial by jury was guaranteed to him by the Constitution of the United States.

Justice David Davis, who had been a law partner of Lincoln's, announced the court's opinion in the Milligan case in April, 1866, a year after the war had ended:

> During the late wicked Rebellion, the temper of the times did not allow that calmness in deliberation and discussion so necessary to a correct conclusion of a purely judicial question. Then, considerations of safety were mingled with the exercise of power; and feelings and interests prevailed which are happily terminated. Now that the public safety is assured, this question, as well as all others, can be discussed and decided without passion or the admixture of any element not required to form a legal judgement . . . [T]he Constitution of the United States is a law for rulers and people, equally in war and in peace, and covers with the shield of its protection all classes of men, at all times and under all circumstances . . . [O]ne of the plainest constitutional provisions was infringed when Milligan was tried by a court not ordained and established by Congress, and not composed of judges . . . [A]nother guarantee of freedom was broken when Milligan was denied a trial by jury . . . Martial law cannot arise from a threatened invasion. The necessity must be actual and present; the invasion real . . . It is difficult to see how the safety of the country required martial law in Indiana . . . Martial rule can never exist where the courts are open, and in the proper and unobstructed exercise of their jurisdiction. (*Ex parte Milligan*, 4 Wall. 2)

Chief Justice Chase concurred:

> The power to make the necessary laws is in Congress; the power to execute in the President . . . But neither can the President, in war more than in peace, intrude upon the

proper authority of Congress, nor Congress upon the proper authority of the President. Both are servants of the people . . . nor can the President, or any commander under him, without the sanction of Congress, institute tribunals for the trial and punishment of offenses, either of soldiers or civilians, unless in cases of controlling necessity, which justifies what it compels, or at least insures acts of indemnity from the justice of the legislature . . . What we do maintain is that when the nation is involved in war . . . it is within the power of Congress to determine to what states or districts such great and imminent public danger exists as justifies the authorization of military tribunals for the trial of crimes and offenses against the discipline or security of the army or against the public safety (*Ex parte Milligan*, 4 Wall., 2).

Thus, the Court declared that the guarantees of fair trial and Fifth and Sixth Amendment privilege are not to be set aside during war. Milligan's conviction by a military commission was overturned. Note, however, that the Supreme Court handed this ruling down *after* the Civil War had ended.

The Court tends to be more complicit with the president during wars. For example, during the Red scare of World War I, the Supreme Court handed down its ruling in *Schenck v. United States* (1919), which involved the secretary of the Socialist Party of Philadelphia. The party leadership was accused of violating the Espionage Act of 1917 which made it a crime to "willfully cause or attempt to cause insubordination, disloyalty, mutiny, or refusal of duty, in the military" (47). Writing for the majority, Justice Holmes argued that Schenck presented "a clear and present danger" to the United States during the war. Holmes refused to accept the argument that Schenck's circular opposing the draft was "speech" or "press," instead Holmes said it was action (Frohwerk v. United States, 249 U.S., 1919, 204). In the same year, the Supreme Court affirmed Burleson's suppressive tactics against Abrams and his four cohorts, who distributed literature critical of the U.S. intervention against the Bolsheviks. In *Abrams v. United States* (1919, 616) the conviction of those who circulated a leaflet condemning U.S. policy in Russia and calling for a general strike was upheld 7 to 2. Crucially, however, Holmes dissented, realizing that these publications were in fact expression, not action. He argued that the "silly leaflets" could not really present a danger in a free "market" of ideas. Holmes, with Louis D. Brandeis, concurring, wrote:

[T]hese pronunciamentos in no way attack the form of government of the United States. . . . I do not see how anyone can find the intent required by the statute in any of the defendants' words. . . . In this case sentences of twenty years imprisonment have been imposed for the publishing of two leaflets that I believe the defendants had as much right to publish as the Government has to publish the Constitution. . . . [T]he best test of truth is the power of the thought to get itself accepted in the competition of the market. . . . [T]he United States through many years had shown its repentance for the Sedition Act of 1798, by repaying fines that it imposed (*Abrams v. U.S.*, 250 U.S., 620, 1919)

Using the majority opinion, however, the New York State Legislature, in January of 1920, did not allow five legally elected socialists to take their seats in the assembly for fear they would spread communist propaganda.

World War II presented the Supreme Court with a national emergency. As had other courts, the Supreme Court of 1941-45 was more willing than usual to permit restrictions on freedom of expression. They upheld the FCC's Mayflower ruling, which prohibited radio and television stations from editorializing. They upheld the incarceration of Americans of Japanese descent. They upheld forcing school children to take an oath of allegiance (*West Virginia State Broad of Education v. Barnette*, 319 U.S. 624, 1943). Not long after the close of World War II, the United States protested the Soviet Union's take over of various Eastern European countries. The Cold War soon underway especially when the threat of internal subversion surfaced.

When the House Un-American Activities Committee began to investigate communist influence in Hollywood, ten writers were summoned before the committee. When they refused to name associates who might be communists, and refused to answer questions regarding their membership in the Communist Party, they were held in contempt of Congress. Among the parties involved, it was agreed to submit a test case to the Supreme Court based on the First Amendment arguments—right to associate, free speech—of Dalton Trumbo, one of the writers. To the shock of Trumbo and the ACLU, the Supreme Court upheld the contempt citation.

In July, 1948, the Federal Bureau of Investigation arrested six members of the Communist Party in their New York City offices. Eventually eleven members of the leadership of the party were brought to trial for teaching and advocating "the overthrow and destruction of the Government of the United States by force and violence," a violation of the Smith Act of 1939 (18 U.S. Code, Section 2385, 1988). The eleven, including Eugene Dennis, secretary of the Communist Party, were convicted despite protests from presidential candidate and former Vice President Henry Wallace and the American Civil Liberties Union. Dennis and his board were fined $10,000 each and sentenced to five years in jail. In 1951 the Supreme Court upheld the *Dennis* decision with Justices Hugo Black and William O. Douglas strongly dissenting (*Dennis v. U.S.*, 341 U.S. 494, 1951.

Chief Justice Vinson argued that the leader of a group who instructed about violent action is as guilty as the group who commits the action. Vinson relied on Judge Learned Hand's theory that the speech is transformed into action at the moment of incitement or instigation. Had we not been at war with Communist China in Korea at the time of this decision, it might have been different. Or had the country not been in the grip of a paralyzing fear of communism because it had spread over half of Europe and a large portion of Asia, the Supreme Court might have returned to its previous position that membership in the Communist Party in America was no different from other party affiliations (*Schneiderman v. United States*, 320 U.S. 118, 1943). In his dissent in *Dennis v. U.S.*, Justice Douglas (1951) wrote:

> Communists in this country have never made a respectable or serious showing in any election. I would doubt that there is a village, let alone a city or county or state, which the Communists could carry. Communism in the world scene is no bogeyman; but Communism as a political faction or party in this country clearly is. . . . The First Amendment . . . . does not mean that the Nation need hold its hand until it is in such weakened condition that there is no time to protect itself from incitement to revolution. Seditious *conduct* can always be punished. But the command of the First Amendment is so clear that we should not allow Congress to call a halt to free speech. . . . the First Amendment makes confidence in the common sense of our people and in their maturity of judgment the great postulate of our democracy. . . . Unless and until extreme and necessitous circumstances are shown our aim should be to keep speech unfettered and to allow the processes of law to be evoked only when the provocateurs among us move from speech to action. (588-590)

Douglas and Black sought to draw a definitive line between speech and conduct, and keep the Congress from crossing it.

Four years after the "police action" ended in Korea and three years after the fall of Senator McCarthy, the Supreme Court ruled in *Yates v. United States* (1957, 298) that fourteen members of the Communist Party who had been arrested in California for calling for the violent overthrow of the government were not guilty of advocating specific illegal activity. They were instead engaged in advocacy of an ideology. Justice Harlan, who believed that there was a significant difference between speech (belief) and action, wrote the crucial decision in Yates. This ruling effectively gutted the Smith Act of 1939, though it remains on the books to this day.

The Vietnam War was the next crisis to put the Supreme Court on guard. Violating a federal law against destruction of draft cards, O'Brien burned his draft card on the steps of a Boston courthouse. He appealed his conviction on the grounds that his act was symbolic speech protected by the First Amendment. When the case reached the Supreme Court, it established a three-part test for determining whether expressive conduct could be punished. The federal government had the burden of proving that it was not suppressing the content of the expression, that it was advancing a compelling government interest, and that the law was no broader than essential to achieve the goal of advancing that interest. The Court found for the government by making a distinction between conduct, which could be regulated, and expression, which could not.[16] The conduct of burning the card violated a specific law that advanced a significant government interest: the Selective Service's ability to check the draft status of citizens.

However, the same Court did rule that students do not "shed" their First Amendment rights at the schoolhouse door even though their protest is non-verbal and endangering. *Tinker v. Des Moines* involved three high school students who were suspended for wearing black armbands as a symbolic protest against the Vietnam War.[17] The Supreme Court held that the suspension violated the students' rights of free expression. The Court limited the scope of the decision, however, by stating that school officials could regulate student expression if it caused substantial disruption or material interference with school functions.

Thus, throughout American history, the Supreme Court has been far more likely to restrict First Amendment freedoms during times of crisis. With few exceptions, it has generally supported the Congress and the executive branch, sometimes reversing its restrictive rulings once the crisis has passed. The terrorist crisis following the attack of 9/11 soon produced legislation that would face constitutional tests. The Bush administration took the initiative in promoting a national security program and led a coalition of nations in a war on the Taliban government of Afganistan. It later entered a war in Iraq on the grounds that "regime change" was essential because the leader of Iraq, Saddam Hussein harbored weapons of mass destruction, had violated UN resolutions, had conspired with terrorists, and had engaged in genocide against Kurds and Iranians.

The Current Crisis in Historical Context

Surely there was palpable evidence of an external threat to the country carried out by operatives of Al Qaeda. A year after the attack, Arab Americans were still held in jail without charges being filed against them. Within weeks of the attack on Pearl Harbor, a congressional committee investigated the event not only in terms of the Japanese attack but in terms of the security breach on the part of the U.S. military. Within days of the assassination of John Kennedy, the Warren Commission was convened to investigate the crime. But no such public investigation was called together regarding the attacks of September 11 until evidence was discovered that the administration might have overlooked signals that an attack was coming.[18] When formal congressional investigations were finally held in the fall of 2002. The Congress then considered whether the whole issue should be turned over to an independent commission.

In his indictment of these terrorists, President George W. Bush told the public that it was in a new kind of war in which terrorists were using American freedoms against Americans. Thus, the president took the initiative in forming a perception of the crisis, converting it into a "war" and then extending into an internal threat. In his address to a joint session of Congress on September 21, 2001 the president described the new threat this way:

Tonight, we are a country awakening to danger . . . [E]nemies of freedom committed an act of war against our country. . . . There are thousands of these terrorists in more than 60 countries. . . . Our enemy is a radical network of terrorists and every government that supports them. . . . These terrorists kill not merely to end lives but to disrupt and end a way of life. . . . They're the heirs of all the murderous ideologies of the 20th century. . . .. Today, dozens of federal departments and agencies, as well as state and local governments, have responsibilities affecting homeland security. . . . Many will be involved in this effort, from FBI agents to intelligence operatives to the reservists we have called to active duty. . . . (760-63).

As this chapter indicates, the second step in inciting the public comes with the development of an internal threat. By November 10, 2001, nearly 1,200 persons were arrested on suspicion of helping the conspirators, of committing related crimes, or of being material witnesses to terrorist activities.[19] Soon stories of abuse of detainees began to emerge. A Pakistani student was beaten by cell mates in Mississippi (Serrano 2002, A16). The Israeli consulate complained that six of its citizens had been handcuffed and forced to take polygraph tests (Serrano 2002, A16). U.S. immigration officials prevented

detainees in Wisconsin, Illinois, and Indiana from visiting with lawyers (Serrano 2001, A4). The INS reported that twenty-six jails across
the country had misapplied INS procedures; the Service began speed-
ing up processing on October 26 (Serrano 2001, A4). At the end of
the summer of 2002, the U.S. Court Appeals for the Sixth Circuit
ruled unanimously that closed hearings violated the First Amendment rights of the press and of detainees on U.S. soil. In order to
hold a closed trial, the INS must demonstrate and judges must cer-
tify that information in the case would harm national security if an
open trial was held. This decision was reinforced on September 17,
2002 by U.S. District Judge Nancy Edmunds, who wrote "An open
detention and removal hearing will assure the public that the government itself is honoring the very democratic principles that the
terrorists who committed the atrocities of 9/11 sought to destroy"
("Detention hearing linked to release" 2002, A18).

Another measure of threats to civil liberties, as we have seen, is
the nature of the legislation passed during the crisis. Congress quickly
passed the legislation proposed by the administration to deal with
the current crisis in the United States. It allows a single federal district court to authorize the "trapping" and tapping of phone numbers
anywhere in the United States.[20] These "roving taps" allow intercep-
tion of electronic evidence such as e-mail and a history of numbers
called from or to tapped phones and e-mail. The legislation gives
wider latitude to the special court that authorizes wiretaps on suspected agents of foreign powers (Lichtblau 2001, A3). The legislation allows information concerning foreign agents in the United States
to be shared among government agencies.[21] The legislation allows
the Immigration and Naturalization Service to detain aliens up to
seven days.[22] It permits the attorney general to detain "terrorist aliens"
and expands the definition of terrorist activity. The district court of
the District of Columbia has been given exclusive jurisdiction over
such cases. The legislation ends the statute of limitation on the newly
defined terrorist activities and increases the maximum sentence to
life imprisonment.[70]

Finally, the new law bans possession of biological agents that pose
a threat to national security unless the possession would serve peaceful
purposes.

The USA Patriot Act was drafted by the White House with the
help of John Ashcroft's Department of Justice. In the Congress it
was considered by the House Judiciary Committee which reported it

out on 36 to none vote. In the Senate it was also favorably reported to the floor as a 187-page document; the Senate voted in favor 96 to 1.[24] Amendments by Senator Russell Finegold (D-Wis.) to protect the rights of "innocent" people were defeated; he cast the lone dissenting vote to the legislation in the Senate. During the debate, Senator Orrin Hatch (R-Utah) argued that the government cannot guarantee total protection of the public "when you have people willing to commit suicide to do us harm. . . . [Those who argue for weakening this law should consider] "the loss of civil liberties of those who died" on September 11 (Jackson 2001, A13). A conference committee quickly worked out the minor difference between the two houses. The bill was stalled over a sunset provision inserted by the House; its negotiators agreed to a four year life span for the key provisions of the bill. The House then decided not to take up its own version of the bill, but to accept the Senate passed measure for debate. It carried 337 to 79.

After the president signed the legislation, Immigration and Naturalization Service Commissioner James Ziglar and Attorney General John Ashcroft held a joint press conference outlining the new rules that had been put in place. The act allows government agents to seek court orders to seize records for investigation to protect against international terrorism or clandestine intelligence activities. The federal government's ability to deny visas to and deport immigrants who "endorse" terrorism was stressed (Lichtblau 2001, A3). The attorney general designated 46 "terrorist organizations" around the world. Any linkage to any of these organizations could be used as a justification to deny a visa or to deport an immigrant or visitor. The legislation's broadened definition of what constitutes a terrorist drew complaints from civil libertarians. Ashcroft attempted to allay these fears by stating that the linkage must establish evidence of "material" support to terrorists. The attorney general also established a task force to track foreign terrorists.

The new rules give the Federal Bureau of Investigation broad latitude to conduct surveillance and information gathering. While these methods are not prohibited by the Constitution, any evidence obtained in violation of the Constitution may not be used in court. For example, the Fifth Amendment provides a right to avoid self-incrimination. However, there is no prohibition per se of the FBI obtaining a confession, for example, to apprehend other terrorists; only the fruits of that confession would be unusable in court. The evidence could be used in a non-criminal case, such as a deportation hearing. Also it should be noted that if a witness were granted "use immunity," nothing confessed could be used against that witness; however, the witness could be compelled to answer questions pertaining to a crime and those linked to it. The due process clause of the Constitution only precludes coercion that shocks the conscience of the court. Thus, if the injection of truth serum could lead to the prevention of a terrorist act, it likely would be upheld, just as extracting blood from a drunk driver has been upheld. Torture, on the other hand, has tended to be of such a shocking nature, that it is prohibited.

Perhaps the most controversial interpretation of the new legislation came on November 9, 2001, when Attorney General Ashcroft announced that federal prison officials would be allowed to eavesdrop on conversations between inmates and their lawyers. According to Ashcroft, as long as officials had a "reasonable suspicion" that useful information was being passed on to an attorney, they could listen in (Savage and Jackson 2001, A5). The American Civil Liberties Union's Washington, D.C. director claimed that the rule violated the right to "an effective and vigorous defense" (Savage and Jackson 2001, A5). Senator Patrick Leahy (D-Vt.) sent a letter to the attorney general demanding a rationale for the rule that appears to violate the Sixth Amendment right to "assistance of counsel" for one's defense.

The next reduction of civil liberties came on November 13, 2001, when President Bush agreed to allow military tribunals to try alleged terrorists (Meyer, Savage and Lichtblau 2001, A1). The order from the president said that those that he designates as terrorists will be "placed under the control of the secretary of Defense," who shall have "exclusive jurisdiction" in these matters (Meyer 2002, A1). These agents of terror may not appeal to "any court of the United States," nor "any court of any foreign nation or any international tribunal." Aside from the infringement on foreign sovereignty implied by this order, it is the starkest restriction of rights during wartime since the Civil War. (See above). The Bush administration claimed it had a precedent for taking such action with the *Quirin* case, wherein Nazi saboteurs were apprehended in the Mayflower Hotel in Washington, D.C. in June of 1942 when two of their members defected. Ten prosecutors tried the saboteurs in the Justice Department building before a military tribunal. Six of the saboteurs were executed on August 8, 1942, and the defectors were sent to prison.[25] If and when terrorists are apprehended, it will be interesting to determine if their circumstances are analogous to those of the Nazi saboteurs, who had been delivered by a German U-Boat to U.S. shores during a declared war. The Milligan case, examined above, would certainly protect American citizens from military tribunals, but foreign nationals might present a different set of circumstances. Under current law, the president must demonstrate that military tribunals are essential because the current system does not allow for the timely prosecution of terrorists. However, the administration could claim that an open hearing might compromise national security. Secondly, the U.S. Constitution applies to "persons" not just citizens who inhabit the country. Almost anyone in the country, as illegal aliens have learned, can file a writ of habeas corpus unless they inhabit an area that has been declared under marshal law or unless they are "military combatants." Others, relying on Taney's ruling in the Merryman case, claim that Congress must legislate the procedure before the president can implement a suspension. In light of these and other arguments, President Bush eventually restricted his tribunals policy to areas of actual conflict overseas, or on bases outside of the United States. That decision was upheld by the U.S. Court of Appeals for the District of Columbia when, in regard to Al Qaeda members and Kuwaitis held in Guantanomo, Cuba, it ruled that "The Constitution does not entitle the detainees to due process. They cannot invoke the jurisdiction of our courts to test the constitutionality or the legality of restraints on their liberty."[26]

In the meantime, Attorney General Ashcroft proceeded to employ the Foreign Intelligence Surveillance Act to his advantage. The act had originally been passed in 1978 to prevent the government from conducting surveillance of political enemies and to establish a wall between surveillance of foreign and domestic criminals. The act establishes a seven judge secret panel to rule on requests regarding national security matters. Any evidence gathered can be used in court but in cannot be passed on to local or state authorities because the secret court, which operates much like a grand jury, can approve search warrants on a lower threshold of suspicion that the "probable cause" standard imposed on the states and other federal agencies. Thus, if during a surveillance the FBI were discovered that someone was in possession of obscene material by the standards imposed by their state, that evidence could not be used in any state prosecution against the individual. The fruits of the surveillance could only be used to prove a national security threat. However, under the Patriot Act investigators may be granted a warrant even if there is no evidence of wrongdoing. In invoking this provision, Ashcroft overstepped his bounds according to the secret court. It rebuked Ashcroft in May of 2002 for letting his criminal investigations pursue too many secret searches. Ashcroft appealed this ruling in September of 2002 to a superior three-judge panel that reviews the use of this legislation. The panel, appointed by Chief Justice Rehnquist, was composed of three Reagan-appointed judges from different Federal Circuit Courts of Appeals. The panel had never been convened before. On November 18, 2002, the three judges, Ralph B. Guy of the Sixth Circuit, Edward Leavy of the Ninth Circuit, and Laurence Silberman of the D.C. Circuit, upheld Ashcroft's appeal and overruled the Foreign Intelligence Surveillance Court. Ashcroft immediately claimed that the decision would revolutionize his ability to investigate and prosecute terrorists. Despite the fears of some civil libertarians, the three-judge panel lowered the wall between intelligence agencies and the FBI, thereby strengthening the authority of the Patriot Act.

The attorney general faced more criticism on August 22, 2002 when it was revealed that federal judges had grave misgivings about the way the Justice Department had handled some of its cases: "The FBI gave false information in more than 75 requests for top-secret warrants brought before the" secret surveillance panel (Lichtblau and Meyer 2002, A1). It was the first time in the twenty-three-year history of the court that it released information about its proceedings.

The State Department kept the crisis alive by announcing in September of 2002 that over 70,000 names of terrorist operatives had been compiled by various international agencies. The Department claimed that Al Qaeda agents remained a threat in the United States (Meyer 2002, A1). Other terrorist groups were targeted. For example, Professor Sami Al-Arian of South Florida University was arrested on February 20, 2003 on conspiracy charges that linked him to the Palestinian Islamic Jihad, which has terrorist cells around the world (Meyer and Dahlburg 2003, A5). Professor Al-Arian was directly linked to seven terrorists of the PIJ when, under the auspices of the Patriot Act, agencies that had been monitoring his activities were allowed to share information.

Furthermore, Ali Saleh Kahlah Al-Marri lost his appeal to be released from Navy custody in South Carolina, when a Federal judge ruled that the Qatari citizen was an "enemy combatant" and thereby subject to a military tribunal. However, the judge criticized the government's moving of the suspect from civilian jurisdiction, where he was charged with fraud, to military jurisdiction, where he was reclassified. The government alleges that the man was part of a "sleeper" cell and that he entered the country in September 10, 2001.

The question of post 9/11 arrests of Middle Eastern men and women was ultimately resolved on January 12, 2004 when the Supreme Court refused to take up a challenge to the practice of keeping the names of the arrested secret. The justices did not comment on the denial of certiorari. Of the 750 people who were arrested, most had been deported or released by June of 2002. The order in *Center for National Security Studies v. Justice Department* narrowed the rights of immigrants, allowing them to be deported for minor violations. Immigrant hearings may be closed to the public. Neither the public nor the media have a right to know who is being detained for questioning in a national security matter.

The Court has taken up the case of the 600 foreign fighters being detained in Guantanamo, Cuba. The question is whether they have a right to hearing at which they would be allowed to assert their innocence. The Court also will decide whether a citizen of the United States can be held by the military without charges if the president designates the citizen as an "unlawful enemy combatant." Yaser Essam Hamdi, of Louisiana, was picked up on a battlefield in Afghanistan; Jose Padilla, of the Bronx, was arrest at O'Hare Airport where he arrived on a flight from Pakistan. These cases were schedule for decisions in the summer of 2004.

TIPS

In the historic crises examined in the first half of this chapter, we saw that citizens often took action on their own to deal with the crisis. The citizens of Boston, among other communities, tried to rid their libraries of certain books during the McCarthy era. French Jacobins were regularly beaten and run out of town during the Alien and Sedition crisis. But most common to a crisis is the citizen as informer. During the current crisis, the administration attempted to enhance a citizen's ability to inform on others with its Terrorism

Information and Prevention Systems, known as TIPS. TIPS was part of the proposed Homeland Security Bill and would have recruited a million volunteers in ten test cities to check on deliveries, e-mail, Internet use, telephone conversation, etc. The volunteers would report what they found to a central database in the Justice Department. The attorney general would then make the information available to appropriate state and local agencies. When House Majority Leader Dick Armey (R-Texas) opposed the provision, it was dropped, then revived after the 2002 mid-term elections as the Total Information Awareness program to be conducted in the Pentagon under the guide of Admiral Poindexter. The system would have access to all computerized information including what you buy, what you watch, and who you talk to.

Finally, it might be useful to assess press restrictions during this crisis in terms of covering the "war" on terrorism. During World War II and the Korean conflict, reporters were allowed to accompany army combat units but had to submit their copy military censorship. During the Vietnam war, much less censorship was employed. However, with the invasion of Grenada during the Reagan administration and the War in the Gulf during the Bush administration, new restrictions were imposed that prevented reporters from traveling with American forces and forced the use of pool reporters where information was shared from a single source. The same policy was followed in the war in Afghanistan. American reporters were forced to rely on the Secretary of Defense or his spokespersons plus any foreign sources the reporters could contact. The administration justified this policy on a number of grounds. First, the use of Internet and satellite communications by reporters might jeopardize U.S. ground troops. Second, the precedent established in the Gulf War worked well and will be followed into the future.

It should also be noted that some members of the Bush administration may have created an environment that has a chilling effect on criticism of the "war" on terrorism. Press Secretary Ari Fleisher was openly critical of commentator Bill Maher's remark that the army's use of missiles in wartime was cowardly. Fleisher later had his remarks deleted from the official transcript. National Security Advisor Condoleeza Rice held a conference call with network news presidents and asked them not to re-broadcast Al Jazeera broadcasts of tapes made by terrorists. While crop dusters were allowed to return to the air, news aircraft were not, which is why when an American Airlines plane crashed in Queens, the news media was only able to show ground shots of the event. The Justice Department abruptly announced in mid-November, 2001 that it would no longer regularly update the number of people being held in association with the September 11 attacks. The Defense Department contracted with satellite operators to prevent them from making pictures available to the media.

In short once it had the legislation it requested in hand, the Bush administration, and particularly the Department of Justice, began to issue orders, regulations, and the like that restricted civil liberties to a greater extent than anticipated. After the initial shock, however, the press began to protect its rights. The media was particularly effective, as we have seen, in bringing suits that forced the Justice Department to release the names of detainees, and forced judges to hold open hearings unless it could be approved that such hearings were a danger to national security. Members of the judiciary, particularly the Sixth Circuit Court of Appeals and the review panel for FISA, were conscientious in holding the Justice Department constitutional standards. Finally, Congress has generally been complicit in fighting terrorism. However, in July, 2003, the House voted 309 to 118 to repeal parts of the Patriot Act that allow for "sneak and peak" searches, which are unannounced. The Justice Department opposed the adjustment to the Act and it has not been taken up in the Senate. The ACLU launched a series of advertisements in favor the House Amendment, and the Justice Department abandoned its plan to introduced Patriot Act II. While these actions and proposals are debated, responsible voices on each side of the civil liberties divide need to keep America's history in mind. Hopefully, it will temper the debate and assure that, in the name of national security, laws are passed that do as little damage to civil liberties as possible.

As in most crises, the terrorist induced crisis in the United States was a real external threat that was shaped in the public's mind by the president's rhetoric. It was also extended into a internal threat to justify legislation pushed the constitutional envelope. As of this writing, the legislation does not appear as dangerous as past threats to the Constitution, such as the Alien and Sedition Acts. Nor does President Bush appear to be exercising the kind of media intimidation used by Lincoln, Wilson, Roosevelt, Lyndon Johnson, or Nixon. However, the interpretation put on the legislation by the attorney general is more troubling and may have to be sorted out by the Supreme Court. If history is any indication, that sorting will be highly dependent on the state of the crisis at the time the Court considers the attorney general's actions.

Notes

1. The USA Patriot Act is 115 Stat. 272.
2. This examination extends my previous work on this subject: Craig Smith, Silencing the Opposition: Government Strategies of Suppression of Freedom of *Expression* (Albany: State University of New York Press, 1996).
3. All sorts of rumors were spread about the Jacobins including that they had evolved from secret societies such as the Knights Templar.
4. Many historians have examined this administration from different perspectives. Some of the more recent that highlight its suppressive nature include Robert H. Ferrell, *Woodrow Wilson and World War I, 1917-1921* (New York: Harper & Row, 1985), 208ff; see also, Christopher C. Gibbs, *The Great Silent Majority: Missouri's Resistance to World War I* (Columbia: University of Missouri Press, 1988); August Heckscher, *Woodrow Wilson* (New York: Charles Scribner's Sons, 1991); Paul Murphy, *World War I and the Origins of Civil Liberties in the United States.* New York: W.W . Norton, 1979), 26-32; David M. Rabin, "The Emergence of Modern First Amendment Doctrine," University of Chicago Law Review 50 (1984): 1217-1219.
5. The "Naturalization Act" extended from five to fourteen the number of years of residence required before full U.S. citizenship could be granted. The "Act Concerning Alien Enemies" authorized President Adams to order the expulsion of "dangerous" aliens during peacetime. The "Act Respecting Alien Enemies" authorized the president to apprehend, restrain, secure, and remove enemy aliens during time of war or undeclared hostilities. The "Sedition Act" prohibited conspiracy against the U.S. government and also prohibited writing, printing, uttering, or publishing false, scandalous, and malicious writings against the U.S. government.
6. Perhaps the most severe measure was the one introduced in the Joint Committee by the ailing Thaddeus Stevens on February 6, 1867. It called for dividing the ten states still outside the Union into five military districts and proposed that habeas corpus be suspended in the districts so that military tribunals could take control. Proponents of the bill claimed that whites loyal to the Union were being driven from the homes and killed, that new black citizens needed to be protected, that the South had arrogantly rejected the Fourteenth Amendment, and that they had established illegal governments. Opponents of the bill said it was unconstitutional, unduly harsh, and imperialistic. In the capital, the *National Intelligencer*, a newspaper that supported the president, said it was "treason enveloped in the forms of law." With their newfound, lopsided majority, Republicans were able to pass the bill 109 to 55 in the House. On February 14, the Senate took up the bill and rehearsed the arguments of the House, making only slight changes in the bill. The law took effect soon after.
7. Under the law, current and former communists, as well as homosexuals, anarchists, and those whom the State Department deems "prejudicial to the public interest," may be excluded. The McCarran-Walter Act, a comprehensive codification of the immigration and naturalization system, was amended by Congress in 1987 to say that aliens may no longer be denied entry into the United States on the basis of "past, current, or expected beliefs, statements, or associations."
8. In June of 1953, speaking at commencement at Dartmouth, Eisenhower did attack some of the excesses. He told his audience not to join the book burners, a response

to McCarthy's call for the burning of certain books recommended by the Voice of America. After McCarthy attacked Eisenhower's beloved Army, the president went on national television to attack McCarthy.

9.   Just after the fall of Fort Sumter, Lincoln wrote to General Winfield Scott, "You are engaged in repressing an insurrection against the laws of the United States. If at any point on or in the vicinity of the military line, which is now used between the City of Philadelphia and the City of Washington, via Perryville, Annapolis City, and Annapolis Junction, you find resistance which renders it necessary to suspend the writ of *Habeas Corpus* for the public safety, you, personally or throough the officer in command at the point where the resistance occurs, are authorized to suspend that writ" in Don E. Fehrenbacher, *Abraham Lincoln: Speeches and Writing, 1859-1865* (New York: Library of America, 1989), 237.

10.   Eugene Debs, the Socialist, would be incarcerated under these acts, and Justice Oliver Wendell Holmes would speak for the majority of the Supreme Court in condemning Debs anti-war rhetoric. After the war, Wilson refused to pardon him; it took a Republican President, Warren G. Harding, to release Debs.

11.   The Creel Committee's attempt to shut down a movie that contained a brutal scene involving the bayoneting of a baby by a British soldier resulted in *United States v. Motion Picture Film "The Spirit of '76,"* 1917. The government argued that the producer of the film had violated Sections 1 and 3 of the Espionage Act by attempting to "cause insubordination in the army. [H]e was sentenced to ten years in jail and fined five thousand dollars. . . . [T]wo years later [it was] upheld by the Ninth Circuit Court" in *Goldstein v. United States*, 258 Fed. 908, 9th Cir., (1919). Imagine the chilling effect these decisions must have had on the motion picture industry in its infancy. Donald Fishman and Joyce Lindmark, "George Creel and the Strategy of Benign Censorship during World War I," paper presented at the annual meeting of the Western States Communication Association, 1994.

12.   This act is in force with only one substantive change: states no longer have the jurisdiction to deal with enemy aliens.

13.   These acts were directed primarily against anti-Federalist editors of French and English heritage, such as Thomas Cooper, Joseph Priestly, James Callender, Benjamin Bache, Count de Volney, and others. For further information on the Alien and Sedition Acts, see Frank M. Anderson, "The Enforcement of the Alien and Sedition Laws," *American Historical Association Reports: Annual Report for the Year 1912* (Washington, DC: American Historical Association, 1914):113-126. 113-126; Claude Gernade Bowers, *Jefferson and Hamilton*. St. Clair Shores, MI: Scholarly Press, 1925), chapters 16 and17; Henry S. Commager, *Documents of American History*, (Englewood Cliffs, NJ: Prentice-Hall, 1973), 175-78.

14.   President Nixon used the same argument during the Watergate crisis.

15.   Vallandingham had been an Ohio congressman who ran for governor of his state. His inflammatory remarks in support of the South resulted in his arrest. The president eventually exiled him to the South. After the war, he became the famous "Man without a Country."

16.   The Court revisited this issue in *Texas v. Johnson*, 491 U.S. 397, (1989). During the 1984 Republican Convention in Dallas, Gregory Johnson burned a U.S. flag to protest the policies of the Reagan administration. His act violated a Texas law against burning the U.S. flag. In a five to four decision, the majority of the Court overturned the Texas law as it would later overturn a U.S. law on the same subject. Writing the majority, Justice Brennan claimed that Johnson's case differed with that of O'Brien because Johnson's action was expressive and no compelling government interest would be advanced by suppressing it: "The state need not worry that

our holding will disable it from preserving the peace." Furthermore, unlike the law under which O'Brien was prosecuted, the Texas law was not content neutral.

17.   *Tinker v. Des Moines Independent Community School District*, 393 U.S. 503 (1969). Justice Black, an absolutist on First Amendment issues, was also a literalist. He voted against Tinker on the grounds that the First Amendment was not meant cover symbolic speech. A year before the Tinker decision, Justice Warren had articulated a compromise position in *U.S. v. O'Brien*: "We cannot accept the view that an apparently limitless variety of conduct can be labeled 'speech' whenever a person engaged in conduct intends thereby to express an idea. . . . This Court has held that when 'speech' and 'nonspeech' elements are combined in the same course of conduct, a sufficiently important governmental interest in regulating the nonspeech elements can justify incidental limitations on the first amendment." *United States v. O'Brien*, 391 U.S. 367, 369 (1968).

18.   These charges were not unlike those that plagued the Roosevelt administration during and after the Pujo Hearings into the attack on Pearl Harbor. After September 11, 2001, some congressional hearings on other matters, employees of the Justice Department and the FBI have been questioned with regard to homeland security. However, their answers have been evasive. Floyd Abrams, a leading First Amendment attorney who, for example, defended the *New York Times* in the "Pentagon Papers" Case, claimed recently that the "American intelligence community" foiled an attempt to hijack fourteen planes from Los Angeles Airport and crash them into the Pacific Ocean, but that they claimed to have been unprepared for what happened in New York and Washington, D.C. on September 11, 2001. Abrams, Floyd. "Remarks for the Cornerstone Project." Washington, DC: The Media Institute. November 16, 2001. President Clinton appearing on "The David Letterman Show" (September 11, 2002) confirmed that many attacks had been foiled by the United States, including the planned attack on Los Angeles Airport.

19.   By May 10, 2002, 752 of the 1,200 were still being held in the custody of the INS. By the end of June all but eighty-one of them had been deported. There were 129 accused of criminal wrongdoing, of which seventy-two pleaded guilty, and eight more were convicted in trials. Six cases were dismissed. The remainder was pending. By August 10, 2002, at least two American citizens apprehended during the military action in Afghanistan were still being held in United States. Yasser Esam Hamdi and Jose Padilla (see below) were being held in military prisons in Norfolk, Virginia and Charleston, South Carolina respectively. See Richard A. Serrano, "A Swift, Secretive Dragnet after Attacks," *Los Angeles Times* (September 10, 2002): A16.

20.   A "pen register" allows determining who was called by cell or other phones, and deciphers the number of the person called by a suspect in a criminal investigation. Before the Congress acted, if the government sought to "trap" numbers, it needed to obtain court permission in the state of origin.

21.   The supposed firewall between the CIA and FBI is regularly breached de facto. The new acts authorized the practice de jure.

22.   The limit before the legislation was two days.

23.   The Internal Security Act of 1950 allowed the attorney general to detain aliens who were members of the Communist Party. They were not allowed bail.

24.   The legislation on money laundering was also ironed out. Only sixty-six House members and one Senator voted against the bill. The president signed it on October 26, 2001.

References

18 U.S. Code, Section 2385. 1988

Abrams v. U. S., 1919. 250 U.S. 616.

Agnew, S. 1970. *Frankly Speaking*. Washington DC: Public Affairs Press.

Binney, H. 1862. *The Privilege of the Writ of Habeas Corpus under the Constitution.* Philadelphia, PA: C. Sherman and Son.

Bush, G. 2001. "Address by George W. Bush, President of the United States Delivered to a Joint Session of Congress and the American People, Washington, DC, September 20, 2001." *Vital Speeches of the Day.* LXVII: 760-763.

Creel, G. 1972. *How We Advertise*. New York: Arno Press.

Dennis v. U.S. 1951. 341 U.S. 494.

Ex parte Merryman. 1861. 17 Federal Case 144.

Ex parte Milligan. 1866. 4 Wall 2.

Frohwerk v. United States. 1919. 249 U.S. 204.

Hollihan, T. 1984. Propagandizing in the interest of war. *Southern Speech Communication Journal* 49:239-51.

Jackson, R. L. 2001. Senate oks anti-terrorism program. *Los Angeles Times.* 12 October.

Johnson, D. 1962. Wilson, Burleson, and censorship in the First World War. *Journal of Southern History.* 28: 46-58.

Johnson, L. 1971. The president's Thanksgiving Day message to members of the armed forces, 24 November 1965. *Public Papers of the Presidents.* Washington, DC: GPO.

———. 1971. Remarks at Doughboy Stadium, Fort Benning, Georgia, 10 November 1967. *Public Papers of the Presidents.* Washington, DC: GPO.

Larson. C. and J. Mock. 1939. The lost files of the Creel Committee of 1917-19. *Public Opinion Quarterly.* 3:5-29.

Levy, L. and M. Peterson. 1962. *Major Crises in American History.* New York: Harcourt, Brace & World.

Lichtblau, E. 2001. Justice officials introduce tighter immigrant policy. *Los Angeles Times.* 12 October.

——— and Josh Meyer. 2002. Terror probe feuds revealed by secret court. *Los Angeles Times.* 22 August.

Link, A., ed. 1991. *The Papers of Woodrow Wilson.* Princeton, NJ: Princeton University Press.

Los Angeles Times. 2002. Detention Hearing Linked to Release. September 18.

McCulloch. H. 1889. *Men and Measures of Half a Century.* New York: W.W. Norton.

Medhurst, M., R. Ivie, P. Wander and R. Scott, eds. 1990. *Cold War Rhetoric.* New York: Greenwood.

Meyer, J. 2002. 70,000 terrorist suspects worldwide on U.S. list. *Los Angeles Times.* 22 September.

Meyer, J., D. Savage, and E. Lichtblau. 2001. Bush to allow terror trails by military. *Los Angeles Times.* 14 November.

Meyer, J. and J. Dahlburg. 2003. Florida professor charged in terrorism case. *Los Angeles Times.* 21 February.

Nixon, R. 1971. Statement on campus disorders, 22 March 1969. *Public Papers of the Presidents* . Washington, DC: GPO.

Parmet, H. 1972. *Eisenhower and the American Crusades.* New York: Macmillan.

Randall, J. 1951. *Constitutional Problems Under Lincoln.* Urbana: University of Illinois Press.

Rashin, A. 1953. What communists can and can't do. *New York Times.* 26 April.

Roosevelt, F. 1942. *Memo to J. Edgar Hoover.* President's Secretary's File. Justice Department, J. Edgar Hoover Folder, Roosevelt Library, Hyde Park, NY. 21 January.

Savage, D. and R. Jackson. 2001. Ashcroft eavesdropping rule assailed. *Los Angeles Times.* 10 November.

Scheiber, H. 1960. *The Wilson Administration and Civil Liberties, 1917-1921.* Ithaca, NY: Cornell University Press.

Schneiderman v. United States. 1943. 320 U.S. 118.

Schenck v. U.S. 1919. 249 U.S. 47.

Serrano, R. 2001. Some held in terror probe report rights being abused. *Los Angeles Times.* 15 October.

_____. 2002. A swift, secretive dragnet after attacks. *Los Angeles Times.* 10 September.

Small, M. 1988. *Johnson, Nixon and the Doves.* New Brunswick, NJ: Rutgers University Press.

Spear, J. 1984. *Presidents and the Press: The Nixon Legacy.* Cambridge, MA: MIT Press.

Suter, J. and J. Samosky. 1994. Uneasy Reading: Censorship in Woodrow Wilson's Wartime Administration. Paper presented at the annual convention of the Western States Communication Association.

Trefousse, H. 1989. *Andrew Johnson: A Biography.* New York: W.W. Norton.

Turner, K. 1985. *Lyndon Johnson's Dual War: Vietnam and the Press.* Chicago: University of Chicago Press.

Washburn, P. 1985. FDR versus his own attorney general: The struggle over sedition. *Journalism Quarterly.* 62:722.

West Virginia State Board of Education v. Barnette. 1943. 319 U.S. 624.

Yates v. U.S. 1957. 354 U.S. 298.

5

The Death and Re-Birth of Irony:
The *Onion's* Call for Rhetorical Healing
in the Wake of 9/11

Daniel J. O'Rourke III and Pravin A. Rodrigues

On September 11, 2001, America awoke to the threat of a terrorist attack. For generations, this nation saw itself as an isolated, impenetrable castle protected by oceanic moats. Now, however, the fortress of democracy had been assaulted from within and the weapon of choice was a domestic airliner. Few who witnessed the first plane crashing into the World Trade Center will ever forget that sight. Some observers wondered how such a tragedy could occur. A frightful clue came moments later when a second plane exploded into the adjacent tower. Reports soon followed of an attack on the Pentagon and a plane crash in Pennsylvania. It seemed that a systematic assault had been waged on America. Confusion swept over the nation like the dust billowing through the streets of New York City. Was this an act of terrorism? Had America witnessed another Pearl Harbor? A dazed nation cried, prayed, and grieved as one.

In his September 20 address to Congress and the nation, President Bush identified those who attacked the country and declared a "war on terrorism." (*www.whitehouse.gov*). He warned, however, that this would be a war unlike any the United States had ever known. In the twentieth century, the United States fought world wars, civil wars, and engaged in a protracted cold war with the Soviet Union, but this nation had never declared war on such a ubiquitous enemy. One columnist from the *New York Times* observed that since 1968, there had been 500 international hijackings and 400 bombings by terrorists. The problem was that this terrorist enemy occupied sixty countries but had no official state (Ferguson, 2001, A31). The United States had suffered previous domestic terrorism at the hands of Timothy McVeigh and been the victim of foreign assaults on embassies and warships but had never been drawn into the global war on terrorism. Now, President Bush placed the United States at the forefront of this twenty-first-century conflict.

The seeming challenge for the world's remaining superpower would be to endure a "war of resolution, not solution." There would be no "unconditional surrender" (Hikins, 1983) in the war on terrorism. Each victory or capture of a terrorist leader had the potential to inspire the next generation of ideological leaders. Thirty years ago, the United States struggled to find an exit strategy in the Vietnam War. Engagement in that civil war left scars on the American psyche that have not yet healed. Now the nation was headed into the uncharted waters of a conflict against an enemy that was neither bound by borders nor inspired by one political agenda. Military and political leaders alike wondered how and even if a war on terrorism could be won.

The magnitude of this war on terrorism was lost on many Americans in the wake of 9/11. Our attention was focused on the glaring gap in the New York skyline and the victims of terrorism across the country. "Ground Zero, " as the site of the bombed Trade Center became known, quickly became a sacred symbol of our collective loss. Citizens from around the country and the world raised millions of dollars in relief funds and supplies to aid the victims and their families. Social commentators and news reporters sought to put the initial assault on America in some kind of context to define the first stage of this new war. Feelings of patriotism swelled as flags appeared on long-empty poles, office buildings, and even automobiles. Attendance at religious services increased while, unfortunately, mosques and Arab-Americans were targeted unjustly for retribution. These were confusing times in which many answers were offered to the questions: "how and why could such an attack occur?" One theme that gained some currency was a declaration of the "death of irony." In the essay, "The Age of Irony, " Roger Rosenblatt wrote: "For some 30 years—roughly as long as the Twin Towers were upright— the good folks in charge of America's intellectual life have insisted that nothing was to be believed or taken seriously" (Rosenblatt, 2001, 79). Rosenblatt asserted that the 9/11 attacks might puncture the surreal cocoon of popular culture that enveloped America and lead to a return of traditional values. The hope was to find some good that might come out of these heinous acts.

The death of irony, to paraphrase Mark Twain, seems to have been greatly exaggerated. The first clue in this premature pronouncement may have come only a few weeks after 9/11 in the form of the satirical publication, the *Onion*. More importantly for this chapter, the analysis of satire and humor in the *Onion* reveals that irony does not conceal reality, but can, in fact, reframe it as a source of healing. Americans historically have used humor as a response to difficult times. The era of the depression brought escapist fantasy in films while the threat of the cold war invoked satire as a means of coping (Kakutani, 2001). The purpose of this chapter is to explore the challenge to irony set forth by Rosenblatt and his contemporaries. Next, the authors offer a brief analysis of the role of humor in reporting political news. Finally, this chapter examines irony as a rhetorical tool for healing in times of tragedy. The authors offer the post 9/11 edition of the *Onion* as evidence of their claims.

The End of the Age of Irony

Roger Rosenblatt, columnist for *Time* magazine, was clear in his assessment of irony post-September 11. He wrote (2001, 79), "History occurs twice, crack the wise guys quoting Marx: first as tragedy, then as farce. Who would believe such a thing except someone who has never experienced tragedy." The tone of his remarks revealed an association of irony with falsehood and frivolousness. In his view, Americans in the gilded age of irony had become accustomed to leaders who professed "to feel their pain" and child actors who "saw dead people" (Rosenblatt, 2001, 79). He wondered now how the citizens of this country would deal with the real pain and real deaths of this attack.

Stephen Goode notes in a cultural review of the year 2001 that criticism of irony was brewing even earlier. In 1999, a twenty-four-year-old Yale law student named Jedediah Purdy authored a book entitled *For Common Things: Irony, Trust and Commitment in America Today*. Purdy (1999, 10) warns, "the point of irony is a quiet refusal to believe in the depth of relationships, the sincerity of motivation, or the truth of speech—especially earnest speech." As trained rhetoricians who have learned the ambiguity of symbols and the difficulty of discerning the intent of a rhetor, we might ask how a law student divined the method of evaluating the truth and earnestness of forensic oratory, but that would be ironic. Purdy would likely respond that the bounty of this country enables privileged classes, including academics and those who shape popular culture, to make light of everything important in life. One of the pieces of evidence for his assault on irony is the popular television program *Seinfeld*. Once characterized as "a show about nothing, " Purdy (1999) believes that this show is emblematic of a popular culture that mocks social institutions and traditions. Since popular culture imitates commercial success rather than life, today we are deluged with television shows, movies, music, and comedians that consistently deride the foundations of our society. One might only think of the dearth of "reality shows" that bear little resemblance to the "real world" that most of us know. History has quickly forgotten that these programs were born not of artistic visions but were responses to a threatened writers' strike. Competitions in the jungle or to marry a millionaire require no scripts; thus, they are inexpensive and have proved to be successful in the ratings. These programs reward treachery, deceit, and undermine the social relationships that are the fabric of our civilization. In this way, social commentators, including Rosenblatt, found these programs to be more than distasteful. They were false, several were sexually suggestive, and they undermined social institutions such as marriage.

This is the American culture that Roger Rosenblatt believed was attacked in 2001. He feared that the fantasies propagated by lying presidents and the purveyors of popular culture had anesthetized the American public into a state where nothing was substantial, where even the attack on the World Trade Center would seem like a movie special effect. Rosenblatt (2001, 79) wrote, "The consequence of thinking that nothing is real—apart from prancing around in an air of vain stupidity—is that no one will know the difference between a joke and a menace."

Indeed, Rosenblatt was not alone in his concern. James Pinkerton of *Newsday* suggested that the terrorist attacks would be "a crushing defeat for irony, cynicism, and hipness" in America (Goode, 2002, 1). Graydon Carter offered a concurring commentary for *Inside.com* that said, "I think it's the end of the age of irony.... Things that were considered fringe and frivolous are going to disappear" (Goode, 2002, 1). Bret Begun (2001, 86) of *Newsweek* wondered specifically how young Americans would respond to the crisis. He wrote,

"We *have* been in a slumber resting under a blanket of satire and irony. It was comfortable there, a safe harbor from having to take anything seriously, our greatest worry." Prior to World War II, a generation of Americans wondered if they had grown too soft and indulgent to fight a foe as formidable as the German army. Would our citizen-soldiers be able to defeat the Nazis? In 2001, most Americans believed that victory was inevitable for our armed forces, the question seemed to be, "How would our citizens deal with the new threat of terrorism among us?"

Rosenblatt's essay was indeed a criticism of contemporary American society and the perceived levels of "falseness" that pervades our popular culture, but it was also a call-to-arms. In the end, he believes that the reality of September 11 was not only the death and destruction caused by attacks but also the acts of bravery and the hope they inspired for the future. Rosenblatt (2001, 79) writes, "In short, people may at last be ready to say what they wholeheartedly believe. The kindness of people toward others in distress is real.... Honor and fair play? Real.... The greatness of the country: real. The anger: real. The pain: too real." In reality, Rosenblatt sees threat and hope. His fear is that irony will mute the former and mock the latter.

Humor

There was little to laugh about on September 11, 2001. As one comedian in New York said, it seemed like "the least funny day in our history" (McKinley, 2001, E1). Standup comedian David Brenner was surprised to find 100 people in his Las Vegas audience that evening. He said that he addressed the morning's events and explained to the audience that in deference to the attacks he could not perform a series of jokes on flying or any political humor that evening (McKinley, 2001, E 1). Comedy clubs across the nation closed, movies were pulled from release, and television networks adapted programming to reflect the somber mood of the nation. CBS and NBC replaced *Late Night with David Letterman* and *The Tonight Show* with news programming, in part, because the nightly comedy monologue would seem inappropriate in the midst of such tragedy. Even the irreverent newspaper the *Onion* ceased publication for a week. One comedian ran the risk of his sardonic wit and quickly felt the consequences of his words. On September 17, 2001, Bill Maher, host of the show *Politically Incorrect*, raised the ire of viewers and sponsors when in a discussion of terrorism and martyrdom he declared that the military policy of massive air strikes was cowardly (Rutenberg, 2001). The fallout from the incident, despite Maher's clarifications and apologies, eventually lead to the withdrawal of major sponsors and the cancellation of the show.

As in all good humor, the key seemed to be: timing. Michiko Kakutani (2001, E 5), writing in the *New York Times*, observed that Americans historically have turned to humor as a release from difficult circumstances. In 1933, in the midst of the Depression, five of the top ten box office stars were comedians. The Cold War saw the publications of Joseph Heller's *Catch-22*, Kurt Vonnegut's *Slaughterhouse Five*, and the production of Stanley Kubrick's film *Dr. Strangelove or: How I Learned to Stop Worrying and Love the Bomb*. Kenneth Burke (1937/1984, 41) has written that the shift from the tragic to the comic frame of reference lies in the humane reconceptualization of a *criminal* act as mere *stupidity*. For Burke, the comic frame requires a transition from seeing acts as evil to perceiving them as the human foibles that each of us commits. An act of evil is not funny; there is no humor in the terrorist hijacking of a plane. However, if a terrorist attempted to capture a police car with a box cutter, there might be humor in the absurdity of the act. For Burke, humor is the opposite of the heroic. Tales of heroism magnify the character of the champion to meet the challenges that lie ahead. Humor, on the other hand, "reverses the process; it takes up the slack between the momentousness of the situation and the feebleness of those in the situation by *dwarfing the situation*" (Burke, 1937/1984, 43). Bob Hope entertained troops on the front lines of four wars not by telling heroic tales but by mocking the mundane elements of military life. Soldiers could be facing imminent danger but would laugh at jokes about "bad Army food" or "inept officers who knew less than the enlisted soldiers." In this way, Hope downsized the scope of the war from geopolitical conflicts and the threat of life and death to stories about pretty girls and the military bureaucracy. Burke (1937/1983, 43) notes that humor is ultimately not a "well-rounded" frame of acceptance because it gauges the situation falsely.

The application of theory and historic precedent to the study of humor and September 11 suggests several points. First, that despite Rosenblatt's contempt for the idea, Marx was right. Before one can attempt to satirize a tragedy, it must be defined and understood as a tragedy. Even in the era of instantaneous news and global information, it took time for the events of 9/11 to unfold. The demand for information tempts media to report rumor and innuendo as fact. Days, not minutes or hours, passed before the scope of the attack was put into context. The first narratives that resonated among Americans were tragic tales of lives lost and the heroic efforts of fire fighters and police officers aiding the victims. These were defining moments in the tragedy. The lack of understanding of what had happened limited the effectiveness of irony and satire because there was no common ground upon which to build. Second, once the scope of the tragedy was defined, Americans were not prepared to downsize or minimize the situation. This was an attack unlike any other in American history that left citizens confused, afraid, and angry. Ground Zero became a hallowed site, sacred ground that contained the remains of thousands of the victims of the assault. As one of the greatest single acts of destruction on American soil, the momentousness of the situation grew in the middle of September 2001. Politicians, celebrities, and average citizens made pilgrimages to Ground Zero that kept the story in the public consciousness. In the days following 9/11, Ground Zero became a national shrine; it was not to be minimized. Finally, the dramatic and violent nature of this first foreign terrorist attack on American soil cast it as pure evil. Americans lack of knowledge about Islam and its followers facilitated propagandistic responses against Arabs and even Arab-Americans. Some of the first attempts at humor after September 11 were cartoons and jokes that sought to release aggressive feelings through scapegoating. The Internet, in particular, circulated hostile humor that scapegoated Osama Bin Laden, stereotypical Arabs, Afghanistan, and, even, Saddam Hussein as the sources of all evil (2001, www.butlerwebs.com). America was not prepared for a shift from the tragic to the comic frame of reference because emotions were running high and the moral indignation of the country could not accept the attack as anything but "evil."

A discussion of humor and tragedy in light of the events of September 11 might seem odd at first, but as previously stated, humor has served as a source of diversion or healing for Americans in the past. In contemporary American society, humor has also become a source of information about complex issues. During the 2000 presidential campaign, a survey commissioned by the Pew Research Center for People and the Press found that 47 percent of all Americans between the ages of eighteen and twenty-nine received at least part of their news from late-night comedy shows (Sella, 2000, 74). Moreover, 25 percent of all Americans reported that the monologues of comedians such as David Letterman, Jay Leno, and Jon Stewart were a source of political information (Sella, 2000, 74). Marshall Sella (2000) in his article, "The Stiff Guy vs. The Dumb Guy, " suggests that comedy simplifies and magnifies the elements of the campaign to offer a more honest portrait of the candidates. Late night monologues are not held to the same journalistic standards of objectivity required of news reporters. Therefore, hyperbole, stereotyping, and irony are the coin of the realm for comedians trying to satirize the news of the day in a five-minute monologue. Both the Gore and the Bush presidential campaigns monitored the late night lambastes of their candidates to gauge swings in public opinion. Chris Lehane, Gore's campaign press secretary, said, "We read the transcripts of those shows and watch them. The monologues are evidence of when a story breaks through. If it makes Leno or Letterman, it *means* something (Sella, 2000, 74).

In an era when Americans are reading less and watching more, humor has become a way for Americans to sift through the cacophony of sound bytes, white papers, and photo-ops to distill an image of a presidential candidate. Indeed, if one-fourth of all Americans view late-night comedians as a source for political information, it is fair to assume that they were also listening for news about the events of 9/11. In the aftermath of the attack, comedy slowly and cautiously returned to the late night airwaves. Mayor Rudolph Giuliani appeared on *Saturday Night Live* and was asked by producer Lorne Michaels, "Is it okay to be funny?" "Why start now?" Guiliani replied. In his first show after September 11, David Letterman replaced his comedic monologue with a personal statement, "If we are going to continue doing shows, I need to hear myself talk for a few minutes" (2001, *http://edition.cnn.com/2001/SHOWBIZ/TV/09/17*, 1). Letterman praised New York as the greatest city in the world and cited Mayor Giuliani's request for a return to normal activities as a reason for resuming the broadcast of the program. The Center for Media and Public Affairs (2002, *http://www.cmpa.com/pressrel/2001latenightjoke.htm*) reported that political jokes dropped by 54 percent on late night television in the month following the attack and that serious guests (i.e., Dan Rather, Madelaine Albright, and columnist Thomas Friedman) were featured twice as frequently in the fifteen weeks after September 11 as they had been in the previous fifteen weeks. It is interesting to note that the lingering impact of

9/11 has actually led to an *increase* in late night political humor. In February of 2002, (http://www.cmpa.com/pressrel 2001latenightjoke.htm), the Center indicated that Letterman's level of political humor was ten times higher than September 2001 and exceeded the pre-9/11 average by 65 percent. Similarly, Leno's average number of political jokes was 27 percent above pre-9/11 levels and Conan O'Brien, host of *Late Night with Conan O'Brien*, increased his use of political humor by 32 percent over the same periods (2002, http://cmpa.com/pressrel/ 2001latenightjoke.htm)

From the front pages of America's leading newspapers to late-night monologues, increased interest in political issues beget increased political humor in nightly monologues. Sella (2000) states that late night comedians have turned their nightly monologues into a national dialogue about the significant issues of the day. The rise of humor as a source of political information, he continues, demonstrates that more and more, "Americans prefer to take their news sweet" (Sella, 2000, 74).

Irony

Irony, like rhetoric, has suffered a definitional setback in the vocabulary of the American public. Communication scholars confront the popular perception that the ancient art of rhetoric is little more than "empty words" or "the antithesis of action." Similarly, students of irony now face the contention that irony implies "falsehood, negation, or contradiction." The *Merriam-Webster Dictionary* (1997, 400) defines "irony" as "the use of words to express the opposite of what one really means." The simplicity of this definition may be functional for everyday speech, but like its counterpart "rhetoric, " this usage denies the history and creative range of the literary device. McGrath (2000, 9) notes that the origin of irony lies in the word "dissemble" and was used by the ancient Greeks "in that abiding preoccupation of theirs, the gap between appearance and reality or between truth and belief." The *Compact Oxford English Dictionary* (1971/1994, 453) illumines this understanding of irony in its definition of the word "dissemble": "To alter or disguise the semblance of (one's character, a feeling, design, or action) so as to conceal, or deceive as to, its real nature, to give a false or feigned semblance to; to cloak or disguise by feigned appearance." Herein lies the secret, to those who believe that reality is "knowable, " irony and indeed all language conceal the true nature of the world. Any symbolic representation conceals the nature of the thing it seeks to describe. Thus, all irony, indeed all language, could be characterized as false and deceptive. Kenneth Burke (1966) counters that all humans are "Bodies that learn language, " physical beings separated from the natural realm by devices of our own making. Symbol-making animals use and misuse symbols to create a "re-presentation" of the world as they understand it or choose to characterize it. The sharing of these symbols enable individuals to create communities with other like-minded symbol-users, in this way, humans are physical beings that exist in symbolic communities of their own creation. For Burke, symbols can reveal or conceal one's perception of the world. Symbols are tools that are neither false nor true. It depends on how a rhetor chooses to use them.

The move from the popular to the scholarly realm requires a leap of faith that recognizes the full symbolic potential of irony. Luigi et al. (2002, 2) refer to irony as "a meaningful mask." In this context, critics would not view the mask as simply a device hiding the "true face, " but, rather, examine the choice of mask, its style, and character to understand how the individual chooses to present herself to the public. Wayne Booth (1974, xiv), one of the preeminent authorities on the subject of irony, writes that the "mask" of irony may take many forms and be used in "tragedy, comedy, satire, epic, lyric poetry, allegory, congressional speeches—to say nothing of everyday speech." He observes that it is not enough to say that irony allows one to "say" one thing and "intend" another, because the same could be written of metaphor, simile, allegory, metonymy and synecdoche (Booth, 7). Let us turn, therefore, to Wayne Booth's seminal work on the subject of irony to establish a working conception of the rhetorical form.

In 1974, Booth offered his text, *A Rhetoric of Irony*, to the scholarly community. In the opening words of his preface, the author notes that "For both its devotees and those who fear it, irony is usually seen as something that undermines clarities, opens up vistas of chaos and either liberates by destroying all dogma or destroys by revealing the inescapable canker of negation at the heart of every affirmation" (Booth 1974, ix), Booth, on the other hand, offers a surprisingly upbeat conception of irony that features cooperation, construction, and community. He calls this form stable irony and identifies its four chief characteristics. First, stable irony is "*intended*, deliberately created by human beings to be heard or read and understood with some precision by other human beings." In this way, irony is cooperatively constructed by a rhetor and an audience. One may not impose irony on another's actions. Second, it is *"covert, intended to be reconstructed with meanings different from those on the surface."* Third, they "are all nevertheless *stable* or fixed, in the sense that once a reconstruction of meaning has been made, the reader is not then invited to undermine it." Finally, stable ironies are *"finite in application"* (Booth 1974, 5-6).

For Booth, the key term in the formation of irony is "reconstruction." He asserts that the starting point for creating a new ironic perspective must be grounded in a shared point of view by the author and reader. This common ground, or commonplace, was defined by Aristotle as *topoi* and was the basis from which all persuasion could occur (Booth 1974, 34). To create an ironic vision of this commonplace, it is necessary to build a platform from which the author and reader may jointly view their shared beliefs. In a somewhat ironic vision for this essay, Booth portrays irony as twin towers standing side-by-side. The second building is slightly taller than the first and represents a reconstructed platform from which one may look down upon the smaller building. The taller building is a "reconstruction" of the initial tower built of the same materials, values, ideas, or commonplaces, as the first. The rhetorical "architect" of the second structure then offers a covert invitation in the form of an ironic statement to all those dwelling in the first building. Those who accept the invitation and make the "leap of faith" upward to the new building now possess a better vantage point, a new perspective, from which they may view the former platform. In this way, the rhetorical "architect" and his audience now share an ironic view of the commonplace they once occupied (Booth 1974, 35-37).

Critics of irony would use this metaphoric vision of reconstruction to offer two critiques of the rhetorical form. First, it is elitist. The invitation to move to the second building is covert and therefore is only offered to a select few. Second, a consequence of the elitist nature of irony is that those who do not make the "leap of faith" upward become victims of the new ironic vision. As victims, they are looked down upon and judged by the elitist caste occupying the taller building. Booth rejects the former charge noting that the architect and audience began in the same place, sharing the same commonplaces or values. Irony begins in understanding and seeks to offer the collective a better vision of their commonly held beliefs. Moreover, Booth (1974, 43-44) argues: "... reconstructions are seldom if ever reducible either to grammar or semantics or linguistics. In reading any irony worth bothering about, we read life itself, and we work on our relations to others as they deal with it. We read character and value, we refer to our deepest convictions."

In response to the second critique, it would be true that those who did not make the "leap of faith" would become the victims of the ironic rhetoric of the reconstructed community. To which Booth might ask, "Why would someone not make the leap?" Ironic statements rooted in fundamental values are invitations *to move together* to higher ground. Shared vision, cooperation, and the aspiration to improve are the hallmarks of a healthy, vibrant community. Irony is not a singular act; it is cooperative and rooted in the bond of commonly held values. The rhetor attempts to persuade the audience of the correctness of his vision because without their support there is no reformation. Booth believes that irony should strengthen communities not tear them apart. Organizations, communities, and cultures evolve and grow or they die. Irony is a tool that invites communities to grow together and adapt to changes in the environment. To understand how irony can help a collective even in times of tragedy, let us turn to our analysis of the *Onion's* post 9/11 coverage.

The Onion

The *Onion* is a relatively obscure, satirical news weekly that humbly bills itself as "America's Finest News Source." In the wake of 9/11, the *Onion* followed the trend of comedy television shows and clubs and suspended publication for a week. On September 26, the paper returned with its understated, "The Holy Fucking Shit Issue: Attack on America." The irony of the *Onion* usually savages politically powerful figures and the pretentiousness of popular culture. The terrorist attack on the United States presented a new challenge for our nation's finest news source.

The circulation for the *Onion* is relatively small and youth-oriented as one might expect. Still, in the era of global communication, the *Onion* has found a much broader presence on the World Wide Web. The *Onion* (2003, *http://mediakit.theonion.com*) reports receiving five million visits a month from Internet users. This first ripple is then extended exponentially by those who forward a funny story to a friend, colleague, or co-worker. This is how one of the authors of this essay was first exposed to the *Onion*. It was the first funny story he remembered reading after the tragedy.

Critics of irony charge that it conceals reality, glamorizes vacuous popular culture, and undermines social values and institutions. Therefore, it should not surprise readers of the *Onion* that the newspaper accepted the challenge of satirizing a national tragedy by addressing the topics of popular culture, politics, and religion. This essay will examine the four feature stories in the first post-9/11 edition, one story respectively on politics and popular culture and two on religion.

In his essay, Rosenblatt (2001) argued that popular fantasy films blur the distinction between "seeing dead people" and dealing with the thousands of deaths cause by the terrorist attack. The *Onion* addresses this premise in the story, "American Life Turned Into A Bad Jerry Bruckheimer Movie." Bruckheimer is the producer for such explosive action films as *Top Gun*, *Armageddon*, and *Pearl Harbor*. The article "American Life" uses the films *Independence Day*, *Armageddon*, and *Passenger 57* as examples to differentiate between the special effects of movies and the tragic events of September 11. The irony comes in the realization that such films are not reality-based. Mock interviews are poised against pictures of the September 11 attack with captions that read, "An actual scene from real life" and "Another scene not from a movie" (2001, *http://www.theonion.com/onion3734*, 1-2). New Yorker Bradley Martin is "quoted" as saying, "I always thought terrorists blowing shit up would be cool. ... Like, if the Pentagon was bombed, I figured they'd mobilize a special elite squadron of secret-agents and half of them would be babes"(2001, *http://www.theonion.com/onion3734*, 1-2). Dan Monahan concurred, "Terrorist hijackings, buildings blowing up, thousands of people dying, these are things I'm accustomed to seeing. ... In movies like "Armageddon, " it seemed silly and escapist. But this, this doesn't have any scenes where Bruce Willis saves the planet" (2001, *http://www.theonion.com/onion3734*, 1). Time and again the extraordinary events of 9/11 are compared unfavorably to the ordinary stories and stars of recent films. The *Onion* notes that the unbelievable events of September 11 would have been rejected as too implausible for even a Sylvester Stallone film. Still, there is a hint of disappointment in the article when it reports that the president who rose heroically to address the nation was not Harrison Ford but George W. Bush. Bush, for his part, did not even kiss a leggy blonde reporter at the conclusion of his speech. Clearly, the story concludes, the tragic events of September 11, 2001 are nothing like the sensational disaster films Americans have come to know and enjoy. There were not even "Attack on America" cups at Taco Bell the next day (2001, *http://www.theonion.com3734*, 2).

On the morning of September 11, 2001, the authors of this essay sat before a television where a young undergraduate said bewilderingly, "It looks like a bad special effect." As America searched for answers and a way to define what was happening, it was not surprising that such a highly popular film as *Independence Day* found its way into the national dialogue. The plot of *Independence Day* included an alien attack on the White House. As rumors swirled and reports of the evacuation of the White House surfaced, the visual imagery of the movie probably crept into the minds of many young people. Critics of irony should realize that media events are commonplaces shared by millions of people, but no sentient being would confuse the two events. The *Onion* used the absurdly heroic scope of movie actors and the crystal clarity of disaster-film-plots to address the confusion we all felt on the morning of September 11. The reconstruction of the tragedy of 9/11 in terms of the plots of recent disaster films demonstrated the complexity of the issues being addressed. As the article concluded, "The collective sense of outrage, helplessness, and desperation felt by Americans is beyond comprehension. ... But one thing *is* clear: No Austrian body builder, gripping Uzis and striding shirtless through the debris, will save us and make it all better" (2001, *http://www.theonion.com/onion3734*, 3). Unfortunately, life is not as simple as a heroic movie plot.

The second topic addressed by the *Onion* was the anticipated response of the United States to these acts of terrorism. On September 13, 2001, *New York Times* columnist Thomas Friedman (2001, A31) wrote, "Does my country know that this is World War III?" Friedman asserted that the religious fervor of the terrorists did not afford negotiation or compromise. This would, in his opinion, be an all-out battle for survival. There was some public discussion of whether terrorism was a crime or an act of war but all that was put to rest when President Bush declared war on terrorism on September 20. As stated at the outset of this chapter, however, this was a war unlike any America had ever fought. How would we attack an enemy without a country? Fortunately, the *Onion's* "in-depth" reporting went to the heart of the matter.

In the article, "U.S. Vows To Defeat Whoever It Is That We're At War With, " the *Onion* reconstructed reality with the help of several high-placed sources. President Bush was "quoted" as saying, "America's enemy, be it Osama Bin Laden, Saddam Hussein, the Taliban, a multinational coalition of terrorist organizations, or any of a rogue's gallery of violent Islamic groups, or an entirely different, non-Islamic aggressor we've never heard of...be warned...the United States is preparing to strike, directly and decisively, against whoever you are" (2001, *http://www.theonion.com/onion3734*, 1). The highly visible Secretary of Defense Donald Rumsfeld, ironically explained to the American public that this would be a war unlike any in its history. He stated:

> We were lucky enough at Pearl Harbor to be the victims of a craven sneak attack from an aggressor with the decency to attack military targets, use their own damn planes, and clearly mark those planes with their national insignia so that we knew who they were. ... Since the 21-st century breed of coward is not affording us any such luxury, we are forced to fritter away time searching hither and yon for him in the manner of a global easter-egg hunt. (2001, *http://www.theonion.com/onion3734*, 2)

Questions were asked in the *Onion* about the kind of enemy we would face. Senator Tom Daschle wondered out loud, "[W]hat if we declare war on Afghanistan and they didn't send anyone to fight us? It's plausible that we would declare war on them, but they wouldn't go to war with us, since they weren't the ones who actually attacked us" (2001, *http://www.theonion.com/onion3734*, 2). Senator John McCain took the ironic conjecture even further, "Christ, ... what if the terrorists' base turns out to be Detroit? Would we declare war on Michigan? I suppose we'd have to" (2001, *http://www.theonion.com/onion3734*, 2). The *Onion* even discovered that those opposed to the war were confused. The paper reported that after President Bush's address to the nation, two dozen protestors gathered across from the White House with placards that read "U.S. Out of Somewhere" and "No Blood For Whatever Those Murderous Animals Hope To Acquire" (2001, *http://www.theonion.com/onion3734*, 3). Terrorism was a new enemy for America. The *Onion* accurately reflected the fear and confusion that an enemy that strikes from within can engender.

In the days after September 11, most Americans were introduced to the names Osama Bin Laden and the terms "the Taliban" and "the Axis of Evil." The uncertainty of "who had attacked us" and "why" left the country confused and frightened. The *Onion* identified that uncertainty and even addressed the very real threat that terrorist cells might still exist in this country. The use of irony in this instance allowed readers the opportunity to see leaders struggling with the same questions they faced. Comparisons of 9/11 and Pearl Harbor were offered in most media as a means of defining the moment in the genre of national crisis. In this parody, the *Onion* reminds readers how easy it was to define an enemy in the twentieth century and how the actions of modern warfare did not seem quite so clear.

Finally, the most contentious issue after 9/11 was that of religion. Little was known about the nineteen terrorists except that they were religious zealots who believed they were performing a sacred mission. Americans general lack of knowledge about Islam and the Arab world lead to an immediate backlash against Middle Eastern culture. Mosques were attacked, Arab-American citizens threatened, and the first delineation of "us" versus "our enemy" was drawn along religious lines. The *Onion* tackled the topic of religion in two stories. The first was "Hijackers Surprised to Find Selves in Hell."

The promise of heavenly rewards for martyrs was said to be one of the motivations of the terrorists. In an interview from the lowest plane of Na'ar, Islam's hell, Mohammed Atta, one of the terrorists, confirmed that:

> I was promised I would spend eternity in Paradise, being fed honeyed cakes by 67 virgins in a tree-lined garden, if only I would fly the airplane into one of the Twin Towers. .... But, instead, I am fed the boiling feces of traitors by malicious, laughing Ifrit. Is this to be my reward for destroying the enemies of my faith? (2001, *http://www.theonion.com/onion3734*, 1)

Iblis The Thrice Damned, conscription officer for new arrivals in Na'ar, explained, "There was a tumultuous conflagration of burning steel and fuel at our gates and from it stepped the hijackers, the blessed name of the Lord already turning into molten brass on their accursed lips" (2001, *http://www.theonion.com/onion3734*, 1). A litany of tortures awaiting the terrorists was described in some detail for the reporters of the *Onion*. Finally, Praxitas, Duke of Those Willingly Led Astray, suggested, "It might actually be the most painful thing we can do, to show these murderers the untold pleasure that would have awaited them in Paradise, if only they had lead pious lives" (2001, *http://www.theonion.com/onion3734*, 2).

On the other end of the religious continuum, reporters from the *Onion* also covered a press conference by God in the story, "God

Angrily Clarifies Don't Kill Rule." In a rare appearance in the physical world, God appeared before the media to clarify His views on the taking of life. The Supreme Being said, "I tried to put it in the simplest terms for you people, so you'd get it straight, because I thought it was pretty important," said God, called Yahweh and Allah respectively in the Judaic and Muslim traditions. "I guess I figured I'd left no real room for confusion after putting it in a four word sentence with one syllable words, on the tablets I gave to Moses" (2001, *http://www.theonion.com/onion3734*, 1). God continued, "Not only did I not want anybody to kill anyone, but I specifically *commanded* you not to" (2001, *http://www.theonion.com/onion3734*, 1). God acknowledged that in the holy books of the Bible, Torah, and Qur'an there were some contradictory messages caused by misinterpretations of inspired human agents. Still, God emphasized His main point to the press. "I don't care how holy somebody claims to be... If a person tells you it's My will that they kill someone, they're wrong. Got it? I don't care what religion you are, or who you think your enemy is, here it is one more time: No killing in My name or anyone else's, ever again" (2001, *http://www.theonion.com/onion3734*, 1).

God declared that His Muslim followers are, on the whole, "wonderful, pious people." (2001, *http://www.theonion.com/onion3734*, 2). He said, "The vast majority of Muslims in this world reject the murderous actions of these radical extremists, just like Christians in America are pissed off over those two bigots on 'The 700 Club' (2001, *http://www.theonion.com/onion3734*, 2) Rather than separate religious traditions, God chose to speak of their similarities, "...the basic message is always the same: Christianity, Islam, Judaism, Buddhism, Shintoism...every religious belief system under the sun, they all say that you're supposed to love your neighbor, folks" (2001, *http:// www.theonion.com/onion3734*, 2). The reporters noted that God seemed to be growing increasingly agitated, until finally, He broke down and wept.

he tears of God shed over man's inhumanity to man. Irony allows the writers of the *Onion* to recast religion not as a rationale for martyrdom but rather as the reason to love your neighbor. In this political satire, writers invoke the voice of God and interview demons from the depth of hell to make their case. Few mainstream journalists have such latitude or the creative freedom to introduce such extreme images and powerful language. The themes of religious piety, tolerance, and the sacredness of life are reconstituted in brusque, hard-biting humor. Still, the fundamental theme of both essays is as old as the ancient commandment; "Thou shalt not kill."

Conclusion

In the November 2003 issue of the *Quarterly Journal of Speech*, Denise M. Bostdorff (2003) offers a most insightful analysis of President Bush's post 9/11 rhetoric. In her article, Bostdorff asserts that Bush employed a form of epideictic rhetoric known as "covenant renewal" to engage Americans and create a new sense of community after the terrorist assault. She found that Bush successfully invoked messages of traditional values and the mission of America in the light of the terrorist attack to renew the covenant between a people and its leadership. Bush's post 9/11 rhetoric not only engaged Americans in the themes of faith and renewal but challenged a new generation of Americans untested by tragedy to rise to the threat of terrorism just as its forefathers had confronted the threat of World War II. Bostdorff helps us "make sense" of a critical moment in contemporary history by explaining it in terms of past historical and rhetorical responses to crises.

In the chaos that followed the events of 9/11, many politicians and social leaders sought to explain the attack as America's entrance into a very different world. It has been suggested that journalism is "the first draft of history." So it was that Roger Rosenblatt and his colleagues wrote in the moment hoping that some real and lasting good might come from this crisis. Many calls for change went out post 9/11. Cultural critics asked Americans to reject the false prophets of popular culture and return to traditional values. Social agencies were overwhelmed by the generosity of people around the world in response to their urgent requests for aid. President Bush, for his part, asked relatively little of average citizens. In previous wars, presidents called for citizens to sacrifice and conserve resources to help defeat the enemy. In the war on terrorism, President Bush asked for tolerance in dealing with Arab-Americans, a return to our normal lives, and to go shopping to stimulate the economy. As our collective sense of compassion and community wane in the years after 9/11, one must wonder if President Bush could have asked for and received a greater sense of personal investment and commitment from the American public.

For its part, the *Onion* asked more of its readers. Satire and irony do not merely question events but seek to reform them into a new rhetorical vision. Boldly addressing the themes of religion, reality, terrorism, and intolerance, the *Onion* offered a form of "comic renewal" that celebrated American values and challenged readers to look forward. Bostdorff's conception of covenant renewal and the *Onion's* irony are both forms of epideictic rhetoric that transformed America's perceptions after 9/11. Covenant renewal affirmed leadership in a time of crisis and empowered the president to declare war on terrorism. Irony, or comic renewal, reminded its audience of their shared values and invited them to move to a higher ground together. Readers and Internet viewers of the *Onion* created a community of like-minded individuals who celebrated the ironic perspective of the publication. The satirical messages of the *Onion* reverberated through a network of Americans seeking some way to understand what happened. The audience may have been separated by time and space as they laughed at "The Holy Fucking Shit Issue" in their hands or on-line. Nonetheless, a community of millions shared its anger, fear, and hope as it reconstructed the image of the attack. The audience was most likely young and conditioned to seeking information from satirists and comedians about politics and world events. The *Onion* addressed 9/11 not as tragedy but in an ironic perspective. This enabled its audience to think of the attack in a new way and begin the process of healing.

Political leaders and journalists are constrained by the proprieties of convention and good taste; satirists and comedians are not. Americans have always found the value of humor in difficult times. The cataclysmic events of 9/11 were no exception. In our complex lives and media saturated world, Americans can be overwhelmed with information. As a result, some choose to reject the bounty of data altogether and live in ignorance. Others, particularly young people have found that reconstructed images offered by humor and satire clarify issues and make them more palatable. Satirists and comedians generally make people laugh and help them move through their daily lives. Jokes are more likely to address mundane issues such as relationships, life at work, or dealing with the kids. These are the localized communities that most of us deal with on a daily basis. Comedians forego the grays of the spectrum to paint the world in vivid hues. More and more, young Americans are turning to these same colorful sources for unambiguous, subjective, and simplistic portraits of the more significant issues in life.

The attacks of September 11, 2001 and the subsequent war on terrorism are complex issues that are still being studied by politicians, journalists, and academics. As time passes and we gather more evidence about the events of those fateful first days, investigators from all fields are helping us gain a better understanding of those almost incomprehensible acts of terrorism. Scholars, unlike politicians and journalists, have the luxury of time in formulating their analyses. It is hoped that volumes like this one will provide more understanding of what happened and how Americans dealt with the tragedy. Sadly, we believe that this rhetorical analysis could provide some insight into the responses that we offer to our *next* national crisis.

Shortly after the attack of 9/11, a few brave voices offered absurd accounts of God's appearance at a press conference and an interview with the hijackers in hell. The *Onion's* satirical take on 9/11 was not an attempt to belittle the tragedy or the heroes who responded to it. Rather, it was a celebration of American faith, tolerance, and our ability to cope with unimaginable events. Irony did not die on September 11, 2001, but it had no place in the national narrative of the moment. The terrorist attack on America was first and foremost a tragedy; it took time and investigative effort until we could articulate that shocking story. Americans mourned our collective sense of loss while celebrating the heroic deeds of firefighters, police officers, and average citizens whom sacrificed so much to help others. Irony takes time to develop. It requires information and a communal sense of where we are and what we believe before the ironist and audience can reconstruct the vision. Americans have historically used their sense of humor to overcome tragedy. Wars, economic depression, and assassinations have challenged the innate optimism of this immigrant nation. Yet somehow we have banded together in laughter and in tears to move forward. The sense of Manifest Destiny that lead our ancestors to explore a nation now leads us to Mars and beyond. Still, the most important journeys in our lives may not be to a physical destination. The challenge to overcome tragedy and move beyond the grief and horror of 9/11 were real obstacles for the American public. Irony is one of the rhetorical tools that enabled us to overcome the difficulties of that journey. The rhetorical reconstruction of irony invites us to see our world and ourselves in a new way.

If the critics were correct and irony had died on September 11, 2001, a piece of the American character and dream would have died with it. Irony will never die; Americans have a long way to go in their collective narrative journey and many obstacles yet to overcome.

References

Begun, B. 2001. The end of irony. *Newsweek: The Spirit of America* (Commemorative Issue), 3 December.

Booth, W. C. 1974. *A Rhetoric of Irony*. Chicago: The University of Chicago Press.

Bostdorff, D. M. 2003. George W. Bush's post-September 11 rhetoric of covenant renewal. *Quarterly Journal of Speech*, 89: 293-319.

Burke, K. 1937. *Attitudes Toward History*. Berkeley: University of California Press.

Burke, K. 1966. *Language as Symbolic Action*. Berkeley: University of California Press.

Ferguson, N. 2001. The war on terror is not new. *New York Times*. 20 September.

Goode, S. 2002. Tragedy spells 'the end of irony.' *Insight*, 14 January, *http://www.insightmag.com/news/160706.html*

Hikins, J. W. 1983. The rhetoric of 'unconditional surrender' and the decision to drop the atomic bomb. *Quarterly Journal of Speech*. 69: 379-400. http://edition.cnn.com/2001/SHOWBIZ/TV/09/17/gen.letterman.return/

http://www.butlerwebs.com/tragedy/humor.htm

http://www.cmpa.com/pressrel/2001latenightjoke.htm The Center for Media and Public Affairs. Late Night Humor Bounces Back from September 11th.

http://www.theonion.com/onion3734/american_life_turns_into.html

http://www.theonion.com/onion3734/god_clarifies_don't_kill.html

http://www.theonion.com/onion3734/hijackers_surprised.html

http://www.theonion.com/onion3734/us_vows_to_defeat_whoever.html

http://mediakit.theonion.com

http://www.whitehouse.gov/news/releases/2001/09

Kakutani, M. 2001. The age of irony isn't over after all. *New York Times*. 9 October.

Luigi, A., C. Rita, and M. I. Giaele. 2002. Behind dark glasses: irony as a strategy for indirect communication. *Genetic, Social and General Psychology Monographs*, 128: 1-21.

McGrath, C. 2000. No kidding: Does irony illuminate or corrupt? *New York Times*. 5 August.

McKinley, J. 2001. Comedians return, treading lightly. *New York Times*. 26 September.

Merriam-Webster's Compact American English Dictionary. 1995. Springfield: Merriam-Webster, Incorporated.

Purdy, J. 1999. *For Common Things: Irony, Trust and Commitment in America Today.* New York: Alfred A. Knopf.

Rosenblatt, R. 2001. The age of irony comes to an end. *Time*, 24 September.

Rutenberg, J. 2001. Bill Mahrer still secure in ABC slot, at least for now. *New York Times*. 8 October.

Sella, M. 2000. The stiff guy vs. the dumb guy. *New York Times Sunday Magazine*. 24 September.

Simpson, J. A. and E. S. Weiner, eds. 1971. *The Compact Oxford English Dictionary*. Oxford: Clarendon Press, 1994.

6

Sport and the Healing of America after 9/11

Robert S. Brown

The World Trade Center bombing of September 11, 2001, is most assuredly one of the worst, if not the worst, tragic losses of life to occur in American society. The death of thousands of people and the televised collapse of one of the country's most recognizable architectural landmarks caused a tremendous shock to the nation that will be felt for years to come.

Much has been written about the impact of the 9/11 tragedy and America's response to it. Media critics continue to dissect the role of the press during and after the initial attack. It has been well documented how the nation rallied from the disaster, guided by political leadership from President George W. Bush and New York Mayor Rudolph Giuliani, heroic efforts from New York City police and firefighters, and thousands of volunteers nationwide who contributed in ways both big and small. America's response, most prominently military engagements in Afghanistan and Iraq, are still ongoing as U.S. foreign policy foreign policy addresses the threat of global terrorism.

It is the point of this essay to investigate the role of American popular sport in post-9/11 America. Despite its status as a major American social institution, sport is often dismissed as somehow more trivial and less socially significant than most other aspects of society. This is understandable, as the very notion of playing games during a time of crisis appears antithetical and in poor taste. However, to dismiss out of hand a cultural mainstay engaging the attention of millions of citizens is to overlook one of the major confluences of people and ideas in American society.

This chapter examines the role of sport in the post-9/11 healing of the America. The debate over the place of sport during crises will first be examined to establish the significant weight sport carries during these tragic times. Once the appropriateness of sport has been examined, the essay will focus on the performance of sport in reaction to crises, with specific attention paid to the post-9/11 World Series and Super Bowl, as a significant communication source of healing messages.

To Play or Not to Play

Since President Roosevelt's "Green Light Letter" to baseball after the bombing of Pearl Harbor, recommending that baseball carry on despite the outbreak of war, sport has not only continued after major American crises, but in fact have argued that it was their solemn duty to continue. The list is long: World War II, Korea, Vietnam, the Kennedy assassination, the Munich Olympic tragedy, the Challenger explosion, President Reagan's shooting, the Gulf War, the 1996 Olympic Park explosion, the Columbine shootings. Sport may have paused for a day, but picked right up soon thereafter behind the cry of "home life must return to normalcy" and/or "sports can be a great spirit boost to those who put their lives on the line."

Out of feelings of honor and the desire to keep up good public relations, sports have changed their basic presentations after tragedies. After gaining support from Roosevelt to play their games during World War II, owners decided to start each game with the singing of the national anthem, gave reduced ticket prices to those who brought in scrap metal and other materials needed for the war effort, and held pre-game ceremonies on the field to honor various soldiers, inductees, and other military contributors (Brown 2002). The weekend after the assassination of President Kennedy, National Football League [NFL] Commissioner Pete Rozelle and team owners loaded up their games with moments of silence, flag ceremonies, the singing of hymns, and other tributes to honor the fallen leader (Brown 1996). Within weeks of the start of the Gulf War the Super Bowl was played before a huge crowd in Miami, where pre-game parties were cancelled out of respect to the war but the game continued without delay.

Unexpectedly, there was a shift in policy after 9/11. September 11, 2001 was a Tuesday, and understandably all sport was postponed that evening and the next day, as was most of everything else in the country. The NFL, however, was scheduled to play the next weekend, some five days after the tragedy. Based on previous history, it was reasonable to expect that the NFL would play, and that the other sports would follow in their steps and resume play that weekend as well. President Bush, following the same pattern as Presidents Roosevelt and Bush before him, urged the NFL and all sports to play "to show that terrorists can't alter the way we go about our lives" (Clayton 2001, 1). A survey revealed that 90 percent of the owners favored playing (Mortensen 2001, 1). Instead, Commissioner Tagliabue announced after a few days of consideration that the NFL would postpone their schedule and take the weekend off. Once this was announced, other sports such as Major League Baseball followed suit and announced they would not play that weekend (Pasquarelli 2001, 1).

I argue that this decision was based on three factors. The first factor was the threat of terrorism. People were worried that terrorists might try to crash a plane into a crowded football game. This fear was reinforced throughout the media as there were multiple mentions of the 1977 movie "Black Sunday," where terrorists planned to crash the Goodyear Blimp into the Super Bowl. The NFL relies in large part on fan attendance, and they could not risk losing their fanbase because people were afraid to enter stadiums.

The second factor was the legacy of the Kennedy Assassination. Kennedy was assassinated on November 22, 1963, a Friday afternoon. The American Football league decided to postpone their schedule, but NFL Commissioner Pete Rozelle announced that their games would be played Sunday afternoon as scheduled. Each game presented tributes to President Kennedy in well thought out ceremonies. Each stadium was packed despite the threat of boycotts, and fans leaving the stadiums commented how stirring and emotional the tributes had been and how much better they felt after being at the games (Brown 1996). However, from comments made after 9/11 by the media and by the NFL Commissioner and owners, the only thing remembered about that 1963 weekend were the protests, threats of boycotts, and Commissioner Rozelle's comments that the decision to play was the worst mistake he ever made in his twenty-five years as head of the NFL. The current NFL management did not want a repeat of what their memories told them had happened.

The final factor was the threat of a boycott by NFL players. Players Union Representatives voted 17-11 against playing. The New York Jets were very vocal about not playing, understandable since they could still see the smoke rising from the World Trade Center site from their stadium. Other players expressed a fear of flying across the country to game sites so soon after the tragedy. Rozelle had ordered players to play after the Kennedy assassination, but Tagliabue appeared unwilling to do the same and risk a player revolt.

This decision was certainly not an easy one, and was not universally welcomed. Sport, though basically an unproductive, albeit popular, entertainment, is viewed as important by millions of Americans. Audiences for sporting events, counting live gate and television viewer ship, are larger than audiences for anything else in society. Fully twenty percent of all media is dedicated to sport news. The amount of money spent on the broadcast rights for sporting events and the sale of sport-related merchandise are both measured in the billions of dollars. It is no surprise then that many people were upset with the decision to cancel weekend games. Florida State football coach Bobby Bowden stated before the weekend decision "I hope we play this game; if we don't it's playing right into their [the terrorist's] hands" ("Should sports" 2001, 1). These sentiments were echoed by Baltimore Ravens coach Brian Billick, who stated "From a personal standpoint—not as a coach but as an American—we want to play. I don't want cowards to dictate what we do in this country" ("League Decides" 2001, 2). Frank Deford, columnist for both *Sports Illustrated* and National Public Radio, wrote "A stadium is crucial for a democratic society, because it's where all classes and types of people come together, to mix and share in a common public space. Calling off the games denied us the opportunity for that precious and comforting assembly" (Martin 2001, 2).

So, in breaking with the traditional response of sport after crises, American sport delayed a return to their playing fields a week longer than usual. However, once the games returned, rather than offering escapist retreats from the tragedy, they communicated a wealth of messages directly addressing the tragedy and its impact. While almost any post-9/11 sporting event could serve as an example for this study, baseball's playoffs, featuring the New York Yankees, and the Super Bowl have been selected as the primary centerpieces of the following analysis due to their huge viewing audiences.

Baseball Contributes to Healing

As mentioned, in the immediate aftermath of the Trade Center destruction, sport decided to go with an unprecedented long-term postponement of games. Despite this decision, it was clear that sport understood its potential role in the healing of society. Tagliabue conceded as much when he said, "at a certain point playing our games can contribute to the healing process. Just not at this time" (Freeman 2001, c13). Gene Upshaw, executive director of the NFL Players Association, echoed these sentiments by agreeing, "We need to pause, stop, and reflect and we need to grieve. Part of that was not playing this weekend . . . . Next week we will play football. That will also be a part of the healing process" (Myers 2001, 121).

While the NFL set the tone for postponing sport, it would be baseball that started the healing process. The New York Mets would be the first team to hold games in New York City on September 21. A smaller-than-normal crowd of more than 35,000 fans, perhaps a sign of fear of more terrorism, stood through twenty minutes of pre-game ceremonies involving color guards from city fire and police departments, Diana Ross singing "God Bless America," and a moment of silence and twenty-one-gun salute honoring the victims and their families (Hill 2001, 20). The seventh-inning stretch featured Liza Minnelli performing "a stirring rendition of the city's unofficial anthem New York, New York" (Justice 2001, 1). From this game forward both New York baseball teams would wear hats featuring the logos of the New York City police and fire departments. All baseball teams would use the seventh-inning stretch time to sing "God Bless America" or other patriotic songs in place of their usual entertainment.

Baseball's contributions to the healing of America culminated during their October 2001 play-offs. Barely a month after the 9/11 tragedy, the New York Yankees made a run through the American league play-offs and World Series before eventually falling in seven games to the Arizona Diamondbacks. New Yorkers had become accustomed to the Yanks making trips to the World Series, but under the current circumstances, the games took on more of an air of importance than ever before. These games were also nationally televised, drawing huge audiences of both baseball fans and curious viewers interested in the recovery of New York and the nation as a whole. Said one fan before game three of the series, "This is a special night for New York and a big game for the whole country. I bet you half the people watching on television in Arizona are rooting for the Yanks. And if they aren't rooting for them, they are rooting for this city" (Klinkenberg 2001, a6).

The opening game of the post-season featured the Oakland Athletics visiting Yankee Stadium. A sell-out crowd of over 56,000 people led mayor Giuliani to say of the game, "It's important for the spirit of the city. The fact that all of these people showed up unafraid, undeterred, I think it's absolutely terrific" (Shifrel 2001, 7). Visible safety measures abound as National Guard troops surrounded the stadium, bomb-sniffing dogs investigated the interior, and all fans were searched before being allowed to enter the stadium - a practice not uncommon since the "Gulf War Super Bowl" of 1991 but increased in thoroughness after 9/11.

Game two of the play-offs, scheduled to begin at 8:00 P.M., would be delayed for a televised speech by President Bush. Another sell-out crowd stood at attention watching the speech broadcast on the center field scoreboard, leading columnist Mike Lupica to comment "So many times the Stadium has been called a cathedral of baseball. Now the stands were as quiet as a cathedral as they all listened to the President talk again about his war, our war, against terrorism" (10). Caught up in the swell of patriotism and anger, the crowd broke into a cheer as Bush declared that "We must defeat the evildoers wherever they hide" (Lupica 2001, 10). Immediately after the speech ended, the baseball establishment continued to build on the feelings started by the President with a stirring version of "The Battle Hymn of the Republic" while uniformed soldiers displayed an outfield-sized flag (Lupica 2001, 10).

Similar ceremonies would be held at every game, but on a larger scale, as the Yankees won their play-off series and moved into the World Series. Besides the typical flag and military ceremonies, Game one of the Series in Arizona featured a re-enactment of firemen raising the flag over the World Trade Center site side-by-side with a re-enactment of the famous flag raising at Iwo Jima from World War II. These two mirror images served to recreate two stirring moments of American triumph while also building a connection between one of the country's greatest military successes and its ongoing war on terrorism. For the seventh-inning stretch, a pre-taped message from President Bush drew cheers when he declared, "we will prevail against the evil ones" just before Vanessa Williams sang "God Bless America" (Harrington 2001, c6).

By game three—the first Series game played in New York—the president decided to make a personal appearance. In the first appearance by a sitting president at a World Series since Eisenhower in 1956, President Bush disregarded any safety concerns and walked across the field from the Yankee dugout wearing a New York Fire Department jacket and after giving the thumbs-up sign to the crowd, threw out the ceremonial first pitch much to the delight and admiration of the crowd (Moran, 2001, 1a). As Bush left the mound to watch the game from the owner's box he was followed by chants of "U-S-A, U-S-A" (Baker 2001, c05). It is apparent that baseball, and the president through his own historic actions, were sending out the desired messages. Commented one fan, "to be honest, I feel pretty safe tonight because the president is here" (Klinkenberg 2001, a6). Yankee manager Joe Torre commented, "We can't allow people to change the fact that we need to live our lives. I thought the president, being here, put his money where his mouth is" (Moran 2001, 1a). Mayor Giuliani echoed these sentiments, saying the president's appearance "shows we're not afraid, we're undeterred and that life is moving on the way it should" (Baker 2001, c05).

Football Contributes to Healing

While he was behind the decision to postpone all of the games, NFL Commissioner Paul Tagliabue was still a strong believer in the positive role his league's games could play. "The NFL is part of American life," the commissioner said, "We play one role in the healing process by playing our games, honoring the victims and heroes, and by saluting brotherhood, diversity and tolerance" (Zipay 2001, a103). Like Major League Baseball, the NFL altered their standard game presentations to deliver healing messages for post-9/11 society. For the resumption of their games on September 24, 2001, the NFL purchased one million miniature American flags to distribute to all fans entering stadiums (Mihoces 2001, 1c). Field-sized flags held by players, police officers, firefighters, and military personnel were used as part of pre-game ceremonies in San Francisco, Dallas, Seattle, and Chicago. Red, white, and blue bunting with the words "United We Stand" were on display along the sidelines and in each end zone of every football venue (Zipay 2001, a103). The NFL arranged for all hats worn by players and coaches to be adorned with American flag details, while the two New York teams remembered their city's efforts by wearing caps displaying the logos of the local police and fire departments (Caesar 2001, c9).

The NFL also arranged for special pre-game ceremonies at every stadium. Two short films, one a sixty-second video chronicling the events of the previous week and the other a tape featuring numerous popular recording artists performing "America the Beautiful," were distributed and played as part of the opening for every game (Hermoso 2001, d6). The League distributed pamphlets to all fans with the words to "The Star-Spangled Banner," "God Bless America,"and "America the Beautiful" to allow for more fan involvement following dignified moments of silence (Mihoces 2001, 1c). In New England, introduced before the game were the honorary captains—the four brothers of Patriot offensive lineman Joe Andruzzi, all New York firemen who had responded to the Trade Center crisis (Farmer 2001, 4-1).

Fox Sports, who owned the broadcast rights to the Super Bowl that season, working in conjunction with Commissioner Tagliabue, readily altered the format for their big game to address social issues brought about by the 9/11 tragedy. Originally designed with a Mardi Gras theme, Fox created a new spectacle based on the theme of "Heroes, Hope, and Homeland" (Hiestand 2001, 1c). Fox Sports Chairman David Hill admitted that Commissioner Tagliabue wanted the original theme changed to be more "respectful and patriotic" and that the new format was intended to "touch the heartstrings of the whole country" (Hiestand 2001, 1c).

For anyone who watched the Super Bowl—and that included well over one hundred million people—the intended messages were clear from the start of football's penultimate game.[1] Host James Brown, in opening the Super Bowl broadcast, announced "We are united more than ever as we fight the war against terrorism." Actor John Travolta then introduced the pre-game ceremonies, giving tribute to everyone who helped the nation through the recent tragedy, from firefighters to "regular people" everywhere. Barry Manilow, along with a host of fellow pop stars, performed his tribute to America, "Let Freedom Ring," while surrounded by dozens of flag bearers, dancers dressed as red, white, and blue Statues of Liberty, more dancers dressed in costumes that can best be described as flag butterflies, while young children representing World Trade Center volunteers from all walks of life escorted a giant Liberty Bell float.

After a commercial break, James Brown was back. He spoke of the Declaration of Independence as the cornerstone of American spirit, and introduced a video where actors dressed as American founding fathers read stirring patriotic comments. This was followed by a reading of the Declaration by past and present NFL stars, including Jim Brown, Roger Staubach, Marshall Faulk, Jack Kemp, Steve Largent, and Don Shula. Brown also mentioned the presence of an original copy of the Declaration on the field, proudly supplied by Home Depot.

After another commercial break, The Boston Pops presented a performance of Aaron Copland's 1942 composition "Lincoln Portrait." In introducing this piece, a combination of Lincoln's words with Copland's music, James Brown said Copland had written it to remind Americans "still reeling from the Japanese attack on Pearl Harbor of their country's history and to inspire us to continually defend liberty and equality." Note the way Brown moved from the post-Pearl Harbor country to the modern post-Trade Center "us" in the same sentence. The Pops then began the music, while former Presidents Ford, Carter, Bush, and Clinton, as well as Nancy Reagan substituting for her ailing husband, read Lincoln's word via videotape with a background montage of patriotic images and scenes from the World Trade Center site. Amidst applause and chants of "U-S-A," the ceremonies slid seamlessly into a performance of "America the Beautiful" sung by pop stars Mary J. Blige and Marc Anthony.

Following Paul McCartney's performance of his Trade Center inspired hit "Freedom," Fox aired a pre-taped package of players from both Super Bowl participants reading inspirational passages from many former presidents, ending the video with Kennedy's famous "ask not what your country can do for you" quote. Mariah Carey then took to the field to sing the National Anthem, joined by a host of New York City police and fire fighters, a navy color guard, and a New Orleans police officer who signed the Anthem for the hearing impaired. As Carey reached the conclusion of the song, the flag-raising ceremonies from Iwo Jima and the Trade Center were again re-enacted side-by-side as they had been at the World Series. To conclude these ceremonies, "U.S. Naval Academy and Hall of Fame legend" Roger Staubach was joined on the field by "World War II hero" George H. Bush for the coin toss.

Without any attempt at subtleness, the NFL used their championship game—the highest rated program on television every year—to provide a plethora of pro-American symbols for millions of viewers. At half time the band U-2 performed their hit song "Where the Streets Have No Names" while the names of all of those lost on 9/11 scrolled behind them on a giant screen. By the end of the game, as red, white, and blue confetti fell from the ceiling of the Superdome, some people jokingly suggested that the game itself had been rigged by the NFL to allow the underdog and aptly named Patriots to win, thus bringing a perfect close to the whole event.

Conclusion

How does sport function after a crisis? Many believe that sport offers a chance to escape from the problems of every day life (e.g., Araton, Halberstam). However, for one to escape from a tragedy, it is logical that a person must continue as if nothing was wrong and that all references to the tragedy need to be avoided. Clearly, sport does not go on with a "business as usual" approach. Games are altered to include various reminders of recent events, from the subtle moment of silence to the grand visions of the World Series and the Super Bowl. Hardly offering an escape from tragedy, sport often directly addresses the nation's pain, inviting spectators to deal with their feelings from a number of perspectives.

As can be seen in the examples examined here after 9/11, sport in America reflects social issues directly, exposing spectators to numerous messages to help them address the recent tragedy. *USA Today* writer Erik Brady, reflecting on the 9/11 events one year later, commented "Ballparks became home to sacramental ceremony. It seemed natural to salute and sing and cry and then settle in for a game that meant exactly nothing and everything all at once" (1c). From the analysis provided in this essay sport can been seen as providing solemn opportunities to mourn the dead, patriotic messages to inspire, salutes to honor the life-saving efforts of all involved, messages to re-enforce unity amongst Americans and remind everyone that life must go on. There were also not so subtle messages of supporting the war against terrorism and gaining victory against those who would attack the country. Dismissed by many as "trivial" or at best "escapist," sport must be recognized for the powerful influence it can have, especially in light of the messages of healing and inspiration for millions of Americans provided after the tragic events of 9/11.

Note

1.   All Super Bowl quotes and event descriptions were taken directly from the broadcast.

References

Araton, Harvey. In time, games can offer escape. *New York Times* 13 Sept. 2001: c9.

Baker, Geoff. Bush strikes a blow for freedom. *Toronto Star* 31 Oct. 2001: c05.

Brady, Erik. Continuity of sports helped heal the times. *USA Today* 11 Sept. 2002: 1c.

Brown, Robert S. Football as a rhetorical site of national reassurance: Managing the crisis of the Kennedy assassination. Ph.D. diss., Indiana University. 1996.

Brown, Robert S. Baseball carries on. In *Take Me Out to the Ballgame: Communicating Baseball*, edited by Gary Gumpert and Susan J. Drucker, 149-167. Cresskill, NJ; Hampton Press, Inc., 2002.

Caesar, Dan. Players take the field amid much poignancy, patriotism, reflection. *St. Louis Post-Dispatch* 24 Sept. 2001: c9.

Clayton, John. Choosing to play would help the nation heal. ESPN.com 12 Sept. 2001.

Farmer, Sam. For NFL it's stars and stripes; Patriotism in full swing as league resumes its normal schedule after postponing last week's games because of terrorist attacks. *Los Angeles Times* 14 Sept. 2001: 4-1.

Freeman, Mike. Pro Football: The games can wait; Tagliabue decides to put off week 2 after much debate. *New York Times* 14 Sept. 2001: c13.

Harrington, Mike. Arizona owner Colangelo stops to smell the roses. *Buffalo News* [New York] 28 Oct. 2001: c6.

Halberstam, David. Sports can distract, but they don't heal. ESPN.com 11 Sept. 2002.

Hiestand, Michael. Patriot Super Bowl; Sept. 11 alters Fox's approach. *USA Today* 10 Jan. 2002: 1c.

Hill, Gary. Baseball: Tears at the ball park as the national game returns. *Independent on Sunday* [London] 23 Sept. 2001: 20.

Hermoso, Rafael. For Giants and Jets, caps honor victims. *New York Times* 21 Sept. 2001: d6.

Justice, Richard. Shea hooray; Mets' return brings life into Big Apple. *Houston Chronicle* 22 Sept. 2001: 1.

Klinkenberg, Marty. President pitches but crowds wary; Bush throws out first pitch at Yankee Stadium. *Ottawa Citizen* 31 Oct. 2001: a6.

League decides not to play after much debate. ESPN.com 13 Sept. 2001.

Lupica, Mike. War & the national pastime. *New York Daily News* 12 Oct. 2001: 10.

Martin, Jurek. Patriotism hits home run in the sporting field. *Financial Times* [London] 6 Oct. 2001: 2.

Mihoces, Gary. Emotional day for NFL. *USA Today* 24 Sept. 2001: 1c.

Moran, Malcolm. Bush makes Series pitch - a strike - in N.Y. *USA Today* 31 Oct. 2001: 1a.

Mortensen, Chris. Mounting issues become too difficult to ignore. ESPN.com 13 Sept. 2001.

Myers, Gary. NFL opts to cancel games for the first time in history; Contingency plans still in the works. *New York Daily News* 14 Sept. 2001: 121.

Pasquarelli, Len. NFL affects decisions of other leagues. ESPN.com 14 Sept. 2001.

Shifrel, Scott and Bill Hutchinson. Fears join cheers as Yanks fall in game 1. *New York Daily News* 11 Oct. 2001: 7.

Should sports step to the sideline. ESPN.com 12 Sept 2001.

Zipay, Steve. Tributes set up by networks. *New York Newsday* 20 Sept. 2001: a103.

7

Patriotism and Political Socialization: Young Adults' Perspectives on the First Anniversary of 9/11

Edward M. Horowitz and Johan Wanstrom

National anniversaries are often times of introspection and reflection in which both individuals and the nation remember acts of heroism, courage, and bravery in the face of marked tragedy. For those who have experienced such tragedies directly, these are occasions to mourn the loss of life and reflect upon what could have been. Yet as time goes on, the harsh and vivid memories we have of those events generally softens, and the pain that was so intense during those immediate moments becomes greatly reduced. Almost immediately as that day's tragic events occurred, most Americans who experienced 9/11 knew that the horrors perpetrated by these terrorist attacks would become events that would be indelibly etched into our collective consciousness—whether experienced directly in lower Manhattan or indirectly watching television.

As America's most painful modern tragedy, our recent memory of 9/11 has been marked by solemn anniversaries and commemorations that have stretched from the original sites of the terrorist attacks—Ground Zero, the Pentagon, and a field outside Pittsburgh, Pennsylvania—across the nation. Yet even as our memories of 9/11 have begun to just barely diminish, these public commemorations have become quieter and more subdued (Reynolds 2003). The anniversary of 9/11 has at the time of this writing become an occasion no longer marked by public events such as the reading of the victims' names and large candlelight vigils, but rather by individual prayer and moments of silence. Even as these annual commemorations of 9/11 have evolved to be more private than public events, each anniversary remains an important occasion to reflect upon the ways America has been affected by these tragic events.

While all Americans were affected in some way by the terrorist attacks of 9/11, what are the long-term effects of these events on young adults? Many Americans still seem to be coping in some ways with the wave of emotions that were triggered by the events of 9/11: intense grief and sadness at the deaths of thousands; anger at the Muslim terrorists, along with Muslims in general; fear that such attacks could happen again; suspicion of foreigners as potential terrorists. In addition, the nationwide resurgence of patriotism brought on by 9/11 continues to be seen in the continued popularity of patriotic music as well as displays of U.S. flags that seem to be hanging nearly everywhere, including homes, businesses, cars, and lapels.

While it may remain difficult on the macro-level to understand how America as a nation is coming to terms with the tragic events of 9/11 and the on-going war on terrorism, it is particularly necessary and important to understand how young adults are coping with the first war of their lifetime. It is during adolescence and young adulthood that individuals begin to make greater cognitive sense of the world around them and try to determine their place in society. In addition, it is the period when young adults' political socialization becomes more manifest. They begin to form political attitudes and begin to develop important patterns of civic participation (e.g., Jennings and Niemi 1981).

Not only do young adults learn these political attitudes, values, and civic skills from parents, school, and the media, but the historical and social environment can be a particularly strong influence on their development (e.g., Flanagan and Sherrod 1998; Horowitz 2001). Periods of history that have been seen as having had profound effects on young adults include such periods as the 1960s in the United States, and the break-up of the Soviet Union and the end of communism in the 1990s—all of which were distinguished by intense conflict, changes, and uncertainty about the future. Research has found that the historical context in which young people live affects their development (Elder 1974; Macek et al. 1998). In college and on their way into the "real world," young adults today may be on their way to becoming "the 9/11 generation" as they are forever-marked by the nation's continuing war on terrorism and the concurring effects it is having upon their socio-political environment.

This chapter examines the reactions and responses of young adults to on-going U.S. war on terrorism on the occasion of the one-year anniversary of 9/11. Are young adults expressing their patriotism through behaviors such as displaying a flag? Are they emotionally affected by the heavy media coverage that occurred on the anniversary of 9/11 and the on-going coverage of the war on terrorism? In what ways does patriotism affect these behavioral and affective measures?

Literature Review

Political Socialization. Political socialization is the process by which a person acquires the necessary skills to function in the political world. In a normative model each of us should be participating fully in the democratic process on a continual basis—following politics in the news, thinking about issues, having discussions with family and friends, forming opinions on these political issues, and then acting on the issues, such as by voting. Political socialization is learning the skills, knowledge, and motivations necessary to do these types of activities. Researchers have primarily focused on how children, teenagers, and young adults learn about politics. Traditionally the main agents of political socialization have been parents, school, and the media. If children and adolescents can learn about and participate in democratic processes and civic life, then hopefully they will continue this civic participation throughout their lifetime (e.g., McDevitt and Chaffee 2002).

Most previous research has looked at political socialization in terms of outcome variables such as political knowledge, political efficacy, and voting behavior (e.g., Niemi and Chapman 1998). However, more recently there has been a shift away from seeing young adults as empty vessels ready and willing to have their political values and attitudes imprinted upon them by the various socialization agents (Niemi 1999). Political socialization is now conceptualized as a much more active and complex process as adolescents and young adults interact directly and indirectly with parents, teachers, the media, and peers (McLeod 2000). In addition, political socialization research is becoming more focused on an understanding of young adults' political processes and attitudes within the broader socio-political domain (Flanagan and Sherrod 1998), examining areas of economic and socio-political change such as post-communist Poland (Horowitz

2001). Research in these areas has found that historical context plays an important role in political socialization (Elder 1974; Horowitz 1998; Macek et al. 1998)

The terrorist attacks of 9/11 and its aftermath of wars on domestic terrorism, in Afghanistan, and in Iraq necessitate a change in our understanding of the political socialization of young adults in the U.S. For the current generation of young adults who spent their childhood growing up in a nation of peace and prosperity, the events of 9/11 have been jarring. While it is still to soon to know whether this will become a defining moment for this generation, students on college campuses across the country were seen to be particularly affected by the events of 9/11 and in the immediate weeks following the tragedy participated in large numbers in the many vigils, memorials, and college "teach-ins" (Kantrowitz and Naughton 2001).

Patriotism. While displays of patriotism—such as displaying a flag—have been seen to have increased since the events of 9/11, the definition of a patriot is still controversial and has changed considerably throughout history from being a revolutionary political activist to a flag-waving non-activist without any ideological considerations. Researchers have examined patriotism primarily from an affective perspective using phrases like "I'm proud to be an American" and "I love my country" that communicate a total love of one's country *independent* of what the country stands for (e.g., Baker and O'Neal 2001; Hurwitz and Pefley 1990; Kosterman and Fechbach 1989; Pan and Kosicki 1994). Others have examined patriotism and its connections with more dangerous forms of nationalism (e.g., Canovan 2000; Nussbaum 1996) that has in recent years burst into ethnic cleansing in Kosovo, Rwanda, and elsewhere.

Rather than examining the affective or nationalistic components of patriotism, Cunningham (1981) and Dietz (1986, 1989) instead focused on the historical concept of a patriot starting in the in the revolutionary era. Sullivan, Fried, and Dietz (1992) argue that "we seem to have traveled a long distance not only from the moment in our historical past when patriotism was forged in revolutionary rhetoric but also from a time when patriotism was linked to a systematically articulated political ideology of 'free world' and anti-communism" (231). A recent Harwood Institute/Gallup survey showed that only 40 percent of Americans thought that a person has to be involved in the political process and the community in order to earn the label patriotic (Harwood 2003). Another poll conducted several months after the 9/11 attacks showed that 37 percent of the nation's youth would try to *avoid* serving in the military service if drafted (*Chattanooga Times Free Press* 2002). A significant number of Americans therefore appear to think that patriotism has little to do with ideas or anything beyond strictly symbolic actions.

What other effects are associated with this type of emotional and symbolic patriotism? Sullivan et al. (1992) analyzed the effects of George H. Bush's patriotic rhetoric in the 1998 presidential campaign and found that people who identify patriotism primarily as something *emotional* and *symbolic* were more susceptible to his rhetoric, while people who identified patriotism in more active terms were more suspicious of the senior Bush's rhetoric.

It was this emotional side of patriotism that seemed to be so strongly present in the immediate aftermath of the 9/11 terrorist attacks. There were few signs of any of the deeper meanings embedded in more complex conceptualizations of patriotism such as "iconoclastic" patriotism that, for example, rejects emotional appeals and identifies working for economic and social justice as patriotic, or "capitalistic" patriotism that admires economic heroes such as Henry Ford and Bill Gates as highly as political figures like Abraham Lincoln in making the U.S. a great nation (Sullivan et al. 1992). Perhaps the only content-based patriotism in the immediate aftermath of 9/11, in contrast to the pure emotional and symbolic patriotism, was seen in expressions of a type of nationalistic-symbolic patriotism where religion and a God-given destiny is seen to play a major role in the success and prosperity of the U.S. (Maraghy 2002; Paulson 2002).

Patriotism also plays an important role in the political socialization of young adults. Research has found that active-learning programs combining mass media, classroom education, and mock-voting can succeed in stimulating interest in election campaigns and teach adolescents the value of participating in the political world (McLeod, Eveland, and Horowitz 1995). This type of "democratic citizenship" (Gutmann 1996) is one that is clearly valued in society as a way to teach young adults to be involved in the political world around them. Throughout the political socialization literature there seems to be an implied focus on teaching patriotism to young adults and the positive long-term effects that such political socialization can have (e.g., Jennings and Niemi 1981). School-based activities to encourage such overt patriotic-based political socialization include the recitation of the Pledge of Allegiance, the raising and displaying of the U.S. and state flag, and the singing of the national anthem before school sporting events. Within the framework of the events of 9/11 and the continuing war on terrorism all of these types of patriotic activities continue to occur in a much more emotional context.

Emotions in the Context of 9/11. There are several different theories to why people utilize emotions when making judgments about what is going on in their lives. The *affect infusion model* (Forgas 1994, 1995) uses *heuristic processes* and suggests that people will use heuristic shortcuts when their mood is used to inform their judgment on an issue that does not involve directional goals for the individual. Emotions from that perspective are used in a less labor-intensive process when an issue does not have direct salience to them. While the amount of importance given to the issues of 9/11 and the war on terrorism may vary among young adults, there are probably other issues that more directly affect a college student's life, such as grades, graduation, and future job prospects.

Taylor (1991), Isen (1987), and Schwarz (1990) all discuss the cognitive strategies that we use to apply judgment. They argue that we are more likely to use heuristic shortcuts involving affect-based judgments when we are in a good mood. Young adults who are generally happy with their lives, with their grades, with family, friends, living arrangements, as well as with America, the political leadership, etc., would have less reasons for utilizing a careful evaluation of an issue that does not directly affect the way that they feel about their overall life situation.

Weiner's (1985) attribution theory argues that people are searching for causal reasons to events that stop them from realizing important personal aims. External, controllable causes are thus associated with anger; we get angry about something that we do not think we have any responsibility for but still find controllable. In other words, young adults may express anger over the events of 9/11 and the war on terrorism because they think that this did not have to happen and that the U.S. is clearly lacking in regard to causality.

The emotional state most interesting to us in this period one year after the events of 9/11 is *suspicion*. Soon after the terrorist attacks of 9/11 many people became suspicious of and acted violently against Arab-Americans and other foreigners in the U.S (*Seattle Post-Intelligencer* 2001). In addition, many people, particularly on college campuses,[1] expressed concerns about the Patriot Act which was passed by Congress six weeks after 9/11 to give the Justice Department greater authority and power to investigate suspicious behavior and potential acts of terrorism (Ensor and O'Brien 2002). In this context it is not surprising to find that research has generally examined suspicious behavior from the perspective of a direct and known threat. For example, Hilton, Fein, and Miller (1993) characterize suspicion "as a psychological state in which perceivers actively weigh the possibility that a target's behavior is genuine against the possibility that it is contrived" (503).

In a different context, Lodge and McGraw (1989) studied the suspicion that U.S. voters felt towards politicians. They argue that the political context in the U.S. involves a great deal of suspicion and that suspicion "is accompanied by cognitive appraisal and scrutiny" (378). Lodge and McGraw further find that negative events (such as 9/11 would be) are more likely to mobilize a more active cognitive analysis in which suspicion becomes a natural component of the scrutiny. However positive events are more likely to be accepted at face value without any suspicion since they do not pose a direct threat to the individual.

What makes the events of 9/11 and its aftermath unique from the context of suspicion is the lack of a direct message or rhetoric to be suspicious about. Other than the few cryptic messages of Osama Bin Laden, there is no apparent rhetoric to scrutinize; there is no direct face of any politician that can be perceived as suspicious in words or actions; and there is no judgment to make about any vote to cast. Prior to 9/11 (and even afterwards) very few people knew about Osama Bin Laden's political intentions regarding American influence in the Middle East in general and in Saudi Arabia in particular. For example, a survey conducted six weeks after the September 11 attacks showed that 91.9 percent of young Americans (age fifteen to twenty-two) wanted to learn *more* about American foreign policies (Rock the Vote 2002). While there was some reporting on the history of U.S. foreign policy in the Middle East in the immediate aftermath of the 9/11 attacks, the majority of the news coverage focused on the disastrous events rather on any national and international politics that may have motivated the events. It is therefore unclear what people could be suspicious about. What could any suspicion be targeted against?

Murray and Meyers (1999) argues that some people have a greater "need" to have enemies to be suspicious about. They analyzed the 1988-1992 Leadership Opinion Project panel data and found that political leaders that were highly suspicious about the Soviet Union were more likely to develop a suspicion about another international nation or institution *after* the collapse of the Soviet Union. This indicates that among some people a general international suspicion exists that does not have to be based on any specific message or political ideas.

Research Question and Methodology

The unique economic and socio-historical conditions of the terrorist attacks of 9/11 and the on-going war on terrorism appear to have affected the political socialization of young adults. These conditions are very different form which prior political socialization research has taken place. The specific goal of this study is to try and identify and explain how young adults are being affected by these conditions in two areas: affect and behavior.

> *RQ1*: One year later, how are young adults affected emotionally by the events of 9/11 and the on-going U.S. war on terrorism?
>
> *RQ2*: How do young adults who display the flag during the 9/11 anniversary differ from young adults who do not display the flag?

Sample

Data for the present study are based on surveys conducted among college students in an introductory communication class at the University of Oklahoma. Surveys were administered on September 12 and 13, 2002, immediately following the one-year anniversary of 9/11. Surveys were purposefully administered on these dates to coincide with the intense media coverage of the one-year anniversary on September 11, 2002 (although there certainly was heavy media coverage of the anniversary during the entire anniversary week). The final sample consists of 532 respondents, 54 percent male and 46 percent female. Although this is not a random sample, this does not limit our ability to determine the relationships between our variables of interest with confidence. Generalization of descriptive statistics to the general population, however, should be done with some caution.

Measurement of Independent Variables

This study used several groups of measures: demographic information; political interest and participation; media use; interpersonal discussion of news, 9/11, and the war on terrorism; patriotism and the patriotic behavior of displaying a flag; political knowledge; affective measures of emotions felt when reading about or watching news coverage of the 9/11 anniversary.

Measures of Young Adult Demographics. The mean *age* of the young adults in our study is 19.8 years (SD = 2.2). As the survey was conducted in the heart of the Bible Belt and given the relationship between the Christian Right and the conservative movement, *religiousness* was measured on ten-point scale (M = 6.7, SD = 2.6).

Measures of Political Interest and Participation. Political interest is a three-item index (á = .80), comprised of items measuring interest in national and international politics, and the war on terrorism. *Political ideology* is measured on a seven-point scale from "very liberal" to "very conservative" (M = 4.3, SD = 1.5). Political participation was measured by asking respondents how likely it would be that they would be voting in the upcoming November 2002 statewide election. *Likelihood to vote* is a ten-point scale from "not at all likely" to "very likely" (M = 6.0, SD =3.4).

Measures of Mass Media. Media use was measured using a total of eleven items assessing attention paid to both news and entertainment in newspapers and on television, as well as coverage of the 9/11 anniversary and the war on terrorism. *Television news* use is a four-item additive index of attention paid to national evening news, national evening cable news, local news at 6:00 P.M., and local news and 10:00 P.M. (á = .70). *Television entertainment* is a four-item additive index of attention paid to television dramas, comedies, reality shows, and crime shows (á = .78). *News of 9/11 and the war on terrorism* is a three-item additive index of attention paid to the war on terrorism and the 9/11 anniversary in newspapers, and attention paid to news coverage and documentaries of the 9/11 anniversary on television (á = .71).

Measures of Interpersonal Discussion. Two types of interpersonal discussion about news and politics were examined: discussion with friends and with parents. Frequency of discussion of national and international news and politics with friends and parents were combined in a four-item additive index measuring *discussion of news* (á

= .85). *Discussion of 9/11 and the war on terrorism* is a four-item additive index measuring frequency of discussion of these two issues with friends and parents (á = .84).

Measures of Patriotism. Two dimensions of patriotism were measured. *Love of country* is a three-item additive index of feelings of love for country, pride in the land, and being proud to be an American (á = .93). Adopted from Sullivan et al. (1992), *symbolic-emotional patriotism* is a three-item additive index of measures assessing patriotic attitudes of serving in the military; seeing "Old Glory" flying on the Fourth of July; and comparing patriotic feelings about the U.S. to a simple, emotional parent-child-like love (á = .75).

Measures of Knowledge. Six items were used to measure general political knowledge and specific knowledge of the events of 9/11. Principal component factor analysis produced two factors accounting for 49.5 percent of variance. The first factor, *political knowledge*, measures knowledge of the chief justice of the U.S. Supreme Court, the political party that controls the U.S. House of Representatives, and the leader of the Palestinians. The second factor, 9/11 *knowledge*, measures knowledge of the locations where the planes crashed on 9/11, the leader of Al Qaeda, and the mayor of New York City during the 9/11 attacks.

Measures of Anti-Terrorism Proposals. Items measured support of governmental monitoring of individual private communication and behavior as outlined in the Patriot Act in three areas (each item a ten-point scale): *monitoring emails* (M = 3.7, SD = 2.6), *monitoring telephone calls* (M = 3.5, SD = 2.6), *monitoring credit card purchases* (M = 4.8, SD = 3.0).

Measurement of Dependent Variables

Affect was measured in four areas: fear, anger, sadness, and suspicion. Each of these is a three-item additive index measuring emotions felt when reading or watching recent news coverage commemorating the anniversary of 9/11. *Fearful* is a three-item additive index of ten-point scales measured from "a little of this feeling" to "a lot of this feeling" of fearful, afraid, and sad (á = .97). *Angry* is a three-item additive index of angry, irritated, and annoyed (á = .76). *Sad* is a three-item additive index of sad, dreary, and dismal (á = .80). *Suspicious* is a three-item additive index of suspicion, distrust, and cautious (á = .84).

Displaying a flag on the anniversary of 9/11 is the behavioral dependent measure. An earlier pilot study found that less than 40 percent of young adults were displaying a flag, and there were no significant differences between those flying a flag on their car, at home, on their clothes, backpack or schoolbag, or elsewhere. As such, a single "yes-no" item was used to measure flag display: "Since the September 11th terrorist attacks many people have been flying or displaying American flags at their home, on their car, on their book bag, on their desk, on their computer, by wearing a ribbon, or in other ways. Are you currently displaying an American flag?"

Results

Hierarchical regression analyses were conducted of young adults' cognitive and affective dependent variables. The first two predictor blocks consist of young adults' demographics [gender, age, and religiousness] and political perspective (political interest, ideology, likelihood to vote). Four additional blocks are entered sequentially: mass media use (attention to television news and entertainment, and to news coverage of the 9/11 anniversary and the war on terrorism); political discussion with family and friends (both of political news and of the 9/11 anniversary and the war on terrorism); patriotism ("love of country" and the "symbolic emotional patriotism"); knowledge (general political and 9/11-specific knowledge). For the behavioral measure, independent samples t-tests were conducted to compare those young adults displaying a flag and those who are not displaying a flag.

Media Use and Interpersonal Discussion

General and 9/11 Media Use. Attention to television news use for young adults is not associated with gender, age, or religiousness (table 7.1). Rather it is the political variables that have most influence. Political interest is the strongest predictor of attention to TV news ($b = .41$, $p < .05$), followed by likelihood to vote ($b = .21$, $p < .01$). Nearly one-quarter of the variance of attention to television news is accounted for by these variables. Attention to television entertainment is predicted by nearly the exact opposite variables. Television entertainment is preferred by women ($b = -.23$, $p < .01$) and younger respondents ($b = -.19$, $p < .01$) who come from somewhat lower socio-economic backgrounds ($b = -.11$, $p < .05$). None of the

Table 7.1
Young Adults' Mass Media Use

	TV News	TV Entertainment	News of 9/11 and War on Terrorism
Demographics			
Gender (m)	.03	-.23**	-.05
Age	.01	-.19**	-.10*
Religiousness	.01	.07	.16**
Incr. R²	0.3	12.4%**	4.7%**
Political			
Political Interest	.41*	.02	.53**
Likelihood to Vote	.21**	.01	-.16**
Ideology (conserv.)	-.08	-.07	-.04
Incr. R²	24.5%**	0.5%	25.7%**
Total R²	24.7%*	12.9%*	30.3%*

N = 532   # = p < .10   * = p < .05   ** = p < .01
All standardized betas are before entry.

political variables have an impact on attention to television entertainment.

Understanding who is paying attention to news of the 9/11 anniversary and the war on terrorism is slightly more complex than understanding attention to television news and entertainment. Neither gender nor socio-economic status predicts to attention to 9/11 anniversary and terrorism news. However, somewhat younger (b = -.10, p < .05) and more religious young adults (b = .16, p < .01) are following such news closely. Political interest is the strongest predictor of attention to 9/11 anniversary and terrorism news (b = .53, p < .01), although these are also the young adults who are a less likely to vote (b = -.16, p < .01). Political ideology does not have any influence. Nearly one-third of the variance is accounted for in this model.

Interpersonal Discussion. None of the demographic variables have an influence on young adults' discussions of news and politics with their parents and friends (table 7.2). As it was with attention to television and 9/11 anniversary news, political interest is also the strongest predictor for news and political discussions (b = .63, p < .01). Young adults who have news and political discussions are also more likely to vote (b = .24, p < .01). Mass media use does not have an

Table 7.2
Differences Between Discussion of 9/11 and News

	Discussion of 9/11 and the War on Terrorism	Discussion of News and Politics
Demographics		
Gender (m)	-.10*	.05
Age -.01	.06	
Religiousness	.13**	.01
Incr. R^2	4.1%**	6.6%**
Political		
Political Interest	.38**	.63**
Likelihood to Vote	.03	.24**
Ideology (conserv.)	-.05	.05
Incr. R^2	15.3%**	29.4%**
Mass Media		
TV News	.26**	.06
TV Entertain.	.15**	-.01
News of 9-11/ War on Terrorism	.61**	-.05
Incr. R^2	22.1%**	0.7%
Patriotism		
"Love of Country"	.01	-.10*
"Symbolic-Emotional"	.16**	.03
Incr. R^2	2.6%**	1.1%*
Total R^2	44.1%**	36.8%*

N = 532   # = p < .10   * = p < .05   ** = p < .01
All standardized betas are before entry.

influence on news and political discussions. Over 36 percent of the variance of political discussion is accounted for in this model.

More female young adults than males are discussing news coverage of the 9/11 anniversary and the war on terrorism with their parents and friends (b = -.10, p < .01). These young adults are also more religious (b = .13, p < .01). Political interest is a strong influence (b = .38, p < .01), but likelihood to vote and political ideology are not. Attention to mass media is a very important predictor to these discussions. While these young adults are paying very heavy attention to news coverage of the 9/11 anniversary and the war on terrorism (b = .61, p < .01), they are also paying attention to television news (b = .26, p < .01) as well as television entertainment (b = .15, p < .01). Young adults engaged in these discussions about the 9/11 anniversary and the war on terrorism also feel greater "symbolic-emotional" patriotism (b = .16, p < .01), although "love of country" patriotism is not an influence. Nearly 45 percent of the variance of discussion of the 9/11 anniversary and the war on terrorism is accounted for in this model.

Political Knowledge

Male young adults have more general political knowledge than females (b = .22, p < .01). All of the political variables have an influence on knowledge: political interest, likelihood to vote, and political ideology (table 7.3). Young adults with political knowledge pay attention to television news (b = .18, p < .01), and have political discussions with parents and friends (b = .20, p < .01). Male young adults also have more knowledge of the events of 9/11, although none of the other demographic variables are associated with knowledge. Political interest is also a predictor of 9/11 knowledge. Young adults who have 9/11 knowledge also engage in more political discussions as well as discussions of the 9/11 anniversary and the war on terrorism.

9/11 Anniversary Affect Measures

Fearfulness. Table 7.4 shows that female young adults are much more fearful after reading or watching coverage of the 9/11 anniversary (b = -.37, p < .01). Young adults who are experiencing fearful emotions also are somewhat more politically interested (b = .11, p < .05), but surprisingly somewhat less likely to vote (b = -.13, p < .05).

Table 7.3
Differences Between Political and 9/11 Knowledge

	Political Knowledge	9-11 Knowledge
Demographics		
Gender (m)	.22**	.23
Age	.07	.01
Religiousness	-.06	-.04
Incr. R²	7.6%**	6.3%**
Political		
Political Interest	.28**	.20**
Likelihood to Vote	.14**	.06
Ideology (conserv.)	.11*	.08
Incr. R²	9.4%*	4.6%**
Mass Media		
TV News	.18**	.05
TV Entertain.	-.05	-.08
News of 9-11/ War on Terrorism	.05	.07
Incr. R²	1.7%**	0.8%
Discussion		
Discuss 9-11/ War on Terrorism	-.03	.10*
Discuss News and Politics	.20**	.18**
Incr. R²	1.4%**	2.8%**
Patriotism		
"Love of Country"	.03	.07
"Symbolic-Emotional"	.01	.03
Incr. R²	0.1%	0.3%
Total R²	20.3%**	14.9%*

N = 532   # = p < .10   * = p < .05   ** = p < .01
All standardized betas are before entry.

Table 7.4
Emotions of Young Adults on the Anniversary of 9/11

	Fear	Anger	Sadness	Suspicion
Demographics				
Gender (m)	-.37**	.05	-.25**	-.09
Age -.02	-.09	-.10*	-.02	
Religiousness	-.02	.01	.03	.13*
Incr. R²	13.5%**	0.8%	8.0%*	3.4%*
Political				
Political Interest	.11*	.01	.05	.16*
Likelihood to Vote	-.13*	.01	-.02	-.08
Ideology (conserv.)	-.01	.01	-.03	-.03
Incr. R²	2.1%*	0.0%	0.4%	2.5%*
Mass Media				
TV News	.05	.03	.06	.18**
TV Entertain.	.19**	.15*	.15**	.15*
News of 9-11/ War on Terrorism	.16*	.12*	.24**	.21**
Incr. R²	5.0%*	3.1%*	5.9%**	5.2%*
Discussion				
Discuss 9-11/ War on Terror	.43**	.18*	.20**	.28**
Discuss News and Politics	-.20*	-.05	-.09	.09
Incr. R²	8.0%**	1.5%*	6.3%*	5.4%*
Patriotism				
"Love ofCountry"	.10#	.20**	.13*	.07
"Symbolic-Emotional"	.03	.13*	.15**	.15**
Incr. R²	0.8%#	3.1%*	2.4%*	1.0%*
Knowledge				
Political Knowledge	.01	.03	-.04	-.01
9-11 Knowledge	-.07	.01	-.01	-.12*
Incr. R²	.05	0.1%	0.1%	1.3%*
Total R²	29.8%**	9.1%*	23.1%*	18.5%*

N = 532   # = p < .10   * = p < .05   ** = p < .01
All standardized betas are before entry.

Fearful young adults are paying attention to news of the 9/11 anniversary and the war on terrorism (b = .16, p < .05), although not paying attention to more general television news. Young adults who are afraid are also having many discussions about the 9/11 anniversary and the war on terrorism (b = .43, p < .01), but having few discussions about news and politics in general (b = -.20, p < .05). Nearly 30 percent of the variance of fear can be accounted for in this model.

Anger. None of the demographic or political perspective variables are associated with feelings of anger (table 7.4). Young adults who are feeling angry are watching and reading news coverage of the 9/11 anniversary and the war on terrorism (b = .12, p < .05) and having discussions about it (b = .18, p < .05). Feelings of anger are associated with both dimensions of patriotism: "love of country" (b = .20, p < .01) and "symbolic-emotionalism" (b = .13, p < .05).

Sadness. Female young adults (b = -.25, p < .01) and younger respondents (b = -.10, p < .05) are experiencing emotions of sadness from the 9/11 anniversary coverage (table 7.4). None of the political variables are associated with feelings of sadness. Sadness is associated with news of the 9/11 anniversary and the war on terrorism (b = .24, p < .01) and television entertainment (b = .15, p < .01), but not with attention to television news. Sadness is also associated with having discussions about the 9/11 anniversary and the war on terrorism with parents and friends (b = .20, p < .01), although not having more general discussions of news and politics. Similar to anger, sadness is associated with both dimensions of patriotism: "love of country" (b = .13, p < .05) and "symbolic-emotionalism" (b = .15, p < .01).

Suspicion. Young adults who are religious (b = .13, p < .05) are feeling suspicious after reading or watching news coverage of the 9/11 anniversary (table 7.4). However none of the other demographic variables are associated with suspicion. Politically interested young adults are more suspicious (b = .16, p < .01), although none of the other political variables are associated. Suspicious young adults heavily attend to mass media news (both television news and 9/11 news) and entertainment. They also have discussions with parents and friends about the 9/11 anniversary and the war on terrorism (b = .28, p < .01). Feelings of suspicion are associated with the "symbolic-emotional" dimension of patriotism (b = .15, p < .01), although not with "love of country" patriotism.

9/11 Behavioral Measure

Displaying the Flag. Independent samples t-tests were conducted to evaluate differences among young adults displaying the flag on the occasion of the one-year anniversary of 9/11 and those young adults not displaying the flag (table 7.5). Of the demographic variables, only religiousness was a significant difference: young adults displaying a flag are somewhat more religious than those not displaying a flag. Those who display a flag also pay more attention to and discuss more often news coverage of the 9/11 anniversary and the war on terrorism. They also have more discussions of news and politics with parents and friends. Young adults displaying a flag are also more patriotic than non-flag fliers in both dimensions of patriotism, "love of country" and "emotional-symbolic." Flying the flag is also associated with support for post-9/11 measures to prevent terrorism, including monitoring email, telephone calls, and credit card purchases.

Conclusions

Looking back on the terrorist events of September 11 sparked different emotions and behaviors among the young adults in our

Table 7.5
Comparing Mean Differences of Young Adults Displaying a Flag
on the Anniversary of 9/11

	Displaying a Flag on 9/11 Anniversary	Not Displaying a Flag
Religiousness	7.3	6.8
Attention to 9/11 and War on Terrorism News	19.3	17.0
Discussion of 9/11 and War on Terrorism	21.1	17.0
Discussion of News and Politics	17.3	14.5
"Love of Country" Patriotism	28.3	25.5
"Symbolic-Emotional" Patriotism	22.6	20.1
Support for Monitoring Emails	4.2	3.5
Support for Monitoring Telephone Calls	4.1	3.2
Support for Monitoring Credit Card Purchases	5.5	4.6

Note: Results of t-tests indicate significant differences ($p < .05$) between reported means.

sample at the University of Oklahoma. What have we learned about the emotions felt by young adults regarding 9/11 and patriotism? How are young adults who fly a flag different from those who do not fly a flag? What do these findings mean for political socialization of young adults?

Fearfulness. It is female young adults who are most afraid after reading or watching news coverage of the first anniversary of 9/11. This fear is associated with attention to news of the 9/11 anniversary and the war on terrorism, although these young adults do not pay any greater attention to mass media than respondents who feel other emotions. However these fearful young adults are engaging in a great many discussions with parents and friends about the 9/11 anniversary and the war on terrorism. Perhaps they are using greater interpersonal communication to seek out support and solace for their emotions. Further research is needed to investigate whether these (primarily female) young adults are experiencing merely a short-term, heightened sense of fear on the occasion of the first 9/11 anniversary, or whether this emotion is more of a long-term effect of 9/11.

Sadness. Female young adults also feel greater sadness on the first anniversary of 9/11 than males. Predictor measures for sadness are nearly identical as those for fear, including attention to mass media and interpersonal discussion. However of all the affective measures, sadness is associated with the *greatest* amount of attention to news of the 9/11 anniversary and the war on terrorism. While causality cannot be established with survey research, these results do seem to suggest that greater attention to mass media during the 9/11 anniversary can increase feeling of sadness, particularly for female young adults. (It seems less likely to us that sad individuals would seek out 9/11 mass media content.) Despite these powerful emotions, young adults feeling sadness engage in less than half as much interpersonal discussions that those who are afraid. Does this mean that they are too sad to even talk about their feelings with parents and friends? Or, do they feel that it is more urgent to deal with fear than with sadness? Does fear as an emotion trigger more actions than sadness? Or, are these differences simply a reflection of a society where expression of sadness are less accepted than expressions of fear? As with fear, further research needs to investigate whether sadness is a short-term or long-term effect.

Suspicion. It is not clear what or whom the suspicion felt by the young adults in our sample is directed to. Of all the four affective measures, only suspicion is associated with religiousness. Young adults feeling suspicious do have political interest, attend to mass media (watching television news and following news of the anniversary of 9/11 and the war on terrorism), and have discussions with parents and friends about 9/11 and the war on terrorism. However, they have no general political knowledge and little knowledge about the actual events of September 11—of the four affective measures, suspicion is the only emotion associated with *negative* 9/11 knowledge.

There seem to be two contrasting areas of concern with our results of suspicion. First, a negative evaluation of suspicion is that it is associated with high levels of absolute claims that are not backed up by actual knowledge. Perhaps actual knowledge is not necessary when beliefs are rooted in faith—greater religiousness is associated with suspicion, as is greater "emotional symbolic" patriotism. Second, a positive evaluation is that suspicion is associated with less attention to the events of 9/11 and the war on terrorism, and more concern about the processes that drives the conflict creating this kind of disaster. Further research is needed to better explain this complex emotion in relation to the events of 9/11 and the continuing war on terrorism.

Anger. There appears to be a considerable difference between young adults reacting with suspicion and young adults reacting with anger. Unlike suspicion, anger is not associated with religiousness, political interest, or attention to television news. However, anger is associated with attention to news coverage of the 9/11 anniversary and the war on terrorism, although at a lower level than discussions associated with suspicion ($â = .12$ vs. $.21$). Young adults who feel angry are having discussions about 9/11 and the war on terrorism, but fewer discussions than those who are suspicious. Anger is also associated with feelings of both dimensions of patriotism: "love of country" and "symbolic-emotional." However the patriotic feelings of "love of country" are more strongly associated with anger than with suspicion.

Unfortunately, of the four affective measures in this study, the least amount of variance was explained by our model for anger. Therefore, it is hard to understand completely where this emotion comes from. None of the demographic or political perspective variables explain anger. Although anger is associated with attention to news coverage of the 9/11 anniversary and the war on terrorism (albeit minimally), it is not associated with attention to general television news. In addition, anger is not associated with either general political knowledge or 9/11 knowledge. Consequently, if anger does not seem to be predicted by news or knowledge, then what causes this emotion?

The fact that anger is not associated with knowledge could be explained with Weiner's (1985) *attribution theory*. Attribution theory says that you will become angry if you find someone else is responsible for something controllable that is happening to you. Then anger is directed at individuals who are thought to be responsible for those actions. For those young adults feeling angry after reading or watching news coverage of the 9/11 anniversary, it is impossible to relate any causality to the U.S. if one does not receive any information from the mass media about America's role in the world. These individuals may also see 9/11 as an isolated, "controllable" event absent of any systematical social problems. In attribution theory anger is caused by events that can or should be controllable—such as isolated individuals from an "axis of evil" who should have been prevented in the first place from getting on an airplane. In contrast, a systematic process feeding hate is hard to control. This would set up the two essential conditions for anger; someone else is to be blamed for a controllable event.

Displaying a Flag. Significant differences were found between those young adults displaying a flag on the one-year anniversary of 9/11 and those who were not. Those flying a flag are somewhat more religious. They also pay greater attention to and have more discussions with parents and friends about news coverage of the 9/11 anniversary and the war on terrorism. They are also more patriotic than the non-flag flyers in both dimensions of patriotism. Displaying a flag seems to clearly be an *expression* of patriotism for these young adults.

More importantly, the association between flying a flag and the support for post-9/11 measures monitoring e-mails, telephone calls, and credit card purchases is conspicuous. These findings are complex because conservative ideology is not associated with flying a flag, none of the affective measures are associated with displaying a flag, and neither is political or 9/11 knowledge. Is flag flying, as Shingles (1981) suggests, simply a passive patriotic demonstration that involves little purposeful initiative? While we agree that flag flying is relatively "easy" to do, the motivations behind such actions may be more complex as the findings here suggest. There seems to be, at least among young adults on the anniversary of 9/11, important differences between those displaying a flag and those who are not—regardless of the difficulty or easiness of the action itself.

The differences among attitudes toward civil liberties between those flying a flag and those who do not fly a flag are particularly problematic. Why are patriotic expressions such as flying the flag associated with support for public policies that curb civil liberties? These results suggest that strong patriotism (as expressed through displaying a flag) predicts to a greater support of measures that infringe upon individual privacy. Does loving one's country mean that individual privacy is a tenuous right? The original definition of patriotism expressed by Socrates before taking his poison was someone who loved his country so much that he was willing to take an unpopular stand for the best of the country. Such a definition of patriotism requires high protection for freedom of speech—which in some ways is the opposite of what many of the contemporary "patriotic" young citizens express.

Effects of exaggerated patriotism becoming extreme nationalism have been experienced in the past decade in Kosovo, Serbia, Rwanda, and elsewhere in the world. Some have said that the events of 9/11 did not so much change the world, but rather changed the U.S., as it now must confront terrorism and violence that is, unfortunately, an almost daily event in some nations. Further research must continue to investigate the relationships among feelings of patriotism, expressions of patriotism such as flying the flag, and support for civil liberties.

Understanding Patriotism. This chapter attempts to build upon the small body of research that examines patriotism from an empirical perspective. Most of these previous studies, as well as other studies that incorporate patriotism as an independent variable, have operationalized patriotism by "love of country" or feelings toward the flag. Instead, here we are able to find several important distinctions between "love of country" and "symbolic-emotional" patriotism. Those young adults expressing greater "love of country" patriotism have fewer discussions of news and politics, and feel somewhat angrier on the first anniversary of 9/11. In contrast, those young adults expressing greater "symbolic-emotional" patriotism have more discussions with family and friends about 9/11 and the war on terrorism, and feel more suspicious. Both dimensions of patriotism are associated with feeling sadness and with displaying a flag on the anniversary of 9/11, and with greater support for measures in the

Patriot Act that allows monitoring of emails, telephone calls, and credit card purchases.

By demonstrating these differences between the two dimensions of patriotism our research supports the findings of Sullivan et al. (1992) in looking at patriotism as a multi-dimensional concept. Yet, similar to the historical perspective that patriotism is a fluid concept and changes with the times, patriotism's meanings must naturally change in the aftermath of the events of 9/11. In the months since the catastrophic events of 9/11 images of patriotism were seen in many guises within the media and elsewhere. Many of the images and rhetoric of patriotism were connected to religion, which was seen as a troubling combination by many (e.g., Stancil 2001). Other images were connected to capitalism and the U.S. market economy (e.g., Cave, Leonard, and Mieszkowski, 2001). Future research needs to more closely examine other dimensions of patriotism, particularly in relation to the historical events of the times. How does patriotism influence cognition and behavior in other political areas, such as speaking out in a public arena or voting? How will our conceptions of patriotism change over time, both individually and as a nation during the ongoing was on terrorism?

Understanding Political Socialization. Finally, this research attempts to position the concept of patriotism more explicitly within the political socialization literature. While understanding patriotism has rarely been the stated objective of political socialization research over the past half-century, it seems that the recent events of 9/11 make it a much more important concept to study. Something dramatically different occurred when in the immediate weeks following 9/11 young adults on college campuses were suddenly expressing interest in politics, wearing U.S. flag lapel pins and red, white, and blue ribbons, and attending memorial rallies and "teach-ins" in the thousands. This distinct change in the political culture of young adults may have the potential to affect their political socialization in a variety of ways yet to be seen or fully understood by researchers. As a University of Michigan graduate student explained it, the events of 9/11 changed the way young adults define themselves:

> Our generation, as long as we've had an identity, was known as the generation that had it easy. We had no crisis, no Vietnam, no Martin Luther King, no JFK. We've got it now. When we have kids and grandkids, we'll tell them we lived through the roaring 90s, when all we cared about was the No. 1 movie or how many copies an album sold. This is where it changes. (Kantrowitz and Naughton 2001)

Further research needs to more fully explore how young adults' patriotic feelings develop and change, and their relationship to political socialization variables such as political efficacy, cynicism, knowledge, and voting. Results here indicated no relationship between either dimension of patriotism and political or 9/11 knowledge. Is patriotism connected to knowledge in other contexts, such as an election campaign? What are the roles that traditional agents of socialization—parents, school, and media—play in developing young adults' patriotism? By further examining patriotism within political socialization we may be better able to understand this "9/11 generation."

References

Baker, William and John O'Neal. 2001. Patriotism or opinion leadership: The nature and origins of the "rally 'round the flag" effect. *Journal of Conflict Resolution* 45: 661-687.

Canovan, Margaret. 2000. Patriotism is not enough. *British Journal of Political Science* 30: 413-432.

Cave, Damien, Andrew Leonard, and Katherine Mieszkowski. September 12, 2001. Is shopping the new patriotism? *Salon.com.* http://dir.salon.com/tech/feature/2001/09/12/consumers/index.html

Chattanooga Times Free Press. 2002. Nation's patriotism still high after Sept. 11 peak. September 11, Lexis-Nexis.

Cunningham, Harry. The language of patriotism 1750-1914. *History Workshop* 12: 8-33.

Dietz, Michael. 1986. Populism, patriotism, and need for roots. In *The New Populism*, edited by H. C. Boyte and F. Riessman, 148-163. Philadelphia, PA: Temple University Press

Dietz, Michael. 1989. Patriotism: A brief history of the term. In *Political Innovation and Conceptual Change*, edited by T. Ball, J. Farr, and R.L. Hanson, 177-193. Cambridge, MA: Cambridge University Press.

Elder, Jr., Glenn. 1974. *Children of the Great Depression: Social Change in Life Experience.* Chicago: University of Chicago Press.

Ensor, David and Miles O'Brien. 2002. *Patriot act worries civil liberties advocates. CNN Saturday Morning News* 07:00, February 2, Lexis-Nexis.

Flanagan, Constance and Leonard R. Sherrod. Youth political development: An introduction. *Journal of Social Issues* 54: 447-456.

Forgas, Joseph. 1994. Sad and Guilty? Affective influences on the explanation of conflict in close relationships. *Journal of Personality and Social Psychology* 66: 56-68.

Forgas, Joseph. 1995. Mood judgment: The affect infusion model (AIM). *Psychological Bulletin* 117: 39-66.

Gutmann, Amy. 1996. Democratic citizenship. In *For Love of Country: Debating the Limits of Patriotism*, edited by M.C. Nussbaum and J. Cohen, 66-71. Boston: Beacon Press.

Harwood, Ronald. 2003. A new kind of patriotism. *Christian Science Monitor,* July 3, Lexis-Nexis.

Hilton, James, Steven Fein, and Dale Miller. 1993. Suspicion and dispositional inference. *Personality & Social Psychology Bulletin* 19: 501-512.

Horowitz, Edward. 1998. *Breaking with the past and facing the future: Challenges of political socialization research in Eastern Europe.* Paper presented to the annual conference of the American Association for Public Opinion Research, St. Louis, MO.

Horowitz, Edward. 2001. *Political socialization in post-communist Poland: Knowledge and attitudes of young adults.* Paper presented to the annual conference of the Association for Education in Journalism and Mass Communication, Washington, DC.

Hurwitz, Jon and Mark Peffley. 1990. Public images of the Soviet Union: The impact on foreign policy attitudes. *Journal of Politics* 52: 3-28.

Isen, Alice. 1987. Positive affect, cognitive processes, and social behavior. In *Advances in Experimental Social Psychology 20,* edited by L. Berkowitz, 203-253. New York: Academic Press.

Jennings, Kent and Richard Niemi. 1981. *Generations and Politics.* Princeton, NJ: Princeton University Press.

Kantrowitz, Ben and Kenneth Naughton. 2001. Generation 9-11. *Newsweek,* November 12, Lexis-Nexis.

Kosterman, Rick. 1989. Towards a measure of patriotic and nationalistic attitudes. *Political Psychology 10:* 257-274.

Lodge, Mark and Ken McGraw. 1989. An Impression-Driven Model of Candidate Evaluation. *American Political Science Review* 83: 399-419.

Macek, Petr and Constance Flanagan. 1998. Postcommunist societies in times of transition: Perceptions of change among adolescents in Central and Eastern Europe. *Journal of Social Issues* 54: 547-561.

Maraghy, Mary. 2002. 9/11, God, and country: Church-state line blurred after 9/11. *Florida Times-Union,* September 10, Lexis-Nexis.

McDevitt, Michael and Steven Chaffee. 2002. The family in a sequence of political activation: Why civic interventions can succeed. *Journalism Communication Monographs,* 4 (1): 7-42.

McLeod, Jack. 2000. Media and civic socialization of youth. *Journal of Adolescent Health* 27S: 45-51.

Mcleod, Jack, William Eveland, Jr., and Edward Horowitz. 1995. Learning to live in a democracy: The interdependence of family, schools, and media. Paper presented to the annual conference of the Association for Education in Journalism and Mass Communication annual convention, Washington, DC.

Morrison, George. 2003. Put down 'War and Peace', Uncle Sam's watching you. *University Wire,* February 27, Lexis-Nexis.

Murray, Shoon and Jason Meyers. 1999. Do people need foreign enemies? American Leaders' beliefs after the Soviet demise. *Journal of Conflict Resolution* 43: 555-569.

Niemi, Richard. 1999. Editor's introduction. *Political Psychology* 20: 471-476.

Niemi, Richard, and Chris Chapman. 1998. *The civic development of 9th through 12th grade students in the United States: 1996.* National Center for Education Statistics, NCES 1999-131. Washington, DC: U.S. Department of Education. http://nces.ed.gov/pubs99/1999131.pdf

Nussbaum, Martha. 1996. Patriotism and cosmopolitanism. In *For Love of Country: Debating the Limits of Patriotism,* edited by M.C. Nussbaum and J. Cohen, 5-24. Boston: Beacon Press.

Pan, Zhonngdang and Gerald Kosicki. 1994. Voters' reasoning processes and media influences during the Persian Gulf War. *Political Behavior* 16: 117-156.

Paulson, Michael. 2002. Spiritual life: A year after 9/11, clergy reflect on the blending of faith, nation. *Boston Globe*, September 14, Lexis-Nexis.

Reynolds, Maura. 2003. Bush plans quiet 9/11 observance. *L.A. Times*, September 5, http://www.latimes.com/news/nationworld/nation/la-naanniversary5sep05,1,5479023.story

Rock the Vote. 2002. Six months later: Young America wants more information on foreign policy post-September 11th. *PR Newswire*, March 15, Lexis-Nexis.

Seattle Post-Intelligencer. 2001. Bush appeals for calm amid incidents of hate: Threats and attacks have targeted mosques, Arab-Americans. September 14, Lexis-Nexis.

Schwarz, Nick. 1990. Feelings as information: Informational and motivational functions of affective states. In *Handbook of Motivation and Cognition: Foundations of Social Behavior 2*, edited by E.T. Higgins and R. Sorrentino, 527-561. New York: Guilford Press.

Stancil, Walter. 2001. When religion and patriotism converge. *Kansas City Star,* September 25, Lexis-Nexis.

Sullivan, John, Amy Fried and Mary Dietz. 1992. Patriotism, politics, and the presidential election of 1988. *American Journal of Political Science* 36: 200-234.

Taylor, Shelley. 1991. Asymmetrical effects of positive and negative events: The mobilization-minimization hypothesis. *Psychological Bulletin* 110: 67-85.

Weiner, Ben. 1985. An attributional theory of achievement motivation and emotion. *Psychological Review* 92: 548-573.

8

Rudy and Gary get Makeovers: Public Attention and Political Reputation Post 9/11

John Llewellyn

On September 10, 2001 Rudolph Giuliani, mayor of New York City, and Congressman Gary Condit, Democrat of California, were sharing a political fate. Both men were under intense and unflattering scrutiny and their political longevity seemed to be in question.

The news media were taking Giuliani to task for at least three shortcomings: a public falling out with his wife and his subsequent "eviction" from Gracie Mansion, his marital infidelity, and a crackdown on minorities through policies of the New York City Police Department. With a harsher tone and more intense scrutiny, the media were hounding Condit with questions about his relationship with a missing government intern, Chandra Levy, and about his candor in answering authorities' questions.

The media treated the Giuliani situation like a bad soap opera. He was cast as inept and unstable—the leader of a city who could not keep his own personal life in order and off the front pages. While no one frontally accused Condit of a role in Levy's disappearance, the media pressed him from all sides to help solve the disappearance as the only person publicly linked to the story.

Although neither man could know it on September 10, 2001, their political fortunes were about to turn; the reason would be too horrific to imagine in advance. Regardless, the fact remains that both men benefited from the shift in public attitudes and attention precipitated by the attacks of September 11, 2001. The terrorist attacks would redefine both men through the tone and volume of media attention they would receive.

The theoretical grounding for this analysis is McCombs and Shaw's theory of agenda setting (1972) as further refined by Entman (1993) through his examination of media framing. Agenda setting theory initially proclaimed that the media do not tell the public what to think, only what topics to think about. Subsequent research has refined and enlarged agenda setting's claims of minimal influence. New studies show that media presentations shape public attitudes. This process of influence is the phenomenon of framing.

The central notion of framing is that when the media direct public attention to a certain topic, some features of that topic are highlighted and others are left in the shadows. The public's reactions to the highlighted features will determine its response to the topic itself. So media accounts do more than select topics for public attention; by the way they discuss those topics the media are helping to shape public response to the person or issue. A similar phenomenon has been documented in the attempts of public relations practitioners and political handlers to influence media coverage of issues, candidates and campaigns (Jackall and Hirota 2000, 112). In those settings the practice is known as "spin." This chapter does not suggest that Giuliani or Condit sought to frame or spin events after 9/11. Rather, chapter documents the stark changes in media coverage of both men—their reframing—after that event.

Representative Gary Condit was a six-term Democratic Congressman from the Eighteenth Congressional District of California. He had served in relative anonymity until May of 2001. On May 15, 2001 an Associated Press story ran with the headline "Detectives interview Congressman Seeking Help in Woman's Disappearance," but police called the interviews "routine." The public would learn that the missing person was Chandra Levy. A May 11 story in the *Modesto Bee* had noted that a $25,000 reward was offered for Levy's safe return—$15,000 from the Levy family and $10,000 from Congressman Condit. As May unfolded, the links between Levy and Condit grew clearer. Her diary was examined and friends were interviewed about her social life. She had told friends of a relationship with someone with connections to Congress though Levy was very circumspect.

The media, however, was hardly circumspect: from June 1, 2001 through September 11, 2001—the full fury of the feeding frenzy—Condit's name was mentioned in 3,014 newspaper articles examined in a Lexis-Nexis search. After the 9/11 events, Condit's mentions dropped from over 200 per week to fifty, with most coming in California papers.

In the week following the attacks, September 12 through 19, Condit's name was mentioned in sixty-eight articles in a Lexis-Nexis search, twenty-six of the articles were in California newspapers. In the period from September 20 through the end of 2001 he was mentioned in 677 news stories on Lexis-Nexis (forty-eight per week), 287 of these stories were in California. Many of these mentions came in year-in-review stories where Condit was used as a pre-9/11 marker of how petty our concerns had been: "At last the '90s are history and Gary Condit is a footnote" (Levins) and "Remember when Congressman Gary Condit's role in Chandra Levy's disappearance was the story of the year?" (Jurkowitz). Even his hometown paper echoed the sentiment: "The Way We Were Before 9/11: Condit, Fluoride, Baseball on Minds" (Sbranti).

Condit's visibility continued to recede. From January 1, 2002 through March 5, 2002, the date of primary elections in California, Condit's name appeared in 355 articles nationally (thirty-two per week), 207 of which were in California papers, according to Lexis-Nexis. On March 5, 2002 Condit lost the primary race in his redrawn district to Dennis Cardoza, a former staffer, by a margin of 55.3 percent to 37.5 percent, effectively rendering him a lame duck. Despite his political demise, Condit was mentioned in 847 news articles (twenty-two per week)—409 in California—from the primary through the general election (November 5, 2002), according to Lexis-Nexis.

Condit was never charged in the disappearance of Levy. He gave four statements to authorities and, in the final analysis, never publicly admitted to an affair with Levy though leaks did suggest that he told police of the affair in the third interview. Condit declined to submit to a polygraph examination by authorities. Clearly, the events of 9/11 wiped Condit from the national agenda. Regardless, his behavior remained a hot topic within his California district where eleven months of drum beating and speculation, including a sophisticated media relations strategy employed by Levy's parents, took their toll.

Two national news interviews, with Connie Chung and Larry King respectively, cemented public opinion about Condit's character. Condit stood convicted as a cad in the court of public opinion. He is hardly the only cad in Washington. The disappearance and extended investigation that followed it broadcast his private morality throughout the nation, including the Eighteenth District of California. Levy was the object of intense concern and sympathy. The fact that she could not tell her side of the story authorized moralists and commentators to think the worst. In the face of this level of visibility, Condit's primary defeat was virtually a foregone conclusion.

In an earlier case, Oregon Senator Bob Packwood was able to obfuscate and deny charges that he was an abuser of women until he had won re-election in 1992. The facts caught up with him and he resigned in 1995. The timing of events made Condit's denials of serious wrongdoing hollow and ineffectual. The *Modesto Bee* wrote Condit's political epitaph following his primary defeat:

> The end came Tuesday. Voters in the 18th Congressional District buried him with a solid vote of no confidence for irrevocably violating the public trust. His behavior after the April disappearance of Chandra Levy of Modesto, with whom he was having an affair, put his own interests ahead of the effort to help find her. She remains missing. His self-absorption was a lapse not only of judgment, but of human decency. ("Condit to blame")

In short, the media's reframing of issues post 9/11 came too late to save Condit's career. By the time Levy's body was found in a Washington area park on May 22, 2002, Condit's career was long over. The conditions at the murder site suggest that Levy may have been the victim of an attack while jogging.

In contrast, the events spawned by 9/11 allowed the transformation of Rudolph Giuliani's image in the media. He went from being presented as a bumbling henpecked mayor with a bad combover to an icon of dignity and resolve for his City and the nation.

Rudolph Giuliani was seen by many as the reincarnation of Thomas Dewey, a politician who sought to ride to national prominence on a reputation as a tough law enforcer. Both Dewey and Giuliani made their initial reputations as prosecutors of underworld figures. Dewey went on to be elected governor of New York in 1942, 1946, and 1950. As the Republican candidate for president, he was defeated by Franklin Roosevelt in 1944 and by Harry Truman, in what was seen as an upset, in 1948.

Giuliani parlayed his crime fighting reputation into election as New York City mayor in 1994. He was reelected in 1998 and was ineligible under term limits provisions to serve a third term. There was a short-lived movement for a third term in the wake of 9/11.

Once in office, however, he discovered that running the city was a far cry from chasing the Mob. He won praise for significant crime reduction though there are some who credit his predecessor, David Dinkins, for initiating important programs. Under his watch, critics said that schools and social services did not get adequate attention.

He came under intense criticism for allegations that his police department was heavy handed in its law enforcement practices. Three cases were emblematic of these criticisms: the 1997 abuse of Haitian immigrant Abner Louima at the hands of police; the 1999 shooting of Amadou Diallo, an unarmed African immigrant, by plainclothes officers as he reached for his wallet; and the killing in 2000 of an unarmed African-American off-duty security guard, Patrick Dorismond, by an undercover officer trying to locate drug dealers. A 1999 *New York Times* editorial sums up Giuliani's mixed record:

> The simple fact is that New York closed out 1998 with fewer homicides than any year since 1964. New York ended the year with fewer homicides than Chicago, which has four and a half million fewer people. These kinds of statistics are what enable the Mayor to get away with policies and behavior that offend decency, undermine democracy and ought to be widely denounced and curtailed. (Herbert)

On a lighter note—but still in the realm of significant damage to his image—comes media coverage of the dissolution of his marriage, the publicly acrimonious separation, and his acknowledged relationship with a local media figure. The dispute even reached the level of Giuliani's being evicted from Gracie Mansion, the mayor's official residence. As the *New York Times* reported in a year-end retrospective: "Last summer, the mayor's marital problems had become so public and so tawdry that some supporters worried about his future in politics. . . . Then came Mr. Giuliani's metamorphosis into the city's heroic leader. His personal life remained a mess, but nobody seemed to care" (Murphy).

Unlike Condit, Giuliani was not associated with unlawful behavior. However, he faced an image problem nearly as severe and as politically damaging—becoming a running joke for news media, editorialists and talk show hosts. On September 10, 2001, Giuliani was headed into the abyss of political irrelevance that was about to claim Condit.

From June 11th, 2001, through September 10 of that year, Giuliani's name had been mentioned in 270 newspaper articles, 268 of them in New York papers, according to Lexis-Nexis. He challenged for the Senate seat eventually won by Hillary Clinton, withdrawing from the race with the disclosure that he was being treated for prostate cancer. So, on September 11, 2001, with his second term on the wane and electoral sentiments about him definitely mixed, Rudy Giuliani was a politician with his career in the balance.

Then came a moment of horror and a period of crisis. These events would redefine his reputation as mayor and frame his public image for years to come. On September 11, while the president and vice-president were spirited away to undisclosed locations, Giuliani was on-scene and even, the public would later learn, in harm's way. For the public and the media Giuliani became a tangible symbol of stability and determination. Although he was not the president for those days, he was the nation's most visible leader.

In the week of September 12 through 19 Giuliani's name was mentioned in sixty-three news articles, fifty-nine of which were in the northeast, according to Lexis. The essence of these stories is reflected in this *New York Times* story from September 14:

> From the moments after the first plane rammed into the World Trade Center on Tuesday morning, Mayor Rudolph W. Giuliani has taken an orderly control of how the city would respond, even when trapped in a building near the fiery towers as the first collapsed to the ground, engulfing him in smoke and debris. . . . The horrific situation illuminated how the mayor, who is known to explode over seemingly small slights, maintains an almost unparalleled sense of calm and control in the most stressful of times, literally embracing his political enemies in the process. (Steinhauer)

From September 20 through the end of the year, Giuliani was mentioned in 574 newspaper articles, 550 from the northeast. For calendar 2002, through November 15 he was mentioned 482 times with all but 10 articles in northeastern papers. As of mid-November 2002 Giuliani had the number one best seller on the *New York Times* non-fiction list with *Leadership* (with Ken Kurson). The marketing blurb says the book "discusses what it takes to be a leader and addresses subjects like the crime rate and 9/11." In May 2002 Giuliani was named "consultant of the year" in a profession he had entered five months before; *Consulting* magazine praised "the unique origins of Giuliani's leadership" (Barron).

The transformative power of media framing in Giuliani's handling of 9/11 is well captured in this September 20 *New York Times* article:

> While is was unlikely just two weeks ago that many people outside the five boroughs were terribly interested in glimpsing the soul of Rudolph W. Giuliani, it is now undeniable that the mayor has become an international celebrity. . . . All this attention to the man whose press aides were needling reporters a month ago to write a few lines on his latest health care initiative during a news conference in a sporting goods store. (Steinhauer)

A September 15 letter to the editor exemplifies Giuliani's stature with the public. The author, a lifelong Democrat, noted that he would write in the mayor's name whenever the primary was held: "No matter who is elected, after this week, Rudy will be my mayor for life" ("America Mourns").

Conclusion

After 9/11 the spotlight of scrutiny ceased to shine on Gary Condit; that change did not come in time to save his career in politics. Observers have noted that he might have been able to save himself with some forthright and contrite admissions—admissions he was unwilling or unable to make. Conversely, prior to 9/11 Rudy Giuliani seemed headed for decidedly mixed reviews as a two-term mayor of New York City and the awkward status of politician with no political prospects. However, Giuliani met and exceeded public expectations in the crucible of the terrorist attacks and their aftermath.

The media attention that either waxed or waned after 9/11, reframed and thus redefined these two politicians. It is interesting to consider one other politician who was reframed after September 11th. President, George W. Bush navigated a different political landscape in 2002 through 2004 as a result of the 9/11 attacks. Troubles with corporate accounting, the economy, education and health care took a backseat to national security. The cases of Condit, Giuliani, and even Bush reinforce the persuasive power of the media's presentation of circumstances. These presentations frame and define issues and in doing so shape public perception of political figures.

References

America mourns, and looks at the path ahead; the Giuliani balm. *New York Times* 15 Sept. 2001, SA: P22.

Barron, James. Boldface names. *New York Times* 29 May 2002, SB: P2.

Condit to blame for his political self-destruction. *Modesto Bee* 6 Mar. 2002, SB: P4.

Detectives interview congressman seeking help in woman's disappearance. Associated Press 15 May 2001, wire story.

Entman, Robert. Framing: Toward clarification of a fractured paradigm. *Journal of Communication,* Vol. 43, No. 3, (1993), 51-58.

Herbert, Bob. In America: The Giuliani m.o. *New York Times* 3 Jan 1999, S4: P9.

Jackall, Robert, and Janice M. Hirota. *Image Makers: Advertising, Public Relations and the Ethos of Advocacy.* Chicago: University of Chicago Press, 2000.

Jurkowitz, Mark. The Best of 2001. *Boston Globe* 30 Dec. 2001, SN: P4.

Levins, Harry. 2001 starts and ends with September 11. *St. Louis Post-Dispatch* 30 Dec. 2001, SB: P1.

McCombs, Maxwell, and Donald Shaw. The agenda-setting function of the mass media. *Public Opinion Quarterly,* Vol. 36, (1972), 176-187.

Murphy, Dean E. Imagine: From hussy to helpmeet. *New York Times* 23 Dec. 2001, S4: P4.

Sbranti, J. N. The way we were before 9/11: Condit, fluoride, baseball on minds. *Modesto Bee* 30 Dec. 2001, SA: P1.

Search is on for woman from valley: Last contact was ten days ago in D.C. *Modesto Bee* 11 May 2001, SA: P1.

Steinhauer, Jennifer. A nation challenged: the mayor; in crisis, Giuliani's popularity overflows city. *New York Times* 20 Sept. 2001, SA: P1.

Steinhauer, Jennifer. After the attacks: the Mayor; Giuliani takes charge, and city sees him as essential man. *New York Times* 14 Sept. 2001, SA: P2.

9

Advertising Responses to September 11: The Crisis Response Ad as a Rhetorical Genre

Katherine N. Kinnick

Within days of the September 11 attacks on the United States, ads addressing the national crisis began appearing in newspapers across the nation, and to a lesser extent, on television. Most were sponsored by large corporations that replaced their traditional product and retail advertising with messages expressing grief and patriotic resolve. For Americans accustomed to incessant product advertising, these ads stood out. Considered "institutional" or "public relations" advertising, the ads' apparent premise was to build public goodwill, not to expand corporate coffers. A content analysis of fifty-five September 11-related ads (Kinnick 2003) found common themes in message and imagery that suggest a unique subset of institutional advertising—advertising that responds to the rare crisis of truly national proportions. But to what extent were these September 11 ads idiosyncratic—and to what extent might they have a recurring form in future national crises? Genre studies suggest a theoretical and methodological framework for answering these questions.

Genre Studies in Communication

The concept of genre is drawn from scholars in literary criticism, who observed that works within a particular "genre" possess a predictable form, style and content. Edwin Black (1965) is credited with first applying generic criticism to rhetoric. Black noted that "there is a limited number of situations in which a rhetor can find himself," and "limited number of ways in which a rhetor can and will respond rhetorically to any given situational type" (133-134). Thus, communicators in similar situations would be expected to communicate in similar ways. An influential 1976 conference on the emerging use of generic criticism in communication scholarship described a genre as possessing "recurring patterns in discourse or action including among others, the repeated use of images, metaphors, arguments, structural arrangements, configurations of language" (Bormann 1978, 165). Herbert Simons' (1978) definition referred to genre as "any distinctive and recurring pattern of rhetorical practice" (36). Simons noted that his definition refers to any symbolic act or discourse designed to influence others, and was not limited to speeches or persuasive campaigns. Foss (1996) further delineates the concept of genre as a family of discourse whose members share interdependent elements, including situational, substantive and stylistic characteristics, and a common organizing principle, or core beliefs, that unite the rhetorical characteristics of the genre.

Over the past thirty years, numerous scholars have identified a variety of genres of communication and their distinguishing characteristics. Most of these studies have focused on types of public address, including the eulogy, apologia, sermons, Jeremiads, political speeches, including inaugural addresses, and "gallows" speeches by those condemned to death. Other genre studies have examined television, film and types of organizational communication, such as business memos. While the mass communication literature includes numerous content analyses of advertising and public relations campaigns, no studies were found which examine these campaigns from the perspective of generic criticism or which attempt to establish particular types of campaigns as genres with distinct rhetorical characteristics.

The value of generic criticism is not just for description and classification purposes, but for prediction and cues to the cultural milieu of the time. Bitzer (1968) contends that prior rhetorical action will influence subsequent discourse in similar situations. With "a special vocabulary, grammar and style...a form of discourse is not only established but comes to have a power of its own—the tradition itself tends to function as a constraint upon any new response in the form" (13). Simons (1978) postulates that "rhetorical genres will emerge most clearly when rhetorical practices are most constrained by purpose and situation" (42). In these situations, "we should be able to predict much of what rhetors will say before they say it. Not always, of course, for one rhetor may respond inappropriately to the constraints of purpose of situation...but ordinarily we may expect considerable conformity" (42).

Generic theory is grounded in a humanist/cultural perspective that emphasizes the importance of situation, as well as form and content. Rhetorical acts do not take place in a vacuum, but in a historical and symbolic context. Rhetorical forms that establish genres "are stylistic and substantive responses to perceived situational demands" (Campbell and Jamieson, 1978, 19). They reveal much about what the rhetor believes to be the appropriate and acceptable rhetorical responses in a given cultural milieu. Because genres "represent conventionalized patterns for thought or structures for meaning, they can serve as an index to the social reality in which they figure" (Foss 1996, 226). Gronbeck (1976) notes that shifts in recognized genres may reveal parallel cultural shifts. According to Campbell and Jamieson (1976), "the critic who classifies a rhetorical artifact as generically akin to a class of similar artifacts has identified an undercurrent of history" (26). They note that charting various genres, the interplay among genres, and the evolution of genres is essential to creating a developmental history of rhetorical acts.

Methodological Approaches to Genre Studies

Harrell and Linkugel (1978) suggested three different foci for genre studies: generic description, generic participation and generic application. Generic description involves the analysis of rhetorical artifacts to determine their characteristics and whether they constitute a distinct genre. Generic participation involves determining whether a particular artifact may be classified as part of an established genre. Generic application involves evaluating a specific artifact based on its adherence to the distinguishing characteristics of its genre, and examining whether its adherence or departure from these characteristics impact its effectiveness (Foss 1996). Reflecting rhetorical research traditions, the body of literature of genre studies is overwhelmingly comprised of qualitative studies, although Simons (1978) contends that a social scientific approach, such as content analysis employing random samples and independent observers, is ideal.

Foss (1996) lays out systematic procedures for generic criticism and appropriate units of analysis for each of the three approaches described above. Each of these involves developing research question(s), selecting artifacts for study, analysis of the artifacts and writing a critical essay. This inquiry will employ Foss' procedures for generic description to investigate whether advertising responses to national crisis constitutes a unique genre with distinctive constructs and characteristics. It begins with a description of the situational demands that may produce unique rhetorical responses, it describes the recurring substantive and stylistic traits of the artifacts examined, and it formulates an organizing principle that unites the various rhetorical strategies employed.

Situational Elements of National Crises

In many ways, the September 11 attacks were unprecedented events in American history. The historical and cultural context of the attacks is marked by the seeming unpredictableness of the surprise attacks, an initially unknown enemy, major loss of life of innocents, destruction of symbolic icons of American identity, and the interruption of major forms of transportation and commerce. While some have suggested Pearl Harbor as the closest comparison to the September 11 attacks, an important distinction is that the latter attacks were designed to target the American psyche, rather than military targets. While the United States may not have been faced with situations of equal proportions in the past, the threat of future acts of terrorism continues to wield important influence on the cultural context to which communicators must adapt their messages.

Conditions in the immediate aftermath of the attacks presented distinct concerns for corporate advertisers, including disruption of their business operations, a slowdown in consumer sales, whether to pull existing advertising, and how to publicly recognize employees or industry colleagues lost in the attacks. Other organizations saw opportunity in the crisis to position themselves as good corporate citizens helping in the recovery effort or cheering America along. September 11 showed that America was vulnerable, and so was corporate America. How to respond to the nation's and their own vulnerability presented a new communication challenge for U.S. corporations. Generic theory suggests that the unique situational demands of a crisis of catastrophic proportions would be expected to generate particular rhetorical responses, responses rooted in the perceived constraints and opportunities presented by the event. Thus, the rhetorical themes and devices employed following the 9/11 attacks would be expected to be recur as a response to future large-scale attacks against the United States and its national symbols, and in other disasters of truly national magnitude.

Substantive and Stylistic Characteristics of September 11 Ads

Generic description requires the observation of similarities in rhetorical responses to certain situations, and creation of a list of the substantive and stylistic characteristics that appear to define the genre. The artifacts analyzed here are fifty-five September 11-related advertisements that ran in a major regional newspaper, the *Atlanta Journal-Constitution*, following September 11, 2001 through the one-year anniversary of the attacks. The ads comprise a census of all ads in this newspaper that made reference to the attacks. They include a mix of national and local ads that would likely be typical of regional newspapers nationwide. Most of these ads (51 percent) were sponsored by manufacturers or retailers of consumer goods, including department stores, grocery stores and car dealers, and more than three-quarters of the ads appeared during the period between September 14 and November 1, 2001.

Similarities in Content

Content of the ads indicates the presence of two common themes: sympathy for victims and victims' families, observed in more than half of all the ads (51 percent); and commentary on unity or patriotism, present in 45 percent of the ads. The expression of sympathy was often found in ad headlines or opening lines of copy. For instance, an American Express ad stated, "Our hearts go out to those who suffered the tragedy of Tuesday, September 11. To our friends, colleagues, their families and everyone else who has been personally affected, we extend our sympathy" (September 16, 2001, P5). Patriotic appeals included a local car dealer's message, "It's in times of tragedy that our nation stands the strongest...our country and its people are a light that will not be extinguished... Today, across the nation, we stand united, embracing the spirit that makes our country the greatest in the world" (September 16, 2004, B4). Mercedes Benz incorporated both expressions of grief and patriotism it its ad copy:

We grieve with the bereaved.
We suffer with those who are missing loved ones.
We rejoice with the rescued.
We pray for those who lost their lives.

We encourage and support the rescuers.
We united in our desire for safety and peace.
We stand as one nation, under God, indivisible, with liberty and justice for all.
    (September 16, 2001, B2).

It is important to note that these two primary themes were found in ads by all types of organizations: mom-and-pop businesses and national chains, retailers, financial service and banking companies, automakers and grocery stores, airlines and other nations. Thus these themes appear to be "grounded in the situation," not merely coincidental.

Four additional message themes were each represented in more than a quarter of the ads. These include mentions of an ad sponsor's charitable activities (29 percent of ads); calls to action to visit a store or website, either to buy something to donate to the relief effort (29 percent of ads); appeals to readers to donate blood or money (27 percent of ads); and calls for readers to resume their daily lives and shopping habits (27 percent of ads). These message themes reveal that advertisers' responses to crisis are not always altruistic, or perhaps have a mixed motive—for instance, combining messages to foster national pride with those to induce sales. For example, The National Restaurant Association equated dining out with patriotic duty: "Dining out is an important way to resume our daily lives, demonstrate our resolve and help keep America's economy strong" (November 1, 2001, C1).

While scholars have identified a number of public relations response strategies that are common in crisis communication, there is little overlap between these response themes, used by organizations facing crises often of their own making, and the themes noted above, which address a crisis of national proportions. For instance, Ledingham and Bruning (2001, 83) compile from the literature seven different crisis response strategies, including attacking the accuser, denial, excuse, justification, ingratiation, corrective action, and full apology. Of these strategies, only ingratiation—reminding stakeholders of corporate good works in order to gain public approval—is reflected in the September 11 ads. Marcus and Goodman (1991) divide crisis responses into two categories: accommodative strategies, that accept responsibility and take corrective action, or defensive strategies, which claim there is no problem or deny responsibility. Clearly, the message themes identified as most common in the September 11 ads do not fit into either of these categories. These comparisons suggest that a national crisis is situationally different from organizational crises, and will generate different rhetorical strategies.

Similarities in Style and Form

The ads examined contained recurring stylistic techniques designed to evoke American pride. These include verbal and visual imagery of American icons; patriotic language, appeals to American cultural premises, quotes from famous American credos, and use of strong, emotionally-charged language.

Three American cultural appeals identified by Reich (1987) occur in the ads: imagery of the United States as a beacon of light and hope; the "mob at the gates" premise, which suggests evil forces (in this case, terrorists) are threatening to extinguish this light; and the premise of the benevolent community, in which Americans pull together to overcome adversity. Imagery of the United States as a beacon of light was a common rhetorical device in ad copy, as well as an accompanying visual image. For instance, a car dealer proclaimed, "Our country and its people are a light that will not be extinguished" (September 16, 2001, B4). The Atlanta Gas Light Company stated, "May the flame of freedom forever glow" (September 21, 2001, A12). The suggestion that evil forces are threatening to extinguish this light is reflective of Reich's (1987) "mob at the gates" American cultural premise. A Merrill Lynch ad was one of many which suggested the cultural premise of benevolent community: "Across the world, thousands of Merrill Lynch people have pulled together to help each other get through this unthinkable experience" (September 16, 2001, A9). Home Depot urged readers, "We can get back to building our own house soon enough. Right now it's time to help our neighbors" (September 16, 2001, A4). In an ad accompanied by a drawing of a marching Statue of Liberty with rolled-up sleeves and a look of fierce determination, General Electric proclaimed, "We will roll up our sleeves. We will move forward together. We will overcome" (September 21, 2001, C10).

Nearly a third of the ads (31 percent) quoted famous America credos, songs or leaders. These expressions included "God Bless America," "united we stand," "one nation, under God, indivisible," "The land of the free and the home of the brave" "in God we trust" and "from sea to shining sea." For the most part, these phrases added little additional meaning to the ad copy, but rather seemed placed in the copy as a technique to evoke patriotic emotions. Lockheed-Martin used an extended quote on patriotism from John F. Kennedy (September 21, 2001, B6) and two ads quoted President George W. Bush.

Emotionally charged language was used in relation to expressions of sadness, expressions of outrage, and expressions of patriotic resolve. The most frequently used terms included "tragic/tragedy," "victims," "strength/strong," "terror/terrorism," "safe/safeguard," "grief" and "freedom/liberty." More extreme, though less frequent examples of emotionally-charged language included "malignant evil," "gross crimes," "deviant extremists," "sinful acts" and "barbaric."

Because these messages were published in the print ad format, message form would be expected to be constrained by the traditional conventions and techniques of print advertising copywriting and layout, including the use of headlines and ending taglines, succinct copy, and eye-catching graphic design. While crisis communication response ads are often published as "open letters" reprinted in the newspaper, or as editorial-like "advertorials," only four of the ads observed used these formats, including two from Saudi Arabia and a two-part series from Merrill Lynch. Instead, the advertisers tended to opt for ads emphasizing spare text and symbolic patriotic images. Similarities in form include the fact that 80 percent of the ads were full page, perhaps in recognition of the magnitude of the event. More than a third of the ads (36 percent) were text only, employing no graphic elements except the sponsors' logos. This suggests the advertisers' perception of the solemn nature of the situational context and national mood. When ads did employ visuals, they almost always included patriotic images, such as the American flag, found in more than a third of all ads. Other commonly used patriotic symbols included the Statue of Liberty or her torch, red, white and blue lapel ribbons and the American eagle. Only seven of the ads pictured products. The impact of the imagery of a flag billowing in the wind (often run in gray scale as background under the text), a torch being lifted high, an eagle soaring, is to reinforce the notion of American supremacy and American resolve. Combined with highly patriotic language in the ads, the overall effect of many of these ads is propaganda-like in its emotional appeal.

To summarize, the characteristics of substance, style and form that appear to define a genre of advertising responses to national crises include:

- Expressions of grief and sympathy;

- Expressions of patriotism;

- "Mixed-motive" content that combines expressions of goodwill with self-serving messages;

- Heavy use of stylistic rhetorical devises, including imagery and language evocative of American cultural values and icons;

- Limited use of visuals except for patriotic imagery;

- Preference for large display ads.

Identifying these characteristics is critical to the development of crisis-response advertising as a rhetorical genre, because genre theory suggests that these elements are not unique to the September 11 tragedy, but will recur in advertising related to future national tragedies of similar scope.

An Organizing Principle for the Genre

The rhetorical strategies observed in the September 11 response ads are united by an overwhelming appeal to patriotism. While sadness and grief may be noted in the opening lines of an ad, it is nearly always followed by powerful expressions of pride in country. The choice to emphasize a positive emotion, even during a time of great grief, is a strategy nearly universal in these ads. These optimistic patriotic appeals offer reassurance of American resolve and capacity, and present America to the world at large as a unified family, unbroken in spirit. In a time of national crisis, when Americans may be tempted to question their nation's standing in the world or its political ideologies, the patriotic tone of the ads functions to brush these doubts aside through reinforcement the nationalistic myths of God-given destiny and supremacy that are cornerstones of America's cultural identity.

Confirming the Presence of a Distinct Genre

Foss (1996, 231-232) offers several criteria which help to determine if observed rhetorical characteristics contribute to a distinct genre. First, she asks, can rules be identified with which other critics or observers can concur if examining the same artifact? The content, form and style features identified previously meet her criteria of being "namable" and discrete variables that other observers of the artifacts should also be able to identify to prove the reliability of these characteristics.

Second, Foss asks, are the similarities in substantive and stylistic strategies clearly rooted in the situations in which they were generated? The fact that the major substantive themes, sympathy and patriotism, are so different from the themes found in organizational crisis communication and conventional product-oriented advertising, suggests that their repeated use is not coincidental, but a strategy linked to the situational demands of a national tragedy. Likewise, the similar rhetorical devices employed by a diverse group of advertising sponsors suggests that these techniques were chosen to meet the creators' perceptions of what would resonate with the American public at this particular moment in time. The similarity in ad content, style and form suggests that the creators of the ads felt constrained by the situation—there were only limited options that audiences would find palatable in this crisis situation. In fact, those ads that deviated from the defining content characteristics of the genre —focusing on products or sales rather than messages of sympathy and patriotism—were rated poorly by coders in a previous study (Kinnick 2003). The similarity in ad content across a year's time span also allows for the possibility that the earliest rhetoric influenced subsequent rhetoric. While advertisers generally pride themselves for taking creative risks, in the sensitive post 9-11 environment, the tried-and-true was preferred over risk-taking.

Ideally, a genre study should compare artifacts from similar situations in different times and places, to determine if rhetorical characteristics are constant in similar situations regardless of time or place. In this case, perhaps because tragedies of truly national scope are rare phenomena in the U.S., a review of literature found no previous studies for comparison. An analysis of advertising occurring after Pearl Harbor, or after a comparable event in another country, for example, might provide an avenue for future exploration of the genre of response ads to national crises and isolation of this genre from other genres

The magnitude of September 11 is reflected in the large number of advertisers who felt it important to invest in crisis response advertising. The attacks and their repercussions challenged American advertisers to break from their traditional sales pitches and find a message appropriate for the mood of the nation. The result was an unusual fusion of advertising form with the rhetoric of condolence and patriotism that is more commonly found in public address. Identifying the characteristics of these ads reveals what business leaders believed was required to heal the American psyche during one of the nation's darkest periods. Their prescription, overwhelmingly, was to embrace and encourage traditional American patriotism. These rhetorical metaphors and images served to simplify the complex and incomprehensible, reinforced a vision of a unified nation, and established unquestioning patriotism as the "normal" response expected of Americans.

The results of this analysis suggest that response ads to national crises represent a previously unidentified genre, one that has not been delineated prior to the September 11 attacks. The ultimate test of this genre may lie in America's next national crisis. Although Americans would like to believe that a September 11 could never happen again, many terrorism experts believe another attack on U.S. soil is an unfortunate inevitability. However, the implications of a distinct genre of response advertising to national crises go well beyond 9/11 and terrorist attacks. Genre theory suggests other widespread crises—such as natural or human disasters that threaten all Americans in all parts of the nation—may also elicit similar responses of patriotism and "pitching in" from advertisers. Advertisers, like government leaders and many ordinary Americans, will adhere to cultural expectations about what is appropriate to say publicly in such a crisis. Whether a week away or decades from now, the new crisis situation would be expected to yield similar perceptions of audience needs and expectations, and advertisers would be expected to generate a recurrence of rhetorical strategies like those that marked September 11.

References

Bitzer, Lloyd. 1968. The rhetorical situation. *Philosophy and Rhetoric* 1, 1-20.

Black, Edwin. 1965. *Rhetorical Criticism: A Study in Method.* New York: Macmillan.

Bormann, Ernest G. 1978. Rhetorical criticism and significant form: A humanistic approach. In *Form and Genre Shaping Rhetorical Action,* edited by K.K. Campbell and K.H. Jamieson, 165-187. Falls Church, VA: Speech Communication Association.

Campbell, Karlyn Kohrs and Kathleen Hall Jamiesen, eds. 1978. *Form and genre shaping rhetorical action.* Falls Church, VA: Speech Communication Association.

Coombs, W. Timothy. 2001. Crisis management: Advantages of a relational perspective. In *Public relations as relationship management,* edited by J. A. Ledingham and S.D. Bruning. 73-93. Mahwah, NJ: Erlbaum.

Foss, Sonja K. 1996. *Rhetorical Criticism: Exploration and Practice* (Second Edition). Prospect Heights, IL: Waveland Press.

Gronbeck, Bruce. 1978. Celluloid rhetoric: On genres of documentary. In *Form and Genre Shaping Rhetorical Action*, edited by K.K. Campbell and K.H. Jamieson, 139-164. Falls Church, VA: Speech Communication Association.

Harrell, Jackson and Wil A. Linkugel. 1978. On rhetorical genre: An organizing perspective. *Philosophy and Rhetoric* 11, 263-264.

Kinnick, Katherine. 2003. How corporate America grieves: Responses to September 11 in public relations advertising. *Public Relations Review* 29 (December): 443-459.

Marcus, Alfred A. and Robert S. Goodman. 1991. Victims and shareholders: The dilemmas of presenting corporate policy during a crisis. *Academy of Management Journal* 34, 281-305.

Reich, Robert. 1987. *Tales of a New America*. New York: Times Books.

Simons, Herbert W. 1978. "Genre-alizing" about rhetoric: A scientific approach. In *Form and Genre Shaping Rhetorical Action*, edited by K.K. Campbell and K.H. Jamieson, 33-50. Falls Church, VA: Speech Communication Association.

10

The Tourism Industry's Reaction in Action: Re-Strategizing Promotional Campaigns in the Wake of 9/11

Lisa T. Fall

Employing effective communication strategies between an organization and its key publics is a rudimentary formula for success. However, there was nothing rudimentary about the September 11, 2001 terrorist attacks on America. This tragedy has caused communication managers to rethink everything they do. Messages are constantly being restructured, communication channels are being retooled, and key publics are being retargeted. The tourism industry has been greatly affected. And the 2003 war in Iraq, coupled with SARS and other health-related outbreaks, has further added to the negative impact on this economic sector.

The Travel Industry Association of America (TIA) has released some updated figures. Since 2000, domestic and international travel expenditures dropped $29.1 billion in 2001 (to $541.1) and $42 billion in 2002 (to $528.5). However, revenue is only projected to decline $24.1 billion in 2003 (to $544.4) and $2.4 billion in 2004 (to $568.1). And, by 2005, revenues are projected to surpass the pre-9/11 revenues by $23.5 billion (to $594.3 billion). Tourism managers continue to work toward meeting a binary, bottom line-oriented goal: (1) to recuperate lost revenues as a result of consumers' hesitation to travel and (2) to enhance potential future revenues by encouraging travelers to visit their destinations. Now, more then ever, the need to implement a sound strategic communication campaign comes to the forefront to serve as a prominent linking agent between the tourism industry and the traveling public; the catalyst for these linking agents is public relations.

Public Relations' Role in the Aftermath

Having assessed consumer trends and market research results, the International Society of Hospitality Consultants (2003) identified the top ten issues tourism managers should focus on. Five of these issues are directly applicable to this study: adaptation to new business realities, worldwide terrorism and safety, global uncertainty, airline issues, and service gaps. Further, TIA's national chair, Bruce Wolff, encourages a four-point travel industry agenda to assist the economy in prospering in spite of varying world events: secure and support a sustained private/public national marketing program to promote increased tourism to the United States; expand the SeeAmerica brand and its various campaign components; enhance travel and tourism's lobbying capabilities in Washington, DC; and expand efforts related to research, including conducting ongoing industry surveys, studies and reports (2004). American Automobile Association CEO and President Robert L. Darbelnet (2003) also defines six trends that must be acknowledged in the industry, three of which are applicable to this study: recognize the diverse segments of the market and tailor your offerings, collaborate to effectively connect all segments of the travel industry, and aggressively promote travel to the United States. In short, all of these industry concerns represent the need for managers to continually re-strategize and readdress their communication programs, while employing stringent research and evaluation mechanisms, on an ongoing basis.

Since the September 11 attacks, society has become more skeptical and more suspicious and watchful. According to TIA, travelers are also experiencing a certain degree of uncertainty. As a result, they continue to be cautious in their planning. Another market research report reveals that Americans still plan to vacation but are staying in their "comfort zones" (e.g., staying closer to home). Further, the concept of "togethering" (engaging in more intimate family- and friend-orientated activities) is apparent. To further demonstrate this "togetherness" behavioral increase, top leisure (vacation activities) include: spending time with friends/family; camping, out/doors/nature trips; adventure and beach vacations; and amusement/theme parks and cultural experiences.

Society, since the attacks, has become more skeptical (Smith 2001) and more suspicious and watchful (Chura 2002; Myra 2002). According to TIA, travelers are also experiencing a certain degree of uncertainty and continue to be cautious in their planning (Amarante 2003). Hence, people may be less apt to pay attention to advertisements and commercials. In combination with consumer skepticism, Ries and Ries (2002) suggest that the crucial ingredient in loyalty and brand building is public relations. Their case study analyses of top companies—to include Starbucks, Wal-Mart, Red Bull, the Body Shop, and Palm—support the premise that most major brands are born with publicity—not advertising.

In the aftermath of the September 11 attacks, both in the long- and short-term, it is apparent that communication continues to play a leading role in the struggle to revitalize the tourism industry. Public relations, which not only establishes, but also strives to maintain mutually beneficial relationships between an organization and its key publics (Cutlip, Center and Broom 2000), serves as a dominant component in the strategic communication mix. Grunig's two-way symmetrical model (e.g., Grunig and Hunt 1984; Grunig and Repper 1992) demonstrates public relations as a process of continual and reciprocal exchange between an organization and its key publics. This model encourages two-way, open channels of communication that provides feedback between an organization and its publics. Advertising, in contrast, provides only a one-way flow of communication from sender to receiver with the goal of selling a product or service (Ries and Ries 2002).

Looking specifically at trends related tourism, travelers are increasingly referring to the Internet when they are planning business and pleasure trips (TIA 2001). Additionally, market research consistently finds that friends and family continue to be the number one source travelers refer to for travel information (July 2001). Taking into consideration these two behavioral trends, increased Internet use among the traveling public illustrates that "word-of-net" is in direct competition with word-of-mouth as related to *how* travelers are obtaining their information. These results reinforce the point that tourism managers strive to offer more mechanisms for their publics to engage in more interpersonal, two-way communication.

This national study illustrates how tourism managers, in the wake of the September 11 terrorist attacks, strategically retooled their communication programs to further support public relations activities. More specifically, the study demonstrates how messages were restructured, primary publics were retargeted, and communication tactics (channels) were retooled among convention and visitors bureau (CVB) managers.

Review of the Literature

Overview of Post-9/11 Communication Studies

Mass Media Focus. Mass media literature regarding the post-September 11 terrorist attacks is as broad as the tragedy itself. But the common denominator among all the studies is the examination of how various communication components been influenced by the attacks. Topics range from court room access (Olson 2002) and crisis management (Ulmer and Sellnow 2002) to travel safety issues depicted via the media (Hall 2002). Greenberg (2002) provides a compilation of social communication issues studies that range from personal issues (e.g., national stress reaction studies and the role communication plays in coping with terror) to mass media-oriented issues (e.g., how television stations covered the crisis and how editorial cartoonists portrayed the enemy, and how news about the attacks diffused).

Still others examine issues such as myth and terror on editorial pages (Lule 2002) how organizations reacted to the 9/11 attacks via their corporate web sites (Gross and Bourland-Davis 2002). Carden (2003) conducted a study in which she sought to determine if public relations activity had increased before and after the attacks. Responses from a survey launched after the September 11 terrorist attacks among public relations practitioners employed in the tourism industry indicated an average of an 8 percent annual increase of public relations efforts among their promotional programs between 2001-2002. On the other hand, advertising decreased an average of 3 percent over the same two-year period.

Wright (2002) learns from his examination that the attacks have increased public relations' role as a significant communication function among corporations. Guth (2003) provides a synthesis of how the public debate over propaganda techniques used during the War on Terrorism closely mirrors issues that took place during the Cold War in 1953. Further, Varisco (2002) studied the use of the Internet as a resource for communicating about the September 11 attacks while Coleman and Wu (2003) analyzed broadcasters' nonverbal communication during the initial twenty-four hours after the terrorist attacks.

Travel/Tourism Focus. Travel, tourism and hospitality researchers have also investigated the September 11 terrorist attacks from an array of perspectives. Like the mass media literature, the travel, tourism, and hospitality literature focusing on 9/11 represents a broad spectrum of subject matter. Analyses range from hotel operations revenue and performance studies (Enz and Canina 2002; O'Neill and Lloyd-Jones 2002) to employee-related issues such as job security and workplace security (Batterman and Fullerton 2002; Cohen 2002; Enz and Taylor 2002), job sharing (Sherwyn and Sturman 2002), workplace privacy (Sproule 2002), and military service and employee rights (Klein, Pappas and Herman 2002). Greer and Moreland (2003) examined United Airlines' and American Airlines' online crisis communication following the September 11 terrorist attacks.

Of special relevance to this study is research that investigates post-9/11 communication issues within the tourism industry. For example, Litvin and Alderson (2003) conducted a case study to find out how the Charleston Area Convention & Visitors Bureau (CACVB) responded. The CACVB employed several special strategies to meet the particular needs of this situation. First, managers immediately started focusing more communication efforts on attracting travelers from their "drive markets" and expanded the six-hour drive radius to a ten-hour radius. Second, advertising expenditures were reallocated from the international travel budget to the domestic drive market budget. Third, advertising copy messages were redesigned to stress the drive accessibility of the city. A new tag line was included: "A short drive down the road. A million miles away." A special holiday vacation advertising campaign was also launched. The CACVB also collaborated with other area organizations to create prepackaged vacation opportunities for travelers.

Frisby (2002) explored how the British Tourism Authority (BTA) responded to the terrorist attacks and the foot-and-mouth outbreaks. BTA managers first identified their most viable key travel markets, then they revamped their communication program accordingly. They redesigned their campaign strategies, objectives, tactics, evaluation and measurement procedures to meet the specific needs of two crises. Enhanced media relations and publicity planning were included in the campaign updates. Disseminating accurate information on a consistent basis to key media served as the crux of the plan. The overarching message goals were threefold: to stress the safety of the destination, to communicate that foot-and-mouth disease was not widespread in Britain, and to highlight the plethora of special activities taking place for would-be travelers.

Hopper (2001) examined how London positioned and promoted itself in the wake of 9/11. The London Tourism Board (LTB) immediately developed the London Tourism Recovery Group, which was taxed with the duty of conducting research during a six-month period to measure the impact the 9/11 attacks were having on the local tourism economy. The research was conducted in phases. Continuous data were collected, leading to timely strategic action planning procedures that were methodically put into place. Marketing expenditures were diverted from the overseas budget to the United Kingdom budget. A special promotional campaign, "The Greatest Show on Earth," was launched to stimulate domestic business to London. Other special promotional campaigns followed (e.g., "Royal London" and "Only in Britain, Only in 2002").

From a hospitality crisis response perspective, Stafford, Yu and Armoo (2002) studied how Washington, DC hotels responded to the attacks. These organizations launched an aggressive public relations program that employed various media relations and publicity strategies. The hotels also worked closely with local, state, and federal government agencies to encourage people to travel—not just to the DC area—but also throughout America.

The results from these studies provide a common theme: strategic communication plays a dominant role in the revitalization process. Among the studies, *none* of the organizations opted do nothing and follow a "business as usual" philosophy. Instead, immediate steps were taken to revamp their communication procedures and programs. Further, the literature indicates that immediate reactive, yet strategic, communication planning was apparent in the wake of the 9/11 attacks—especially among travel and tourism organizations. From the literature review, four overarching themes have evolved. Organizations are (1) restructuring messages; (2) refocusing their primary publics; (3) readjusting communication channels for disseminating key messages; and (4) revamping communication campaigns to include more public relations activities.

Situational Theory of Publics

The situational theory of publics (Grunig 1975; Grunig 1978; Grunig 1979a) focuses on relationships between communication and behavior. This theory accounts for how and when people communicate and when the communications are likely to have an impact. Situational theory predicts communication behavior according to three independent variables: problem recognition, constraint recognition, and level of involvement (Grunig 1978; Grunig 1983; Grunig and Repper 1992). Grunig has since extended the theory (e.g., 1979b, 1983, 1989), as have others (e.g., Aldoory 2001; Hallahan 1999; Major 1998; Heath, Liao and Douglas 1995; Dorner and Coombs 1994; Major 1993; Cameron 1992; Hamilton 1992; Elliott, Mahmoud, Sothirajah and Camphor 1991).

All three of the situational theory of publics predictor variables were evident in the aftermath of the September 11 attacks, providing a valuable opportunity to study this theory as it relates to the tourism industry. According to Grunig's research, *problem recognition* is the extent to which individuals recognize that issues/events are problems to be concerned about. In the case of this study, we recognize and acknowledge the fact that since the 9/11 terrorist attacks, the level of danger associated with traveling has dramatically heightened. *Constraint recognition* is the extent to which individuals see their behaviors as limited by obstacles or barriers beyond their control. In this case, we have concerns about the uncontrollable dangers associated with traveling. Finally, *level of involvement* represents the extent to which an issue is personally relevant to individuals. In this case, as United States Americans, we are all involved—whether we care to be or not.

In short, regarding the 9/11 terrorist attack, here in the United States we recognize the situation (problem), we are constrained by the situation, and we are involved in the situation in some facet or another. Communication researchers should not negate the opportunity to learn from such a volatile atmosphere. Therefore, this situation, although traumatic, offers an isolated opportunity to further study the situational theory of publics.

Relationship Management Perspective

Supporting Grunig's work is the relationship management perspective (Ledingham in press; Ledingham 2003; Ledingham and Bruning 2003; Bruning and Ledingham 2000; Ledingham and Bruning 1998; Ledingham, Bruning, Thomlison and Lesko 1997; Ledingham 1993; Ledingham and Bruning 1997). Within this theoretical perspective, relationship is defined as "the state which exists between an organization and its key publics in which the actions of either entity impact the economic, social, political, and/or cultural well-being of the other entity" (Ledingham and Bruning 1998, 62). This perspective also substantiates the importance of public relations with regard to developing and maintaining relationships among organizations and their key publics. Dozier (1985, 85) points out that communication is "a strategic management function that (that helps) manage relationships with key publics that affect organizational mission, goals, and objectives." The relationship management perspective echoes this statement: "While goals are developed around relationships...communication is used as a strategic tool in helping to achieve those goals," and that "while measurement of communication efficiencies should certainly be part of the evaluation process, their importance eventually may rest upon their ability to impact the achievement of relationship objectives" (Ledingham and Brunig 2000, 63).

The concept of connectivity. Serving as a common denominator among Grunig's situational theory of publics and Ledingham's public relations management perspective is the concept of *connectivity* (Katz, Gurevitch and Hass 1973) between receivers and senders. A strong cohesion between receivers and the actual channel to which they receive the communication can further enhance the information encoding and decoding process. Katz et al. (1973) assert that individuals use mass communication to "connect" themselves with different kinds of others, to include self, family, friends, and the nation. As suggested by McLuhan's (1964, 1967) work, " the medium is the message."

Typology of publics. The notion of connectivity also aligns with Grunig's differentiation among publics (Grunig 1984; Grunig and Repper 1992). Active publics perceive a situation as relevant and are proactive in their behavior to seek out information about it. Latent publics, however, are unaware of the consequences. On the other hand, apathetic publics don't care and do not see the relevance of the situation, nor do they proactively seek out information about it.

One-way vs. two-way flow of communication interaction. Also associated with the situational theory of publics are Grunig's four models of public relations: press agentry, public information, two-way asymmetrical and two-way symmetrical (e.g., Grunig 1984; Grunig and Repper, 1992). The first two models depict a one-way flow of communication from sender to receiver. The latter two represent a two-way flow of communication from sender to receiver, then back to the sender, thereby providing an opportunity for feedback and response from either party. The two-way symmetrical model, which encourages balanced communication between the sender and receiver, plays a critical role in the relationship-building process (Ledingham in press; Ledingham 2003).

Controlled vs. uncontrolled communication. The distinction between "controlled" and "uncontrolled" communication techniques is also relevant to this study. Controlled tactics represent information over which the sender has *total* control of the editorial content, style, placement and timing (Smith 2002; Bivins 1999). An example is paid advertising. On the other hand, uncontrolled tactics represent information over which the sender does *not* have the ultimate decision-making power of content, style, placement and timing (Smith 2002; Bivins 1999). Examples include media relations activities. A media release is sent to a particular outlet (e.g., newspaper, magazine, radio or television station); however, that sender has no control over the final outcome of the story.

Rationale Behind the Study's Objectives

The tourism industry is, more than anything else, a service-driven profession. Hence, it makes financial sense for this particular industry to engage in balanced communication strategies that support relationship-building activities and offer two-way interaction between tourism managers and travelers. Specifically, this study contends that, in the wake of the September 11 attacks, public relations activities, practiced within the framework of the relationship management perspective, will be used more frequently among tourism managers than will advertising methods to enhance travel.

The concept of connectivity, in tandem with what the situational theory of publics explains, supports the premise that active publics will gravitate to sources (channels) that serve as *relationship building tactics*—because these receivers (travelers) have a personal vested interest in the message. Additionally, active publics will attend to messages that are disseminated via *uncontrolled* channels, such as unpaid messages, which tend to lend more credibility due to their unrestrained, "filtered" nature (Ries and Ries 2002). Finally, active publics will be more inclined toward communication tactics (channels) that offer *two-way* interaction.

Tourism managers, who are specifically targeting *active* publics, will employ more uncontrolled channels of communication, which appear to be more genuine with intentions of building relationships as opposed to selling products and services (e.g., marketing, advertising). Further, these managers will employ more channels that offer two-way flow of interaction between their organization and key receivers (travelers). By doing so, the receivers will feel more connected to the messages, as supported by the situational theory of publics.

One overarching question drives this study. In the in the wake of such an enormous tragedy that has greatly impacted the tourism industry's livelihood, how have tourism managers retooled their communication programs? The following research questions are addressed:

RQ1: How has communication tactic use flexuated among tourism managers as a
result of the September 11, 2001 terrorist attacks?

RQ2: How have tourism managers redesigned their promotional messages as a result of the September 11, 2001 terrorist attacks?

RQ3: How have tourism managers redirected their primary publics focus as a result of the September 11, 2001 terrorist attacks?

RQ4: Does frequency of communication tactic use (advertising, marketing, public relations, new media) predict the redesigning of promotional messages?

RQ5: Does frequency of communication tactic use (advertising, marketing, public relations, new media) predict the refocusing of primary publics?

Method

Population

Convention and visitors bureaus (CVB) were chosen for the study because these are the organizations taxed with the primary duty of promoting their city/region as a destination location to external publics (leisure as well as business travelers). The initial sampling frame comprised organizations from three lists: CVBs that are members of the International Association of Convention & Visitors Bureaus, CVBs posted on the official Travel Industry Association of America web site and CVBs listed on each of the fifty state official tourism web sites. These lists were cross-referenced to eliminate duplication.

A total of 800 respondents were randomly selected from the final list. A total of 195 surveys were returned as "undeliverable," diminishing the initial sampling frame to 605 potential respondents. From that 605 sample, 184 usable surveys were returned, resulting in a 30 percent response rate.

Administration Procedures

This study employs a web-based survey distributed via the Internet to email addresses of CVB communication managers across the United States during June and July 2002. Prior to launching the study, tourism managers were sent a pre-notification electronic mail message to let them know the on-line survey was forthcoming. One week later they were sent an electronic mail message that included a brief explanation of the study and the link to the on-line questionnaire. In the letter, it was clearly specified that the study was being conducted within the framework of the post-September 11 terrorist attacks and that all answers should be based on such activity. In the opening paragraph of the letter, respondents were instructed to send the questionnaire to the person responsible for overseeing the organization's communication program if they were not the appropriate contact. Respondents were instructed to click on the link to be immediately directed to the questionnaire. A week before the assigned deadline, the researcher sent a follow-up electronic mail message to remind respondents to complete the survey by the designated date. Again, the link to the online questionnaire was included in the electronic mail correspondence.

Operationalization of the Variables

The primary variables under investigation are message, primary publics, and communication tactics (channels). To address the refocusing of primary publics, respondents were asked if they *changed* their primary publics as a result of the September 11 attacks. If they did shift their primary public focus, they were instructed to indicate *who* these new publics were. To address the redesigning of campaign messages, respondents were asked to indicate *how* they revamped their messages. Questions addressing both of these variables were open-ended, allowing for respondents to type in their answers.

The literature defines communication channels in a variety of ways, including information sources, communication tactics, communication techniques, and communication methods. These terms will be used interchangeably throughout this study. The communication tactics under investigation are based on a thorough review of the tourism literature (e.g., Fall 2000a; Fall 2000b; Fodness and Murrray 1999; Fodness and Murray 1998; Andereck and Caldwell 1993; Snepenger and Snepenger 1993; Fesenmaier and Vogt 1992; Rao, Thomas and Javalgi 1992). As a validity check, the instrument was pre-tested among various CVB managers who were not part of the final random selection. They were also asked to pay close attention to the list of communication tactics, then to make appropriate additions and deletions.

Table 10.1
Communications Tactics Employed at Convention & Visitors Bureaus across the United States

COMMUNICATION TACTICS
Billboard Ads
Magazine Ads
Newspaper Ads
Radio Ads
TV Ads
Internet Web Site
Industry Trade Show
Travel Agent
Highway Welcome Center
Magazine Media Release
Newspaper Media Release
TV Media Release
Auto Club Materials
Direct Mail Appeal

For each communication tactic, respondents were instructed to rate the *present* frequency of use compared to frequency of use *before* the September 11, 2001 terrorist attacks. A Likert-type 1-5 point scale was used: 1=do not use it at all now, 2=use it slightly less now, 3=use it the same, 4=use it slightly more now and 5=use it much more now. Respondents were also provided with an example for clarity: "If you use magazine media releases MUCH MORE frequently now than you did before the September 11 attacks, you would choose *use it much more now.*" Additional blanks were included for respondents to type in and rate any communication techniques not listed in the questionnaire.

Analyses

To address the first three research questions, frequency of use and mean scores were calculated and analyzed. The channels were then categorized based on their communication orientation (e.g., advertising, public relations, marketing tourism, and new media). The tactics were also categorized based on their flow of sender/receiver interaction: one-way provides no feedback mechanism and two-way provides feedback mechanisms. To address the latter two questions, message and primary public variables were categorized thematically. The communication tactics were collapsed into four information source factors. These variables were then submitted to s discriminant function analysis.

Results

Profile

More than half the respondents have bachelors degrees and another 15 percent have masters degrees. Educational backgrounds range from degrees in communications (21 percent) and business, marketing, and management (21 percent) to nearly a third of the respondents who report "other" degrees in English, Journalism, Human Resources, Political Science and Hospitality Management. Approximately 75 percent of the respondents are female, which is characteristic of the tourism profession in general. Geographically, the sample represents various sectors from across the United States, including the West (21 percent), Midwest (33 percent), Northeast (14 percent), and South (32 percent).

Addressing RQ1

Results in table 10.2 reveal that public relations techniques are being used more frequently now than before the September 11, 2001 attacks. The data indicate that Internet web sites (18.6 percent), direct mail correspondence (10.6 percent), newspaper media releases (8.0 percent), newspaper ads (7.4 percent), auto club materials (6.9 percent), and magazine media releases (6.4 percent) represent the *most* increased use. Data also illustrate that paid advertisements (billboard ads, 35.9 percent; radio ads 23.4 percent) and travel agents (19.6 percent) are being the *least* used now, compared to before, September 11, as defined by "do not use it at all now." Overall mean scores among public relations tactics (newspaper, magazine and TV media releases) and the more traditional marketing/tourism specific tactics (e.g., highway welcome center and auto club materials) dem-

Table 10.2
Frequency Scores of Communication Tactic Use: Now Compared to Before September 11 Terror Attacks

Communication Tactics Employed at USA CVBs	Use Much More Now (%)	Use Slightly More Now (%)	Use Same Now (%)	Use Slightly Less Now (%)	Do Not Use At All Now (%)
Billboard Ads	3.2	4.8	48.4	2.7	**35.9**
Magazine Ads	2.1	17.0	59.6	**17.0**	1.1
Newspaper Ads	**7.4**	**24.5**	46.8	**10.1**	6.5
Radio Ads	2.7	15.4	47.9	**5.3**	23.4
TV Ads	5.3	11.2	41.5	1.6	**35.0**
Internet Web Site	**18.6**	**38.3**	39.4	0	0
Industry Trade Show	1.6	11.7	**66.0**	13.8	2.2
Travel Agent	1.1	5.9	59.0	**8.5**	19.6
Highway Welcome Center	4.3	18.1	**72.3**	.5	1.1
Magazine Media Release	6.4	**21.3**	**64.4**	1.1	3.8
Newspaper Media Release	**8.0**	**23.9**	**62.8**	.5	1.6
TV Media Release	2.7	17.0	**61.2**	.5	10.3
Auto Club Materials	**6.9**	1.54	56.9	2.1	**12.0**
Direct Mail Appeal	**10.6**	**24.5**	48.4	1.1	8.5

Bold-face figures indicate the highest scores for each category of use.

onstrate higher use scores than do the traditional advertising tactics, as illustrated in table 10.3. Internet web site has the highest mean score.

For further clarification, table 10.4 provides each tactic's level of control and communication domain. Controlled tactics represent information over which the sender has *total* control of the editorial content, style, placement and timing (Smith 2002; Bivins 1999). An example is paid advertising. Uncontrolled tactics represent information over which the sender does *not* have the ultimate decision-making power of content, style, placement and timing (Smith 2002; Bivins 1999). Corresponding with the data reported in tables 10.1 and 10.2, public relations tactics are being used more frequently and advertising tactics are being used less frequently.

Table 10.3
Overall Mean Scores, Standard Deviation Scores, and
Ranking of Communication Tactic Use: Now Compared to
Before September 11 Terror Attacks

Communication Tactics Employed at USA CVBs	Mean	Standard Deviations	Mean Rankings – (1= highest mean score; 13=lowest mean score)
Billboard Ads	2.33	1.13	13
Magazine Ads	3.02	.69	8
Newspaper Ads	3.17	.95	6
Radio Ads	2.67	1.09	10
TV Ads	2.48	1.25	12
Internet Web Site	**3.78**	.74	1
Industry Trade Show	2.96	.65	9
Travel Agent	2.58	.92	11
Highway Welcome Center	**3.24**	1.00	4
Magazine Media Release	**3.26**	.76	3
Newspaper Media Release	**3.37**	.71	2
TV Media Release	3.04	.88	7
Auto Club Materials	3.04	.99	7
Direct Mail Correspondence	2.58	1.00	11

Bold-face figures indicate highest mean scores

Addressing RQ2

Results addressing RQ2 indicate that nearly half (43 percent) of the tourism managers have re-designed their promotional message as a result of the September 11 attacks while the other half (48 percent) kept the same message; 9 percent did not respond to this question. A thematic analysis of the message changes reported by respondents illustrates thirteen overarching themes. As described in table 10.5, the most frequently reoccurring themes reported focus on drivable destination/accessible location, safety, relaxation/getaway, destination branding, freedom/patriotism, and family.

RQ3 findings demonstrate that more than more than half (63 percent) of the managers have *not* redirected their target publics while one-third (33 percent) have opted to do so.; 4 percent did not respond to this question. A thematic analysis of the primary public shift changes reported in table 10.6 indicates that managers' re-targeting of primary publics fall into categories. "Lifecycle / lifestyle" publics include seniors, families, singles and couples.

Table 10.4
Descriptions of Communication Tactics Under Investigation

Type of Tactic (Channel)	Flow of Communication Interaction	Level of Control	Communication Orientation
Billboard Ads	1-way	Controlled	Advertising
Magazine Ads	1-way	Controlled	Advertising
Newspaper Ads	1-way	Controlled	Advertising
Radio Ads	1-way	Controlled	Advertising
TV Ads	1-way	Controlled	Advertising
Internet Web Site	*Combination:* 1-way / 2-way	*Combination:* Controlled / Uncontrolled	Advertising/ Public Relations/ Marketing: Tourism-Specific
Industry Trade Show	2-way	Uncontrolled	Marketing: Tourism-Specific
Travel Agent	2-way	Uncontrolled	Marketing: Tourism-Specific
Highway Welcome Ctr. Information	1-way	Controlled	Marketing: Tourism-Specific
Magazine Media Release	1-way	Uncontrolled	Public Relations
Newspaper Media Release	1-way	Uncontrolled	Public Relations
TV Media Release	1-way	Uncontrolled	Public Relations
Auto Club Materials	1-way	Controlled	Marketing: Tourism-Specific
Direct Mail Appeal	2-way	Controlled	Marketing: Tourism-Specific

Table 10.5
Message Change Themes Resulting from the September 11, 2001
Terrorist Attacks

*Message ChangeFocus	Frequency of Times Reported
Driveable /Accessible location	18
Safety	10
Relaxation/Getaway	10
Destination Branding	9
Family	7
Freedom/Patriotism	7
Cost (value for price paid)	5
Home away from Home	5
Recreation/Outdoors	4
Meeting Destination	3
State Message	3
Nostalgia/Sameness	3
Special post-911 message	2

*Note: some respondents provided messages with multiple themes, so their message themes were coded in more than one category.

"Geography" publics range from regional and state to driveable markets while "Duration of Stay" publics are represented by day-trippers and weekend travelers. The fourth category, "Type of Traveler," is further divided between business and vacation (leisure) publics. Business publics entail meeting planners, associations, and SMURFs (social, military, educational, religious, fraternal) while vacation publics are represented by golfers/sports enthusiasts, and general leisure. The last category of "Miscellaneous," is represented by domestic and patriotic travelers. As shown, the most frequently reoccurring shift of primary publics focuses on drive markets, regional markets, and families.

Addressing RQ4

To address the last two research questions, the fourteen communication variables were first collapsed into information source factors developed and validated in previous studies (Fall, 2000a; 2000b). Reliability scores indicate acceptable alpha coefficients: advertis-

Table 10.6
Re-targeted Primary Public Resulting from the
September 11, 2001 Terrorist Attacks

*New Primary Public Focus	Frequency of Times Reported
Lifecyle/Lifestyle	
Senior	2
Singles	1
Families	10
Couples	1
Geography	
Regional	15
In-state	9
Drive Market	22
Duration of Stay	
Day-Trippers	2
Weekend Travelers	1
Type of Traveler	
~ *Business*	
SMERF segments(social, military, educational,	
religious, fraternal)	2
Meeting Planners	3
Associations	2
~ *Vacation / Leisure*	
Leisure	8
Sports Enthusiasts/Golfers	2
Miscellaneous	
Domestic	2
Patriotic	2

*Note: some respondents provided primary publics with multiple categories, so their answers were coded in more than one category.

ing, a = .77; public relations, a = .72; tourism marketing, a = .77. (See table 10.7)

When examining which information source factors predict the decision to redesign promotional messages, results indicate that there is a statistically significant difference among the four factors, explaining 63 percent of the variance: Wilk^s Lambda = .941, X (4, 184) = 9.932, p = .042. In particular, the public relations/media relations factor is the largest predictor with a discriminant coefficient of .707, followed by tourism marketing with a score of .575. In other words, increased levels of public relations and tourism marketing tactic use predicts the redesign of promotional messages. Said an-

Table 10.7
Alpha reliability Scores for Information Source Factors

INFORMATION SOURCE FACTORS		
Advertising	**Tourism Marketing**	**Public Relations**
Billboard Ads	Industry Trade Show	Magazine Media Release
Magazine Ads	Travel Agent	Newspaper Media Release
Newspaper Ads	Highway Welcome Center Information	TV Media Release
Radio Ads	Auto Club Materials	
TV Ads	Direct Mail Appeal	
$\alpha = .72$	$\alpha = .77$	$\alpha = .77$

other way, those mangers who have opted to redesign their promotional messages are significantly more likely to increase public relations and tourism marketing techniques as well. (See tables 10.8 through 10.11)

Addressing RQ5

When examining which information source factors predict the decision to redirect the primary publics focus, no significant discriminators were found.

Discussion

An organization cannot successfully provide "service" to its varied publics without the implementation of a well-orchestrated public relations. In support of this premise, several lessons can be learned from this study. First, the results provide further support for the applicability of situational theory of publics and its relevance to the tourism industry. Second, results demonstrate how public relations techniques continue to serve as key components for communicating in the aftermath of a crisis of such magnitude as the September 11 attacks.

Applicability of Situational Theory and Relationship Management

This study illustrates how communication strategies were revamped based on the *situation*. No "cookie cutter" formulas or "how to" crisis manuals could be used for such a rare and unchartered circumstance. The predictions of the situational theory of publics

Tables 10.8-10.10
Summary of Canonical Discriminant Functions

Table 10.8
Eigenvalues and percent of Variance Explained

Function	Eigenvalue	percent of Variance	Cumulative percent	Canonical Correlation
1	.063	100.0	100.0	.244

Table 10.9
Standardized Canonical Discriminant Function Coefficients

	Function
	1
Advertisements	-.353
Public Relations/Media Relations	.707
Tourism Marketing	.575
Internet Website	.211

Table 10.10
Structure Matrix

	Function
	1
Public relations/Media relations	.890
Tourism Marketing	.865
Advertisements	.648
Internet Website	.487

Pooled within-groups correlations between discriminating variables and standardized canonical discriminant functions. Variables ordered by absolute size of correlation within function.

Table 10.11
Functions at Group Centroids

	Function
Message	1
1.00	-.265
2.00	.235

Unstandardized canonical discriminant functions evaluated at group means are substantiated among the details of these findings. Further, results support the relationship management perspective, which encourages more interpersonally oriented communication between an organization and its key publics. Two other theories also assist us in understanding the results. According to the media systems dependency theory (DeFleur and Ball-Rokeach 1975), during particular situations, such as crises, people tend become more dependent on the media for information. The agenda setting theory (McCombs and Shaw 1972), which predicts that the media sets the agenda for what we think about, also helps to understand the findings. In the case of the September 11 attacks, any information related to this situation *was* the agenda. Hence, the results suggest that the CVB managers are making decisions that are compatible with their information seekers. People are both *tuned in* (to the agenda) and *tuning in* (to the media). So, it makes sense – from a cost-benefit standpoint – for these managers to spend money on a channel that provides the most utility benefit to their publics.

Results from this study also demonstrate that tourism managers are actively engaging in media relations as a primary function in the aftermath of the attacks. Since the "traveling public" encompasses a wide variety of people, the media serves as a beneficial vehicle to reach travelers. This finding also speaks directly to the predications made by the situational theory of publics: these practitioners are "matching" their communication channels to those which best fit the needs of their intended publics. In this case, managers are seeking to earn exposure in key newspapers, magazines and on specific television stations to effectively reach them. On the other hand, advertisements, which supply us with controlled information, may not seem as genuine in their attempts to communicate messages.

Public Relations as a Strategic Communication Function

Results from this study also support the premise that, in order to *proactively* react to a crisis situation, communication programs need to be strategically and continually retooled to meet the needs of changing organizational goals and environmental demands. In the case of managers surveyed in this study, they realized that promotional messages appropriate "pre-9/11" were not the most conducive messages "post-9/11" (e.g., they refocused their messages to capture more driving travelers; they emphasized safety, relaxation, and family). Further, the results indicate that managers opted to utilize more "uncontrolled" communication channels than they did advertising (e.g., non-paid messages that are filtered via editors as opposed to paid messages that get published "untouched"). As discussed, these uncontrolled channels tend to project a more genuine undertone. Finally, this re-strategizing process revealed that CVB managers refocused their target audiences based on *who* they deemed most appropriate to receive these messages (e.g., regional and drive-market travelers). To recap, the CVB managers' strategic communication decisions during the post-9/11 crisis phase involved: (1) revamping messages based on the appropriateness /sensitivity of the situation; (2) refocusing of target audiences; and (3) shifting of selected communication channels to disseminate key messages to select audiences/target markets. As the literature suggests, this reassessment of these three critical areas in the communication process are vital to a public relations / promotional program's success in the aftermath of a crisis.

Limitations of the Study

This study has a few limitations. First, it was launched in the summer, which is one of the busiest periods for CVB manages. This timing issue probably diminished the response rate. Second, as with any self-administered survey, one can never be sure if the appropriate person actually completed the questionnaire. Third, the results have limited generalizability to convention and visitors bureaus. Additionally, other research data collection methods should be considered when studying CVB managers in the future. Since many of these tourism managers are located in "high traffic/high profile locations," they probably receive numerous email messages each day. Hence, the on-line survey may have gotten buried among the other messages, therefore diminishing the study's overall return rate. Finally, this study's results cannot fully explain *why* managers chose to retool their communication programs. Although the survey questions were framed within the context of the post-9/11 terrorist attacks, certainly there are other reasons (causes) why some managers opted to retool their communication strategies (e.g., price inflation among some media channels, budget cuts among CVB programs, etc.)

Suggestions for Future Research

While the tourism industry used to traditionally rely more heavily on marketing, this profession is now focusing more attention on public relations strategies. The service industry, as a whole, offers tremendous opportunities for public relations researchers who want to study relationship-building programs. After all, an organization cannot successfully provide "service" to its varied publics without the implementation of a well-orchestrated public relations program (Fall in press, Stacks and Caroll in press; Fall 2000c; Heath 1994). This author contends that good service is, in itself, a strategic form of public relations—and that public relations management serves as a solid foundation for sound customer service.

Additionally, relationship-building programs need more attention. For example, member relations programs, which are prominent among the tourism industry (e.g., frequent participant incentive programs), warrant further study as do special event and corporate sponsorship programs. Finally, much research still needs to be conducted to test for success of various components related to the four-step public relations process, including research, action planning, communication and evaluation methods.

Regarding crisis management, researchers should continue to look carefully at how tourism destinations are responding to catastrophes. Case study analyses to determine what organizations are doing effectively—and ineffectively—to restore consumer confidence among their primary publics in the aftermath of crises is an important area for future research. Even as importantly, researchers need to narrow the scope to extrapolate variables that serve as predictors of strategic communication success during such situations. Another suggestion is to take a closer look at *how* a destination is positioning itself in the tourism the marketplace. Determining which publicity variables serve as better predictors than others do is important to an organization from an image, as well as a financial, perspective.

In terms of publicity and promotions, a subject that deserves further attention is movie placement. Many cities experience tremendous tourism growth after a movie is filmed "on location." Hence, the *venue* itself becomes the variable for examination. Of importance are questions that address *why*—based on *how* the destination was depicted via the file—moviegoers find the destination to be an attractive place to visit.

As an extension to this particular study, it would be of benefit to launch the same survey among the sample (e.g., CVB managers) to compare the results of how they retooled their communication programs (e.g., message change, target public refocus, channel shift) in the *immediate aftermath* to how they are re-strategizing *now*—to test for significant differences. However, even more importantly than the differences, researchers should dig deeper and find out how effective/successful these communication program changes are, from a cost-effective analysis.

Conclusion

The results from this study further support the utility of Grunig's (1978; 1979a) situational theory, providing an even sharper tool that communication specialists can use to carve their messages. However, the message should not be the only component that provides a benefit for the receiver while he/she is engaged in the communication process; the *medium* should also offer the receiver something unique. In the case of targeting would-be travelers to visit a particular destination, the channel should provide a opportunity for receivers to feel personally connected. Public relations communication tactics provide this connectivity. These methods are interactive, uncontrolled, offer two-way flow of communication and encourage relationship-building opportunities between an organization and its publics. This premise is substantiated by Ledingham and Bruning's relationship management perspective.

However, the post-9/11 terrorist attacks demand that communication programs be elaborately, yet strategically revamped. One cannot assume that programs that were successful pre-9/11 will continue to be appropriate post-9/11. Findings from this study reinforce the importance of public relations. It is evident that the tourism industry, like the rest of corporate America, is working assiduously to recuperate its business base. Public relations management continues to play an successful role in the revitalization of the tourism industry.

Note

1.   The researcher would like to thank the College of Communications Research Center at the University of Tennessee for sponsoring the study, both in name and in monetary support, and to Kathleen Kinser for designing the online survey.

References

AAA president offers 6 changes the travel industry can make to prosper, October 21, 2003. *http://www.htrends.com/researcharticle7874.html*

Aldoory, L. 2001. Making health communications meaningful for women: Factors that influence involvement. *Journal of Public Relations Research* 13(2): 163-185.

Amarante, K. 2003. TIA survey shows slow and steady tourism growth, June 6, *http://www.hotelinteractive.com*

Andereck, K. and L. Caldwell. 1993. The influence of tourists' characteristics on ratings of information sources for an attraction. In *Communication and Channel Systems in Tourism Marketing*, edited by M. Uysal and D. Fesenmaier, 171-189. New York: Haworth Press.

Battterman, R.L. and J. F. Fullerton. 2002. Collective bargaining after September 11: What about job security and workplace security. *Cornell Hotel & Restaurant Administration Quarterly* 43(5): 93-108.

Bivins, T. 1999. *Public Relations Writing. The Essentials of Style and Format*. Lincolnwood, IL: NTC Publishing.

Bruning, S. and J. Ledingham. 2000. Perceptions of relationships and evaluations of satisfaction: An exploration of interaction. *Public Relations Review* 29(10): 85-95.

Cameron, G.T. 1992. Memory for investor relations messages: An information-processing study of Grunig's situational theory. *Journal of Public Relations Research* 4: 45-60.

Carden, A. 2003. *The use of persuasive appeals and public relations in the travel and tourism industry post 9/11*. Paper presented at the annual meeting of the Association for Education in Journalism and Mass Communication, Kansas City.

Chura, H. 2002. The new normal. *Advertising Age* 73(10): 1.

Cohen, E.A. 2002. Collective bargaining regarding safety and security issues. *Cornell Hotel & Restaurant Administration Quarterly* 43(5): 109-118.

Coleman, R. and D. Wu. 2003. *More than words: Broadcasters' nonverbal communication in the first 24 hours of the September 11 terrorist attacks*. Paper presented at the annual meeting of the Association for Education in Journalism and Mass Communication, Kansas City.

Cutlip, S., A. Center, and G. Broom. 2000. *Effective Public Relations*. Upper Saddle River, NJ: Prentice-Hall, Inc.

DeFleur, M. and S. Ball-Rokeach. 1975. *Theories of Mass Communication*. New York: David McKay.

Dorner, C. and T. Coombs. 1994. The addition of the personal dimension to situational theory: A re-examination and extension. Paper presented at annual meeting of International Communication Association, Sydney, Austalia.

Dozier, D.M., L. A. Grunig, and J. E. Grunig. 1995. *Managers Guide to Excellence in Public Relations and Communication Management*. Mahwah, NJ: Lawrence Erlbaum Associates.

Elliott, W.R., M. A. Mahmoud, J. Sothirajah, and T. Camphor. 1991. Mass media and the third AIDS epidemic: AIDS knowledge and acceptance in a rural area. Paper presented at the annual meeting of the Association for Education in Journalism and Mass Communication, Boston.

Enz, C.A. and C. Canina. 2002. The best of times, the worst of times: Differences in hotel performance following 9/11. *Cornell Hotel & Restaurant Administration Quarterly* 43(5): 41-51.

Enz, C.A. and M. Taylor. 2002. The safety and security of U.S. hotels: A post-September 11 report. *Cornell Hotel & Restaurant Administration Quarterly* 43(5):119-136.

Fall, L.T. In press. A public relations segmentation study: Using Grunig's nested segmentation model and Yankelovich's generational influences model to distinguish vacation traveler publics. *Journal of Hospitality and Leisure Marketing*.

Fall, L.T. In press. Consumer Relations. Chapter in Robert Heath (ed). *Encyclopedia of Public Relations*, Thousand Oaks, CA: Sage.

Fall, L.T. 2000a. An exploratory study of the relationship between human values and information sources within a tourism framework. *Journal of Hospitality & Leisure Marketing* 7(1): 3-28.

Fall, L.T. 2000b. Segmenting pleasure travelers on the basis of information source usefulness and personal value importance. Dissertation. Michigan State University.

Fall, L.T. 2000c. An exploratory study of the relationship between human values and information sources within a tourism framework. *Journal of Hospitality and Leisure Marketing* Vol. 7 (1): 1-15.

Fesenmaier, D. and K. Vogt. 1992. Evaluating the utility of touristic information sources for planning Midwest vacation travel. *Journal of Travel & Tourism Marketing* 1(2): 1-18.

Fodness, D. and B. Murrray. 1999. A model of tourist information search behavior. *Journal of Travel Research* 37(3): 220-230.

Fodness, D. and B. Murrray. 1998. A typology of tourist information search strategies. *Journal of Travel Research* 37(2): 108-120.

Frisby, E. 2002. Communicating in a crisis: The British tourist authority's responses to the foot-and-mouth outbreak and 11 September, 2001. *Journal of Vacation Marketing* 9(1): 89-100.

Greer, C.F. and K.D. Moreland. 2003. United Airlines' and American Airlines' online crisis communication following the September 11 terrorist attacks'. *Public Relations Review* 29(4): 427-441.

Greenberg, B. 2002. *Communication & Terrorism: Public and Media Responses to 9/11*. Norwood, NJ: Hampton Press.

Gross, D. and P. Bourland-Davis. 2002. Corporate graffiti: An analysis of corporate web site responses to the attacks on America. Paper presented at the annual meeting of the National Communication Association, New Orleans.

Grunig, J.E. 1975. Some consistent types of employee publics. *Public Relations Review* 1(4): 17-36.

Grunig, J.E. 1978. Defining publics in public relations: The case of a suburban hospital. *Journalism Quarterly* 55: 109-118.

Grunig, J.E. 1979a. A new measure of public opinions on corporate social responsibility. *Academy of Management Journal* 22: 738-764.

Grunig, J.E. 1979b. Time budgets, level of involvement, and use of the mass media. *Journalism Quarterly* 56: 248-261.

Grunig, J.E. 1983. Communication behaviors and attitudes of environmental publics: Two studies. *Journalism Monographs* 81.

Grunig, J.E. and T. Hunt. 1984. *Managing Public Relations*. New York: Holt, Rinehart & Winston.

Grunig, J.E. and F.C. Repper. 1992. Strategic management, publics, and issues. In *Excellence in Public Relations and Communication Management*, edited by J.E. Grunig. Hillsdale, NJ: Lawrence Erlbaum Associates.

Grunig, J.E. 1989. Sierra Club study shows who becomes activists. *Public Relations Review* 15(1): 3-24.

Guth, D. 2003. Propaganda v. public diplomacy: How 9/11 gave new life to a cold war debate. Paper presented at the annual meeting of the Association for Education in Journalism and Mass Communication, Kansas City.

Hall, C.M. 2002. Travel safety, terrorism and the media: The significance of the issue-attention cycle. *Current Issues in Tourism* 5(5): 458-466.

Hallahan, K. 1999. Communicating with inactive publics: The moderating roles of motivation, ability and opportunity. Paper presented at the annual meeting of Public Relations Society of America Educators Academy, College Park, MD.

Hamilton, P.K. 1992. Grunig's situational theory: A replication, application, and extension. *Journal of Public Relations Research* 4: 123-149.

Heath, R., S.H. Liao, and W. Douglas. 1995. Effects of perceived economic harms and benefits on issue involvement, use of information sources, and actions: A study in risk communication. *Journal of Public Relations Research* 7: 89-109.

Heath, R., S. A. Leth, and K. Nathan. 1994. Communicating service quality improvement: Another role for public relations. *Public Relations Review* 20(1): 29-41.

Hopper, P. 2001. Marketing London in a difficult climate. *Journal of Vacation Marketing* 9(1): 81-88.

Independent Poll: Americans Still Plan to Vacation But They are Staying Within their "Comfort Zones." April 8, 2004, *http://www.htrends.com/research*article5723.html

International Society of Hospitality consultants top ten issues. Listserv news story. http://www.hotelinteractive.com/news/articleview.asp?articleID=1658

Katz, E., M. Gurevitch, and H. Hass. 1973. On the use of mass media for important things. *American Sociological Review* 38: 164-181.

Klein, J.S., N. J. Pappas, and M. I. Herman. 2002. The userra: Workers' employment rights following military service. *Cornell Hotel & Restaurant Administration Quarterly* 43(5): 75-83.

Ledingham., J. In press. A general theory of public relations, In *Public Relations Theory, Volume II* edited by, Carl Botan and Vincent Hazelton. Hillsdale, NJ: Lawrence Erlbaum.

Ledingham, J. 2003. Explicating relationship management as a general theory of public relations. *Journal of Public Relations Research* 15(2): 181-198.

Ledingham, J. and S. Bruning. 2000. *Public Relations as Relationship Management*. Mahwah, NJ: Lawrence Erlbaum Associates.

Ledingham, J. and S. Bruning. 1998. Relationship Management in public relations: Dimensions of an organization-public relationship. *Public Relations Review* 24(1): 55-65.

Ledingham, J. and S. Bruning. 1997. Building loyalty through community relations, *Public Relations Strategist* Vol. 3(2): 27-29.

Ledingham, J.A., S.D. Bruning, T.D. Thomlison, and C. Lesko. 1997. The transferability of interpersonal relationship dimensions into an organizational setting. *Academy of Managerial Communication Journal* 1: 23-43.

Ledingham, J. 1993. The kindness of strangers: Predictor variables in a public information campaign. *Public Relations Review* 19(4): 367-384.

Litvin, S.W. and L.L. Alderson. 2002. How Charleston got her groove back: A CVB's response to 9/11. *Journal of Vacation Marketing* 9(2): 88-197.

Lule, J. 2002. Myth and terror on the editorial page. *Journalism and Mass Communication Quarterly* 79 (2, Summer): 275-293.

Major, A.M. 1993. Environmental concern and situational communication theory: Implications for communicating with environmental publics. *Journal of Public Relations Research* 5:251-268.

Major, A.M. 1998. The utility of situational theory of publics for assessing public response to a disaster predication. *Public Relations Review* 24(4): 489-508.

McCombs, M. and D. L. Shaw. 1972. The agenda-setting function of mass media. *Public Opinion Quarterly* 36(2): 176-187.

Olson, K. 2002. Courtroom access after 9/11. A pathological perspective. *Communication Law & Policy* 7(4): 461-494.

O'Neill, J.W. and A. R. Lloyd-Jones. 2002. One year after 9/11: Hotel values and strategic implications. *Cornell Hotel & Restaurant Administration Quarterly* 43(5): 53-64.

Rao, S., E. Thomas, and R. Javalgi. 1992. Activity preferences and trip-planning behavior of the US outbound pleasure travel market. *Journal of Travel Research* 30(3): 3-12.

Ries, A. and L. Ries. 2002. *The Fall of Advertising and the Rise of PR*. New York: HarperBusiness.

Sherwyn, D. and C. Sturman. 2002. Job sharing: A potential tool for hotel managers. *Cornell Hotel & Restaurant Administration Quarterly* 43(5): 84-91.

Smith, R. 2002. *Strategic Planning for Public Relations*. Mahwah, NJ: Lawrence Erlbaum Associates.

Smith, W. 2001. Thinking ahead for the week of Oct. 22, 2001. Opportunities in the paradox of community, Yankelovich, *http:www.yankelovich.com*

Smith. W. 2001. Thinking ahead for the week of Oct. 29, 2001. What we'll see more of, Yankelovich, http://www.yankelovich.com

Smith, W. 2001. Thinking ahead for the week of Nov. 5, 2001. New traditions, Yankelovich, http://www.yankelovich.com

Smith, W. 2001. Thinking ahead for the week of Dec. 10, 2001. Marginal changes in consumer behaviors, Yankelovich, http://www.yankelovich.com

Snepenger, D. and Snepenger, G. 1993. Market structure analysis of media selection practices by travel services. In *Communication and Channel Systems in Tourism Marketing*, edited by M. Uysal and D. Desenmaier, 21-36. New York: Haworth Press.

Sproule, C.M. 2002. The effect of the USA Patriot Act on workplace privacy. *Cornell Hotel & Restaurant Administration Quarterly* 43(5): 65-73.

Stacks, D.W. and T. Caroll. in press. Travel-tourism public relations: One step forward, two steps back? *Journal of Hospitality & Leisure Marketing*.

Stafford, G., L. Yu, and A. K. Armoo. 2002. Crisis management and recovery: How Washington DC hotels responded to terrorism. *Cornell Hotel & Restaurant Administration Quarterly* 43(5): 27-40.

Togethering: The new trend in family vacations, October 13, 2003. *http://www.htrends.com/researcharticle7776.html*

Travel Industry Association of America. Press Release (April 9, 2003). Record number of Americans traveling at home; Overseas travel plummets [press release]. *http://www.tia.org/Press/press/pressrec.asp?Item=267*

Travel Industry Association of America. TIA Research: Travel Forecast Summary, http://www.tia.org

Travel Industry Association of America. 2004. TIA's National Chair Sets Tourism Agenda for 2004" [press release], January 13, http://www.tia.org

Travel Industry Association of America. 2001. "More State Tourism Offices Offering Web Sites to Help Travelers" [press release], Feb. 8, http://www.tia.org

Travel Industry Association of America. 2001. "How Americans Use the Travel Media," July, http://www.tia.org

Travel Industry Association of America. 2002. TIA Forecast Shows Slow Road to Recovery for Travel and Tourism Industry [press release], Oct. 14, http://www.tia.org

Ulmer, R.R. and T.L. Sellnow. 2002. Crisis management and the discourse of renewal: Understanding the potential for positive outcomes of crises. *Public Relations Review* 28(4): 361-365.

Varisco, D.M. 2002. September 11: Participant webservation of the "war on terrorism." *American Anthropologist* 104(3): 934-938.

Wright, D.K. 2002. Examining how the September 11, 2001 terrorist attacks precipitated a paradigm shift advancing communications and public relations into a more significant role in corporate America. *Journal of Communication Management* 6(3): 280-292.

11

Politically (In)corrected: Electronic Media Self-Censorship Since the 9/11 Attacks

Bruce E. Drushel

"That's what the First Amendment is for, is to bother people."
— *U.S. Supreme Court Associate Justice Anthony Kennedy (1992)*

"Censorship is the strongest drive in human nature; sex is a weak second."
— *Phil Kerby, editorial writer,* Los Angeles Times *(Hentoff 1999, p. 1.)*

Introduction

At the philosophical heart of the freedoms of press and speech guaranteed by the U.S. Constitution is the so-called marketplace of ideas, in which it is assumed that a robust and unrestrained dialogue on significant issues is essential to public policy formation in a democracy. The media are assumed to have a particularly important role in this process, functioning as they do as essentially a fourth branch of government, and taking the lead in questioning the activities of the other three as well as those of other societal institutions.

At no time is this function more crucial, nor the media's commitment to it more vital, than during times of war or other social upheavals. Sadly, it also is during these times that the media are most likely to fall victim to attempts at government control or their own self-censorship. Reactions to the September 11, 2001 attacks upon the World Trade Center and the Pentagon underscore how effortlessly media personalities and media organizations can be goaded into silence, passive acceptance of popular perspective, or even public renouncements of earlier speech.

In what was perhaps the most widely reported case of a media personality recanting remarks on the attacks, Bill Maher, host of

ABC's late-night discussion program *Politically Incorrect*, reacted to the White House's characterization of the hijackers of the planes that crashed into the World Trade Center and the Pentagon as "cowardly". Maher paid for his candor: stations pulled his program, advertisers cancelled, the White House criticized his comments, and ultimately, his program was cancelled.

Maher's case was the most visible example, but hardly the only one, of media company executives censoring themselves or their employees in the months and years following the September 11 attacks. These incidents have raised concerns among free speech advocates over the potential for a chilled climate of expression at a time when many argue the country needs as much information and analysis from as many perspectives as possible.

This chapter reviews media self-censorship since the World Trade Center and Pentagon attacks, and examines the broader phenomenon of expression inhibition. It then locates the phenomenon within First Amendment thought and theory, and discusses possible implications of chilled speech during times of national crisis for the policymaking process. It concludes with an argument for greater regulation of the marketplace of ideas to ensure the representation of unpopular points of view.

Bill Maher's Ultimate Political Incorrectness

Politically Incorrect was a half-hour political discussion program, hosted by comedian Bill Maher, and featuring a panel of famous and near-famous guests. The program premiered in 1993 and soon became one of cable channel Comedy Central's most successful series. In January of 1997, the program was acquired by ABC to follow *Nightline* as a companion late-fringe time period program (Rutenberg 2001).

Like nearly all broadcast network programs, *Politically Incorrect* was pre-empted on September 11, 2001, and for a full week afterward for continuous coverage of the aftermath of the attacks. When it returned to the air on September 18, Maher addressed the crisis, and, during a portion of his comments, the assessment by the White House that the hijackers, who had perished along with the passengers on the four commandeered flights, were cowards:

"We have been the cowards, lobbing cruise missiles from 2,000 miles away. That's cowardly. Staying in the airplane when it hits the building, say what you want about it, [is] not cowardly" (Marks 2002, p. B-25).

Reaction was swift and pointed. Seventeen ABC affiliate stations around the country pulled the series from their schedules, three of them permanently, including the one in Washington, DC. Sears and Federal Express asked ABC to remove their commercials from the program. White House spokesman Ari Fleischer, who admitted he hadn't actually seen the broadcast, took the unusual step of denouncing it, calling Maher's comments "unfortunate" and "a terrible thing to say." Fleischer added that the incident was a reminder that Americans "need to watch what they say, watch what they do, and this is not a time for remarks like that; there never is" (Armstrong 2001).

Maher apologized and backed away from the remarks on the next evening's program:

> In no way was I intending to say, nor have I ever thought, that the men and women who defend our nation in uniform are anything but courageous and valiant, and I offer my apologies to anyone who took it wrong...My criticism was meant for politicians who, fearing public reaction, have not allowed our military to do the job they are obviously ready, willing and able to do and who now will, I'm certain, as they always have, get it done. (Armstrong 2001)

Perhaps not surprisingly, attention spurred by the controversy led to a dramatic, albeit temporary, improvement in the program's ratings. For the week of September 17, *Politically Incorrect* averaged 2.8 million viewers, up 20 percent from the same period in 2000, and its best audience in more than six months. While ABC/Disney Chairman Michael Eisner was said personally to have disapproved of Maher's behavior, the company itself stood behind the broadcast (Armstrong 2001). A senior ABC executive told a reporter:

> "We're certainly not going to remove the show from the air. It would send the wrong signal. Besides, if you're not going to let people speak their minds, why is this show on the air?" (Rutenberg 2001, p. C-1).

Maher himself predicted, on the other hand, that he soon would be out of a job. He was correct: ABC cancelled the program at the end of June 2002. His exile from hosting political discussion programs would be short-lived, however. In February of 2003, the premium cable service HBO premiered the weekly *Real Time with Bill Maher*. Since HBO, unlike ABC, derives its revenues primarily from subscriptions, not commercials, and need not appeal to ABC's mass audience, it evidently was less concerned with the potential reaction of advertisers to controversial programming.

Other Instances of Self-Censorship after September 11

About five weeks after the start of the *Politically Incorrect* controversy, an executive of Maher's network himself was forced to apologize for a statement he made at the Columbia Graduate School of Journalism. ABC News president David Westin had been asked if he believed the Pentagon could have been considered a "legitimate" target of those opposed to U. S. foreign policy:

> I actually don't have an opinion on that and it's important I not have an opinion on that as I sit here in my capacity right now. The way I conceive my job running a news organization, and the way I would like all the journalists at ABC News to perceive it, is there is a big difference between a normative position and a positive position. Our job is to determine what is, not what ought to be and when we get into the job of what ought to be I think we're not doing a service to the American people. (Kurtz 2001, p. C-1)

After he came in for harsh criticism from the likes of Rush Limbaugh, Matt Drudge, and editorial writers at the *New York Post*, ABC released a statement in which Westin apologized:

> I was wrong. I gave an answer to journalism students to illustrate the broad, academic principle that all journalists should draw a firm line between what they know and what their personal opinion might be. Upon reflection, I realized that my answer did not address the specifics of September 11. Under any interpretation, the attack on the Pentagon was criminal and entirely without justification. I apologize for any harm that my misstatement may have caused. ("Reacting to CyberAlert" 2001)

Westin ultimately kept his job. Two other journalists who had opinions—unpopular ones—were not so fortunate. Dan Guthrie was fired by *the Daily Courier* in Grants Pass, Oregon, after he wrote in one of his columns that President Bush was an "embarrassment" for "hiding in a Nebraska hole" instead of flying straight back to Washington, DC, following the attacks on September 11. And *the Texas City Sun* fired columnist Tom Gutting after he wrote that, on September 11, President Bush was, "flying around the country like a scared child, seeking refuge in his mother's bed after having a nightmare" (Scordato and Monopoli 2002).

More than two years after those incidents, CBS apparently still was reluctant to air material critical of Bush, even if it didn't directly address national security, even if some one was paying to air it, and even if it appeared to depart from prior network practice. In January of 2004, CBS turned down a request from the organization MoveOn.Org to buy time during the Super Bowl for a commercial critical of budget deficits during the Bush presidency. While the network claimed the action was consistent with its longstanding ban on advocacy advertising, a group of two dozen Democratic lawmakers noted that CBS recently had aired commercials on the issues of smoking and drug abuse from the American Legacy Foundation and from the White House Office of National Drug Control Policy, respectively. A few months before, CBS also had come under criticism for moving a dramatic series critical of Ronald Reagan from its advertiser-supported network to its sister subscription network Showtime. The lawmakers claimed both incidents were part of what they called a "disturbing pattern" of the network giving in to complaints by the Republican National Committee (Brown 2004).

At least some media self-censorship has been prompted, not by negative reaction to unpopular viewpoints, but by preemptory cautions from the White House. National Security Advisor Condoleezza Rice asked executives of the major broadcast and cable news organizations to approach carefully stories from Middle East news sources, because they might include coded messages from Osama bin Laden to his associates. Following the warning, CNN and Fox News Channel aired only a brief excerpt from a twenty-minute tape from bin Laden discussing Muslim versus Christian conflicts. On previous occasions, both had aired tapes of bin Laden in their entirety. The Arab satellite channel Al Jazeera, meanwhile, aired the entire tape, as well as a response from a U.S. diplomat (Bodney 2002).

The Pressures Towards Self-Censorship

The period following September 11 is hardly the first time the U.S. media have been faced with determining how best to handle the fallout from unpopular speech. Hentoff (1999) points to the decision by CBS to suspend Andy Rooney from its newsmagazine *60 Minutes* for unflattering remarks he made about gays during a television special and for allegedly racist remarks a magazine reporter says he made during an off-air interview as an instance that was badly handled. On the other hand, Hentoff praised a decision by the magazine the *Progressive* not to bow to pressure from a funding source that objected to its publication of an ad for an anti-abortion group. The shunning by media organizations of screenwriters, journalists, directors, and personalities who were listed in *Red Channels* or otherwise accused of anti-American activity during the so-called

McCarthy period is an oft-cited example of timorous behavior by the Fourth Estate and the entertainment industry (Sterling and Kittross 2002).

Journalists and the organizations for which they work frequently defend unpopular behaviors and media content by referencing dedication to journalistic mission or ethics or the enormous responsibility their profession shoulders in a democracy. They routinely let roll off their backs criticism of alleged distortion and slanting, offensiveness, alarmism and sensationalism, as well as accusations that the financial machinations of their corporate parents impugn their journalistic objectivity. Why, then, would they appear to be much more concerned with reaction to their work in the period following a national crisis?

Expression Inhibition

The answer may lie in an area of study communication theorists refer to expression inhibition, more frequently known as the Spiral of Silence. According to Noelle-Neumann (1984), fear of social isolation is such a powerful force that people will suppress their natural inclinations to honestly express their views rather than risk ostracism: "When people think others are turning away from them, they suffer so much that they can be guided or manipulated as easily by their own sensitivity as by a bridle" (p. 6).

As Noelle-Neumann's colorful assertion suggests, people are keenly aware of public opinion and are remarkably able to sense its direction. Not surprisingly, public opinion is a particularly powerful force when society is in danger.

In the case of the "proper" attitudes and behaviors since the September 11 attacks, it should come as no surprise that someone critical of the White House response, U. S. policy in the Middle East, or, indeed, the unacceptability of such criticism would perceive himself or herself in the minority. A nationwide survey of 1,561 adults immediately following the attacks revealed that 61 percent believed that it might be necessary for the average citizen to surrender some civil liberties for the benefit of the so-called war on terrorism. And more than two-thirds believed it would be acceptable for law enforcement officials to randomly stop individuals for questioning for no other reason than their fit to a "terrorist" profile (Barabak 2001).

As simple and as intuitive as expression inhibition sounds, it likely is a complicated mechanism. While early scholarship on the subject found that people curb their desires to speak in order to avoid overt defiance of authority (Janis 1982) or openly contradicting a presumed majority (Noelle-Neumann 1984), more recent work has suggested the decision to speak one's mind may have more to do with local or even interpersonal factors: one may remain silent so as not to hurt others (Wyatt, Katz, Levinsohn, and Al-Haj 1996); one may speak if he or she senses interpersonal trust; (Wyatt, Kim, and Katz 2000); and one is more willing to argue if the opinion climate seems congenial (Glynn, Hayes, and Shanahan 1997).

Pressure from Government Figures

Another explanation for the media's unusual reticence regarding potentially unpopular ideas may be more overt pressure towards conformity in the form of statements and warnings from officials in the Bush administration. Given his record in the Senate favoring less fettered law enforcement powers over civil liberties, John Ashcroft drew considerable opposition as George W. Bush's nominee to head the Justice Department. In testimony before his former Senate colleagues after the attacks, Attorney General Ashcroft appeared to address his critics, whose tactics he claimed, "scare peace-loving people with phantoms of lost liberty" and who "only aid terrorists, for they erode our national unity and diminish our resolve. They give ammunition to America's enemies" (Gellman 2002, p. 95).

Ashcroft, of course, was hardly the first government official to use threats to national security as a rationale for coercing agreement from the media. Bodney (2002) notes that President John F. Kennedy, speaking to news executives in New York only a few days after the Bay of Pigs fiasco, cautioned, "Every newspaper now asks itself, with respect to every story: 'Is it news?' All that I suggest is that you add the question: 'Is it in the national interest?'" (p. 3).

In the United States, the tradition of government attempts to quash speech potentially at opposition with policy is an old one. Hentoff (1999) notes that the Alien and Sedition Acts of 1791 made punishable criticism of either the President or Congress. Numerous journalists were jailed while the acts were in effect.

But perhaps the ultimate example of a government-induced chilling effect on free expression and criticism in history occurred in the

Greek colony of Thourioi (c. 400-500 B.C.). The system of laws there effectively was self-perpetuating: anyone wishing to advocate a change to them had to speak with his head in a noose. If the advocacy was unsuccessful, the speaker was strangled (Tedford 1985).

Self-Censorship, Free Speech, and Democracy

It may be, as Bodney (2002) argues, that the indeterminate duration and limitless scope of the so-called war on terrorism pose a real threat to First Amendment rights, assuming the government attempts traditional wartime control over press coverage of battles and the overall conduct of the war, and pressure upon dissenting views of its value or necessity. And if, as Bodney argues, the war on terrorism is equivalent to the Cold War, at least in terms of scale and boundlessness, we can expect ongoing pressure from the government on the press to self-censor, much as happened in the 1950s and 1960s.

But while the persuasive power of coercion by government officials cannot be underestimated, First Amendment guarantees notwithstanding, Gellman (2002) contends that legislation and threats of criminal prosecution actually are less of a threat than the social pressure to conform to majority views. And pressure to adopt popular viewpoints and behaviors is even greater in times of crisis, such as following September 11.

In terms of frequency, Gellman (2002) argues, actual attempts by the government to censor or pressure the media have been almost nonexistent, while efforts from private individuals, including those from the media, aimed at self-censorship have been common. For instance, opponents of the White House war on terrorism, as well as those who questioned its feasibility and advisability, were largely absent from news and talk programs in the weeks following the World Trade Center and Pentagon attacks. The exception was those political discussion programs on cable with conservative hosts, where the opponents to the war were held up as subjects of ridicule.

And, Gellman (2002) asserts, even though a legal analysis tends to ignore self-censorship in favor of a focus on instances of state action, from the standpoint of social effects, perceived public sentiment against a dissenting viewpoint is more potent than an attempt by the government to suppress that viewpoint. As an example, the implication and subsequent popular perception he was unpatriotic probably was more effective at quieting Bill Maher than the government could have been.

The Social Value of Dissent

Frequently, the discussion regarding the right to free speech during times of crisis is painted as a contest between individual freedom (dissent) and the good of society (national security). This dynamic tension may be thought of as having its roots in the concept of Social Contract, in which individuals agree to surrender their unfettered ability to act as they choose in exchange for the protections and benefits afforded by membership in a society. The traditional Western ideal has been that there are certain so-called natural rights, such as speech, that one might not be expected to surrender (Carter, Franklin, and Wright 1999). In practice, Hentoff (1999) observes that Western societies frequently have asked their citizens to surrender their natural right of expression, and often for marginal social benefit. Efforts by the Congress in the 1980s to outlaw desecration of the American flag and negative public reaction to the ACLU's defense of a march by Nazis through the heavily Jewish community of Skokie, Illinois in the 1970s are recent examples.

But Harvard Law Professor Zachariah Chafee, Jr. (cited in Tedford 1985) believes the free speech/national security tension to be a false dichotomy. Speech, he contends, can have either an individual interest or a public interest, the latter having as its central purpose the attainment of truth. The search for truth and safety of the public (national security) both are social goods, meaning threats to the latter must be imminent, not just conceivable, before the former is sacrificed.

To illustrate the role of speech as a public good of value equal with the national security or public safety, Bodney (2002) cites the ill-fated decision by John F. Kennedy early in his presidency to provide CIA support in the invasion by anti-Castro Cuban of the Bay of Pigs. Popular knowledge of the role of the government came only after the invasion failed. Bodney questioned whether Kennedy might have been dissuaded from going through with the plan had the press reported what it knew in advance, and had public opinion been against it. Somewhat ominously, he notes that the willingness of U. S. media organizations to succumb to White House pressure to edit tapes purportedly from Osama bin Laden meant that Arab viewers received better information than viewers in the U.S., since the Al-Jazeera satellite service airs both the speeches of bin Laden and U. S. officials unedited.

Beyond State Action

Scordato and Monopoli (2002), in fact, contend that the more potent threats to speech from private suppression than from the government since September 11 raises the question of whether government intervention is necessary to further protect speech. To bolster their argument, the authors rely upon a literal interpretation of the concept of the marketplace of ideas. If the two truly are analogous, there is precedent for intercession by the government: while reliance upon marketplace forces in commercial domains is deeply engrained in American ideology, the government has acknowledged that those forces occasionally are thwarted or otherwise fail, as they did with the appearance of trusts in key industries more than a century ago. Congress's solution was to attempt to restore some equilibrium to the forces through anti-trust legislation.

In much the same way, Congress might promulgate legislation targeted at forces that inhibit free expression. The potential value of such a move extends well beyond sound decision making in times of crisis. One of the basic precepts of representative democracy is that society advances through the free exchange of ideas and, moreover, is hindered by its lack. From the perspective of those elected to positions of leadership, free speech can function as a social safety valve—a cathartic experience (Scordato and Monopoli 2002). A public mollified by having had its say is a public more placid and more easily governed.

But what sources of inhibited expression might be feasibly addressed? Put another way, who might the targets of such legislation be? This paper has identified three likely sources of expression inhibition in the months and years since September 11, 2001: coercive government officials, timorous media organizations, and perceived pressure for conformity from the public at large.

The First and Fourteenth Amendments were intended to circumvent attempts by the government or government officials to censor the press, and, generally speaking, they have been successful. Where the media have caved into pressure from the government, it has not been because of fear of legal sanction, but more over fear of negative public reaction or of the loss of the benefits of being perceived by the executive branch as being friendly: access to officials for interviews, advance word of key decisions and actions, and strategic "leaks" of information and off-the- record statements. "Pressure" is likely too amorphous an activity to regulate reliably, and the unintended result could be less speech from officials worried about the line between advocacy and threat. Obviously, it would be neither possible nor desirable to attempt to control majority public opinion, the expressions of it, or the perceptions of it.

But if one might assume that some media executives bow to perceived pressure from the public, advertisers, and officials more easily than others, the best guarantor of a robust marketplace of ideas would be at least some key media outlets being controlled by executives who are less easily cowed. One solution, therefore, would appear to be ensuring that outlets were controlled by a greater number of different individuals, since more owners would be more likely to include the less timorous. This argument bolsters the case of those who seek more stringent limits on media ownership.

The unmistakable trend in the regulation of media ownership since the 1970s has been to allow companies to own more media outlets nationwide and in individual markets. Frequently, the argument for this approach has been economic efficiency, and concerns for a resultant lessening of diversity in viewpoint have been countered with the claim that new technologies (e.g., cable, satellite, and the Internet) have dramatically increased the channels of speech available. Courts thus frequently have supported challenges to longstanding restrictions, or even to eased restrictions that aren't easy enough.

Another promising approach would be discouraging the natural tendency of profit-driven media organizations to suppress the expression of viewpoints that would be unpopular with advertisers and audiences. There also is precedent for it: from roughly 1949 until 1987, the Federal Communications Commission developed and enforced its so-called Fairness Doctrine, which required broadcasters to cover significant controversial issues, and to do so from all perspectives. Not only did the rule effectively discourage radio and television stations from keeping unpopular viewpoints off the air— it actually encouraged stations to seek them out.

While this is an approach with which society has had some experience, it also is one fraught with peril: generally speaking, it is as constitutionally suspect for the government to compel speech as it is to restrict it. More than thirty years ago, the U. S. Supreme Court endorsed the argument that the public benefit of being exposed to a broad range of ideas outweighed limitations on a press organization's absolute freedom over the messages it disseminated. In fact, in a footnote to the Supreme Court's *Red Lion* case (1969), Justice Byron White noted that Congress doesn't abridge freedom of speech or press just because it limits the power of the owners of media companies by compelling a multiplicity of voices. Law professor Jerome Barron goes further: given what he considers to be a failure of the marketplace ideas due to ownership concentration in the media, he contends that the First Amendment does not just allow, but in fact requires a government-protected access to views other than those media organizations want to disseminate (Carter, Franklin, and Wright 1999). But in recent years, a more conservative Court has been more likely to protect more expansively an organization's speech—even when that speech was entirely commercial in nature, and even when it meant that minority viewpoints were not disseminated.

Those who specifically opposed the original Fairness Doctrine before its repeal in 1987 particularly were concerned over anecdotal reports that it might actually have a chilling effect on speech by media organizations (and, because of the leadership role of the media in public debate, on speech more broadly). At the time, broadcasters claimed they were less like to report on controversial subjects because of the costly legal battles they would have to fight against those who believed their coverage was unbalanced, and whose complaints could slow down the process of getting their station licenses renewed (*Syracuse Peace Council* 1987). Since the Telecommunications Reform Act effectively insulated the renewal process from the complaints of private citizens and groups (*Broadcast Station Renewal Procedures* 2002), this basis for a chilling effect from the Doctrine should have disappeared. To make the Doctrine enforceable, the FCC likely would have to have some penalty available for stations that don't present sides of an issue unpopular with the station ownership, advertisers, and the general public, but the Commission likely could craft both enforcement procedures and penalties that would encourage compliance in both letter and spirit.

Were Congress to resurrect some form of the Doctrine, it should apply to as many media as possible, unlike the broadcasting-specific original. At a minimum, it should apply to both broadcast and cable television and radio, where the preponderance of the public gets its information on public issues. For consistency's sake, newspapers should be included as well, though the U.S. Supreme Court

once blocked an effort by Florida to impose a portion of the Doctrine having to do with candidate endorsements upon newspapers
(*Miami Herald Publishing Co. v. Tornillo* 1974)

Conclusions

The self-censorship of speech assumed to be unpopular by media
organizations in the period following the September 11, 2001 attacks on the World Trade Center and the Pentagon has resulted from
a combination of overt pressure from the government and the perceived threat of negative reaction from audiences and advertisers,
on whom the advertiser-supported media depend for their profit-
ability. While conventional interpretation of the First Amendment is
sufficient to insulate the media from pressure from government officials, the more pernicious threat to free expression lies in the profit
motive of the media themselves. Just as the government must intervene to ensure the proper balance of forces in a free commercial
market, so may it have to intervene when efforts to restrict viewpoint at a critical time threaten a free marketplace of ideas.

References

Armstrong, M. 2001. White House politically corrects Maher. EonLine, September 27, 2001. Available: http://www.eonline.com/News/Items/0,1,8886,00.html

Barabak, M. Z. 2001. America attacked *Times* poll: U.S. keen to avenge attacks. *Los Angeles Times*, September 16, 2001, p. A1.

Bodney, D. J. 2002. War, wisdom, and freedom of the press. *Communications Lawyer 19* (4), pp. 3-6.

Broadcast Station Renewal Procedures. 47 U.S.C.A. § 309(k) (2002).

Brown, S. 2004. CBS defends decision to bar advocacy spots. *Adweek*, January 28, 2004. Available:http://www.adweek.com/aw/national/article_display.jsp?vnu_content_id=2079134.

Carter, T. B., M. A. Franklin, and J. B. Wright. 1999. *The First Amendment and the Fifth Estate*. New York: Foundation Press.

Gellman, S. 2002. Enduring and empowering: The Bill of Rights in the third Millennium—The First Amendment in a time that tries men's souls. *Law and Contemporary Problems 65*, pp. 87-101.

Glynn, C. J., A. F. Hayes, and J. Shanahan. 1997. Perceived support for one's opinions and willingness to speak out: a meta-analysis of survey studies on the "Spiral of Silence." *Public Opinion Quarterly 61* (4), pp. 452-63.

Hentoff, N. 1999. *Free Speech for Me But Not for Thee*. New York: HarperCollins Publishers.

Janis, I. L. 1982. *Groupthink: Psychological Studies in Policy Decisions and Fiascoes*. 2nd ed. Boston, MA: Houghton-Mifflin.

Kennedy, A. 1992. Transcript of Oral Argument, *Lee v. International Society for Krishna Consciousness*, 112 S. Ct. 2701, March 25, 1992.

Kurtz, H. 2001. Objectivity lesson: ABC News chief apologizes. *Washington Post,* November 1, 2001, p. C-1.

Marks, P. 2002. An iconoclast's last days on his late-night soapbox. *New York Times,* June 23, 2002, p. B-25.

Media Research Center. 2001. Reacting to CyberAlert item, ABC News President David Westin has apologized and said "I was wrong" for having "no opinion" on whether the Pentagon was a "legitimate" military target. Media Research Center 6 (171), October 31, 2001. Available: http://www.mediaresearch.org/cyberalerts/2001/cyb20011031_extra.asp.

Miami Herald Publishing Co. v. Tornillo. 418 U.S. 241 (1974).

Noelle-Neumann, E. 1984. *The Spiral of Silence: Public Opinion—Our Social Skin.* Chicago: University of Chicago Press.

Rutenberg, J. 2001. Bill Maher still secure in ABC slot, at least now. *New York Times,* October 8, 2001, p. C-1.

Red Lion Broadcasting Co. v. Federal Communications Commission. 395 U.S. 367 (1969).

Scordato, M. R., and P. A. Monopoli. 2002. Free speech rationales after September 11th: The First Amendment in post-World Trade Center America. *Stanford Law & Policy Review 13,* pp. 185-203.

Sterling, C. H., and J. M. Kittross. 2002. *Stay Tuned: A History of American Broadcasting* (third edition). Mahwah, NJ: Lawrence Erlbaum Associates, Publishers.

Syracuse Peace Council. 2 FCC Rcd. 5043 (1987).

Tedford, T. L. 1985. *Freedom of Speech in the United States.* New York: Random House.

Wyatt, R. O., E.Katz, H. Levinsohn, and M. Al-Haj. 1996. The dimensions of expression inhibition: Perceptions of obstacles to free speech in three companies. *International Journal of Public Opinion Research 8* (3), pp. 229-247.

Wyatt, R. O., J. Kim, and E. Katz. 2000. How feeling free to talk affects ordinary political conversation, purposeful argumentation, and civic participation. *Journalism & Mass Communication Quarterly 77*(1), pp. 99-114.

About the Contributors

Matthew Barton is assistant professor of communication at Southern Utah University and a recent graduate from the University of Nebraska. He is interested in presidential politics, religion and popular culture. He has authored and co-authored numerous convention papers dealing with these and other contemporary topics. He has most recently published in the area of communication education in the basic course.

Robert S. Brown is associate professor and chair of the Department of Communication Arts Ashland University. He specializes teaches in the area of sports communication and information. In addition to numerous articles and book chapters, Brown is the co-editor of *Case Studies in Sport Communication* (Praeger 2004).

Robert E. Denton, Jr. holds the W. Thomas Rice Chair of Leadership Studies and serves as director of the Major General Thomas Rice Center for Leader Development at Virginia Polytechnic Institute and State University. He has degrees in political science and communication studies from Wake Forest University and Purdue University. In addition to numerous articles, essays and book chapters, he is author, co-author or editor of fifteen books. The most recent titles include *Images, Scandal and Communication Strategies of the Clinton Presidency* (Praeger 2003) and *The 2000 Presidential Campaign: A Communication Perspective* (Praeger 2002). Denton serves as editor for the Praeger Series in Political Communication and Presidential Studies as well as Rowman & Littlefield's Series Communication, Media and Politics.

Bruce E. Drushel is an assistant professor in the Department of Communication at Miami University at Oxford, Ohio. He teaches courses in electronic media and broadcast journalism. Recent publications have focused on censorship and telecommunication policy.

Lisa T. Fall, APR, is an assistant professor in the School of Advertising & Public Relations at the University of Tennessee. She earned her Ph.D. in mass media from Michigan State University. Her research specialty is public relations and marketing within the travel, tourism and hospitality management field. Fall has published articles in the *Journal of Hospitality & Leisure Marketing, Journalism & Mass Communication Educator, Iowa Journal of Communication,* and *Journal of Vacation Marketing.*

W. Wat Hopkins is associate professor of communication at Virginia Tech, where he teaches courses in communication law and journalism. He has published a number of articles and books on free speech issues, and is editor of *Communication Law and Policy,* a quarterly law review. He is also editor and co-author of the textbook *Communication and the Law*

Edward M. Horowitz is assistant professor in the Department of Communication at the University of Oklahoma. He has degrees from Franklin and Marshall College and the University of Wisconsin-Madison. Horowitz teaches courses in the areas of media effects and society. His recent focus of study has been the democratic processes in post-communist Poland.

Katherine N. Kinnick is an associate professor in the Department of Communication at Kennesaw State University. She teaches and writes about the societal implications of media content and public relations. Her work has appeared in *Journalism and Mass Communication Quarterly, Public Relations Review, Women's Studies in Mass Communication,* and *Race, Gender and Class.* She is the recipient of the University's Distinguished Teaching Award.

Ronald Lee is professor of communication studies at the University of Nebraska-Lincoln. He teaches and writes about contemporary rhetoric and political culture. His work has appeared in the *Quarterly Journal of Speech, Political Communication, Western Journal of Communication, Communication Studies, Southern Communication Journal, Argumentation and Advocacy,* and *Technical Communication Quarterly.* He is presently completing a book on the rhetorical negotiation of presidential legacies.

John Llewellyn is associate professor in the Department of Communication at Wake Forest University. He teaches a wide range of courses in rhetoric and public relations. Llewellyn's recent publications have focused on corporate public relations campaigns.

Daniel J. O'Rourke is an associate professor of communication arts at Ashland University. He is co-editor of *Case Studies in Sport Communication* (Praeger 2004) and has made numerous presentations at conferences on communication and popular culture.

Pravin A. Rodrigues is assistant professor in the Communication Arts Department at Ashland University, Ohio. He has degrees in mass communication and interpersonal communication from Bowling Green State University. His research interests include intercultural communication, rhetoric and Asian Indian identity.

Craig R. Smith is chair of the Department of Film and Electronic Arts and director of the Center for First Amendment Studies at California State University, Long Beach. Dr. Smith's most recent book is *The Four Freedoms of the First Amendment*. He has also served as a full time speechwriter for President Ford and a consulting writer for George H. W. Bush.

Johan Wanstrom is a doctoral student in the Department of Communication at the University of Oklahoma.

Index